SHAMROCK, CROWN AND CRESCENT

The Remarkable Life of 19th Century Mercenary
Eugene 'Hassan Bey' O'Reilly
(1828-1873)

GERARD RONAN

Staten House

All rights reserved
Copyright © Gerard Ronan 2024.

Gerard Ronan asserts his moral right to be identified as the author of this work in accordance with the Irish Copyright and Related Rights Act 2000.

All rights reserved. No part of this publication may be copied, reproduced, stored in a retrieval system, broadcast or transmitted in any form or by any means, electronic, mechanical, photocopying, recording or otherwise without prior permission in writing from the author.

ISBN: 979-8-89587-930-6

Cover Illustration: 'Encounter Between Cossacks and Bashi-Bazouks', John Charlton RA & JD Watson, England, circa 1880. *The Graphic* (Illustrated Newspaper), England, Great Britain, circa 1880, Museums Victoria Collections, Item HT 22531. https://collections.museumsvictoria.com.au/items/1452784, Accessed 21 December 2023. Colourised by author.

Also by Gerard Ronan:

The Irish Zorro
The Round Towers of Fingal
William Kelly of Portrane
Margaret Evans – Poet of Portrane
Sophia Parnell Evans
The Seduction of Benedict Arthur
The Falsest Rogue
The Killing of Thomas Towson
The Radical Reverend

For the O'Reillys

EDITORIAL NOTES

THE ORTHOGRAPHY OF Ottoman place names during the nineteenth century was far from an exact science and frequently confused by the multi-lingual nature of the empire. In attempting to tell Eugene's story, and to allow the reader to follow Eugene's travels on modern maps, I have opted, where possible, to use the modern names of the villages, towns, and cities he visited, with one exception. I have chosen throughout to refer to the Ottoman capital as Constantinople rather than Istanbul, primarily because, during Eugene's lifetime, the word 'Stamboul' was frequently used to refer to the Islamic/Turkish area of the city, as distinct from the European/Frankish quarter, which was centred around the districts of Galata and Péra. All were considered districts of a greater Constantinople.

There are also several chapters within the narrative where dialogue occurs. These have been transcribed verbatim from published accounts of the conversation, be it the later recollections of one or other of the parties involved, or the contemporaneous notes of a witness. They have not been imagined or altered. For descriptions of landscapes and daily life beyond those already cited in the endnotes, I have relied upon contemporaneous or near-contemporaneous travel diaries and memoirs, such as those listed in the footnote below.[1]

---

[1] *Harper's New Monthly Magazine*, Vol. 16, Issue 93, February 1858, pp.290-303; Amicis, Edmondo de, *Constantinople*, Vol. II, Henry T. Coates & Co., Philadelphia, 1896; Duberly, Fanny. *Journal kept during the Russian War...*, Longman, Brown, Green and Longmans, London, 1856; Perrier, Amelia. *A Winter in Morocco*, Henry S. King & Co., London, 1873

CONTENTS

PREFACE i
THE BLANCHARDSTOWN AFFAIR 1
ARREST AND IMPRISONMENT 17
THE MAKING OF A RADICAL..24
NOVARA TO KOMÁROM 43
CONSTANTINOPLE 54
CROSSING THE BALKANS 59
THE SIEGE OF CALAFAT 67
GALLANTRY AT BUZĂU 78
NINE MONTHS IN ANATOLIA...85
RESENTMENT IN THE RANKS...98
BEATSON'S 'MUTINY'...106
TURNING TURK..119
THE DAMASCUS MASSACRE 123
TRIBUNAL JUDGE...137
MOUKHTARA 144
THE LETTER TO WILLIAM SMITH O'BRIEN 156
THE PRINCE AND THE MATRIARCH 164
The DAMASCUS GENDARMERIE....................................168
THE LAING CONVERSION SCHEME................................181
THE KARAMIST REBELLION 184
A VISIT HOME..189
PUTTING THE TEAM TOGETHER 200
A CONSULAR WEDDING 205
JANE DIGBY 210

CAPTURE!	221
A DIPLOMATIC STORM	233
THE ZAPTIEH PRISON	242
LE GRAND HOTEL DU LOUVRE	253
BOULOGNE-SUR-MER	258
BELGRADE TO FEZ	264
A WIDOW SCORNED	269
MADAME MASSY	275
ACKNOWLEDGEMENTS	283
LIST OF ILLUSTRATIONS	285
INDEX	287

PREFACE

In 1860, the Syrian city of Damascus erupted in a brutal frenzy of sectarian bloodletting that provoked more than one international power to seek to intervene in the region, ostensibly to preserve the safety of the surviving Christian population.

Against this backdrop of internecine strife and international intrigue, a certain Colonel Hassan Bey leapt to global prominence. He did so, not as the swashbuckling mercenary whose reputation for gallantry had seen his name frequently grace the minor columns of the British and Irish press, but as the rescuer of displaced Christians, protector of pilgrims, and, perhaps, as the unlikeliest of appointees to a judicial panel subsequently hailed as a precursor of the International Criminal Court. Within the year, he would also hold the reins of civil and military power in Syria.

Though a trusted official of the Ottoman Empire – soon after to be raised to the rank of *Pasha* – Hassan Bey was not a Turk; nor, indeed, was he a Syrian, Lebanese, Maronite or Druze. He was not even a Muslim. He was, in fact, an Irishman and, at least nominally, a Catholic. A veteran of the Young Ireland rebellion of 1848, and the prime mover behind the notorious 'Blanchardstown Affair', his given name was Eugene O'Reilly. This is his story.

THE BLANCHARDSTOWN AFFAIR

ON THE AFTERNOON of Thursday, 27 July 1848, Thomas Clarke Luby answered the door of his family home at St James's Terrace in Dolphin's Barn, at that time a single-street village in the suburbs of Dublin.[2] He noted with approval the presence on his doorstep of Eugene O'Reilly, a lithe, brown-haired, neatly dressed young gentleman of just twenty years of age. Six years Luby's junior, Eugene had become an unlikely friend of late. They had not met for several weeks.

Eugene had never called to Luby's home before. That he should do so now suggested exceptional circumstances. For the past three weeks, O'Reilly had been traipsing about rural Meath, recruiting volunteers for an armed uprising. Warrants for his arrest were already several days old.[3]

Both Luby and O'Reilly had studied law at Trinity, though not together. Luby had been several years ahead of Eugene and had graduated in 1845. He was currently studying to be a barrister at King's Inns.[4] Eugene, on the other hand, had left Trinity under something of a cloud and without completing his studies. It was rumoured that his political activities were to blame.

As a semi-regular contributor to the *Nation*, Luby's political affiliations were public knowledge. He had never actually been a member of any Confederate club, but he was widely known to be a vocal supporter of armed resistance. Eugene was shown into the sitting room where, without preamble or explanation, he

---

[2] At the time it was called Dolphin's Barn Terrace.
[3] National Library of Ireland, Thomas Clarke Luby letters, MS 332, p.12.
[4] Burtchell & Sadlier. *Alumni Dublinenis*, p.514.

blurted out his news. He was, he declared, about to 'make a bold stroke' and wanted Luby to come with him.

A call to arms ought really to have been made with a surfeit of confidence, but there was a hesitant look in O'Reilly's eyes that was far from reassuring. Luby hesitated.

'I'm in a devil of a fix,' said Eugene. 'I am to meet two hundred armed club men tonight and I'm not sure that a regiment of soldiers won't be on the spot to surround and capture us the moment we get there.'

Questioned as to the reason for his pessimism, Eugene related an encounter he'd had earlier that morning with the attorney, Charles O'Hara. A leading light in the Confederate movement and expected, following the uprising, to be named in the provisional government, O'Hara was a man of substance and influence. Curious as to what Eugene had been up to of late, he drew from the youngster details of his plans to attack Blanchardstown barracks and his recruitment campaign in County Meath.

> The garrison of Dublin, he assumed, would have work enough found for it immediately in the South; but if a formidable force could be despatched to Meath, he would cross the Boyne and take up a position in the more defensible country beyond, among a population already effectually armed and organised in the agrarian societies known as the "Molly Maguires." If he could muster two hundred volunteers at Blanchardstown on the borders of Dublin and Meath, the remainder of the adventure he considered hopeful, and even easy.[5]

It was only when he relayed his decision to delegate the mustering of Dublin Confederates to one Patrick Joseph Barry, commonly known as 'P.J.', that a look of alarm crossed O'Hara's face. An ostentatious law clerk who held the role of secretary to both the Dublin

---

[5] Duffy, Charles Gavan. *Four years of Irish history, 1845-49*, Cassell, Petter, Galpin & Co., London, 1883, p.672.

Remonstrants and the Grattan Club, P.J. Barry was widely perceived as a loose-tongued braggart who had a tendency, when drunk, to trumpet his largely imagined importance. Ubiquitous in the Confederate movement, he personally knew almost every enrolled member in Dublin.[6]

In the peculiar stuttering manner for which he was famous, O'Hara cautioned Eugene against having anything to do with Barry. The man, claimed O'Hara, was 'suspected of giving intelligence to the Castle'.[7] Perplexed as to what he should do, the arrangements for the night having already been made, Eugene had sought out Luby, whose judgement he esteemed highly.

'Could the gathering still be countermanded?' asked Luby.

It couldn't. The clubmen of Navan were prepared to take the town that night and were confident, should they receive support from Dublin, that most of the hundred soldiers defending the town would be willing to 'fraternise'. Taking Dunshaughlin would be child's play after that. With a proclamation from the provisional government in Munster expected 'at any moment', aborting the Blanchardstown attack could have direct consequences for the rising throughout Meath.[8] Eugene didn't know what to do for the best.

Luby asked Eugene what he knew about Barry. Apart from what O'Hara had told him, Eugene had to admit, it was very little. From the brief contact he'd had with the man, he'd formed the impression of 'an ardent, exceptionally zealous and active member of the Confederate organisation.' It had been purely by chance, he said, that their paths had crossed and that they had fallen into conversation about how best to arrange a rendezvous of Dublin club men.[9] Barry's

---

[6] N.L.I., O'Donoghue's Narrative of 1848, 28 August 1848, MS 770, pp. 1-2.
[7] Duffy, Charles Gavan, *Four years of Irish history*, p.674.
[8] National Library of Ireland (NLI), Thomas Clarke Luby letters, MS 332, p.1.
[9] Ibid., p.6.

offer to help had, at the time, seemed heaven-sent.

Luby attempted to reassure Eugene. 'After all,' he theorised, 'there is probably nothing in Mr. O'Hara's suspicions. These impressions of a man get abroad without any reasonable grounds. Anyway, it seems to me you must take your chance and go with the adventure at all hazards. I suppose you have come for me?'

'Yes,' replied Eugene.

'Am I merely going out with you temporarily, or am I now going with you altogether?'

'You're to come with me for good.'

'Very well, I'll go and get ready.'

Luby descended the stairs and told his mother to get a few things ready as he would be leaving in a few moments. Catherine Luby complied without complaint but with a sinking heart and through a veil of tears. Pulling on his black frock coat, Luby bid her farewell and climbed the stairs to his father's bedroom.

The Rev. James Luby was bedridden, courtesy of a stroke he had suffered some years previous. Explaining that he was going away, Thomas asked for the money his father had been putting away for this very moment. James Luby pulled a purse from beneath his pillow. Bidding his father a hurried farewell, Luby descended the stairs and rejoined Eugene in the sitting room.

'The people in this house must be greatly attached to you,' Eugene observed. 'I heard them crying'.

Luby did not reply. He had no wish to reveal that he still lived with his parents. It would take too long to explain; almost as long as it might to explain how his Catholic father had become a Protestant minister; how his mother had persisted in her Catholicism; and how her son, just six at the time of his father's conversion, had been raised in both faiths and emptied of all desire to fully subscribe to either.

Leaving the house, the pair walked in silence. They had reached Cork Street before Luby recovered his spirits. Anxious and excited in equal measure, they fell into a jocular mood. This night might well be their last, but it might also be historic. Neither possibility was lost on them.[10]

> It was with high hopes and youthful ardor, that I sallied forth with my friend Eugene that morning. Never in any of my revolutionary adventures during more than twenty-eight years since have I gone forth for Ireland with similar buoyancy of heart. Never has the same glow of faith and enthusiasm returned.[11]

Hailing a covered hackney cab, they went in search of P.J. Barry to O'Hara's Shellfish Tavern on the corner of York Street and French Street.[12] Failing to find him, they pressed on to a house in Stoneybatter where, as the cab pulled up to the kerb, Eugene was greeted by his father's law clerk, an unctuous young man of diminutive stature.

The clerk shared some murmured intelligence with Eugene and received by return some instructions regarding money and a request to fetch Eugene's rifle. The clerk's demeanour worried Luby. Eugene reassured him.

'He is one of the best creatures in the world, and would do anything for me'.

From Stoneybatter, they drove next to the Drogheda Tavern on Amiens Street, where Eugene had taken a first-floor room.[13] Waiting for them was a pair of 'zealous and highly intelligent' secretaries of the Navan clubs: a one-eyed man named Mullen, and his cousin, a callow youth by the name of Murray. They had come to discuss the plans for the night ahead.

P.J. Barry had left by the time Eugene and Luby arrived, but the sight of his discarded prayer book on the table prompted Eugene to share O'Hara's

---

[10] Ibid., p.2.
[11] Ibid., p.22.
[12] Afterwards the Royal College Tavern.
[13] Most likely Dublin and Drogheda Railway Hotel, 46 Amiens St.

intelligence. Mullen leapt immediately to Barry's defence, questioning the grounds on which O'Hara had impugned the man's integrity. At the same time, he couldn't help but relate the curious nature of Barry's behaviour prior to his departure. Claiming that he hadn't long to live, Barry had indulged in an effusively ostentatious display of 'religious fervour'.

Following further discussion, Eugene despatched Murray to Navan with orders to hold off on any attack until the Dublin auxiliaries could join them. Mullen was next to take his leave, claiming some private business about town. The O'Reillys' clerk arrived shortly after, bringing Eugene's rifle, a newly forged pike head without a staff, and a sum of money in gold coins.[14] Having safely delivered them, he left without delay.

Luby, meanwhile, had hit on a means by which they might further swell their numbers. He had a friend, James Hayes, a civil engineer who was vice-president of the Clontarf club. With Eugene's approval, he scribbled a note to Hayes, sent it off by messenger, and settled himself by the windows to watch for Hayes' arrival. Hayes arrived within the hour, accompanied by a handful of young men who appeared somewhat anxious about what they were being asked to do.

The secretary of the Clontarf club, James O'Rorke, was especially skittish, driven to nervous distraction by the 'incautious' volume of Luby's voice. After some gentle persuasion and a communal dropping of voices, the Clontarf men agreed to participate and a cordial toast was drunk to the success of the night's endeavour.

The Clontarf men had only just taken their leave when Michael Barry, brother of P.J., arrived. Undersized and slight of frame, Barry possessed the calmness and inflated eloquence of a barrister and Luby took an instant dislike to him. Eugene, on the

---

[14] N.L.I., Thomas Clarke Luby letters, MS 332, p.3.

other hand, appeared reassured by his arrival, and the pair spoke privately for a while. He was to be the last of their visitors that night. His departure left O'Reilly and Luby with an empty room and time to kill.[15]

> We talked lightly and gaily of a hundred things. O'Reilly talked of some ladies, with whom he had enjoyed flirtations. These soft reminiscences seemed to put him, for a moment or so, into a comic state of depression. Of course he had also the responsibility of our grand expedition weighing on his mind, while I was comparatively free from such heavy cares. I walked up and down the room romancing in an easy fluent strain, doubtless absurd, but probably rather amusing.
>
> With a slight air of nervous excitement and anxiety, surely quite natural under the circumstances, my intended companion in arms rubbed his forehead rapidly with his white hand, after which process he said with a gentle smile:- "After all, isn't it a devil of a thing to think of? How is it, Luby, that you are taking it all so very coolly?"[16]

There followed an absurd exchange on the matter of shirts as Luby wondered where they might get fresh ones when their night's work was done. Eugene suggested they confiscate some from the wardrobe of a local landlord after they had taken Navan.

'Ay,' laughed Luby. 'Fine cambric shirts.'

Later that night they enjoyed a meal of mutton chops and bass, chased down with a glass or two of punch. Outside of the hotel, the city's poor were being decimated by famine and disease. For those who still had money, however, there were few shortages worthy of the name.

As they consumed what might yet prove to be their last meal, they picked over the plan for the night, which was first to take Blanchardstown, then Dunshaughlin, and finally, to march on Navan and Trim. At Dunshaughlin, they would acquire handles for

---

[15] Ibid., p.4.
[16] Ibid., p.5.

the pike heads that Eugene had commissioned, one of which he had given to Luby. No matter what happened, they would stick to each other, and should the adventure turn sour, Eugene promised, they would escape together and find commissions in some continental army.

Military commissions, however, were expensive and far beyond Luby's limited income. Diplomatically, he chose not to enlighten his comrade as to the gulf in their respective incomes, being more concerned at that moment about what they might do should the rumours about P.J. Barry be proven true and they arrived at the mustering point near Blanchardstown Wood to find the police or army waiting for them.[17]

'Oh, in that case,' said Eugene, 'we'll fall back on the County Cavan among the Molly Maguires.'[18]

Upon the appointed hour, Mullen rejoined them, and Eugene promptly paid the bill and hailed a covered hackney. In his haste and distraction, he left behind him his copy of *The Artillerist's Manual and British Soldier's Compendium*. It would be found in his bedroom the following day.[19]

On reaching Parnell Street,[20] Mullen held the cab while Eugene and Luby entered a public house to collect P.J. Barry. They found him at the counter paying for drinks. Eugene pressed a hand to his shoulder.

'I suppose this is Mr. Luby,' said Barry as he turned and offered a friendly hand.

A middle-sized man, about thirty years of age, Barry's greeting was effusive and fawning. The mood was not reciprocated. As they climbed into the cab, an

---

[17] Ibid.
[18] The 'Molly Maguires' were a secret and largely agrarian subversive organisation who blackened their faces during raids.
[19] Griffiths, Frederick Augustus. *The Artillerist's Manual and British Soldier's Compendium of Sword Exercise, Artillery Exercise, Equipment &c. Fireworks. Fortification. Mathematics. Gunnery &c. &c. &c.*, E. Jones, Woolwich, 1840.
[20] Then called Great Britain Street.

unexpressed tension settled on the company, and as they drove along Cavendish Row and past the Rotunda Hospital, Eugene could contain himself no longer.

'Do you know what, Barry?' he said boldly. 'I was thinking of shooting you this morning. I was told you were an informer.'

'Surely this is unnecessary,' Luby protested forcibly. 'Quite uncalled for!'

Eugene was not to be deflected. 'But now I'm glad I didn't,' he added, 'for now I find you're true, and things are all right.'

Mullen said nothing. Luby fidgeted with a nervous intensity. Barry seemed genuinely mortified.

'Now this is too bad,' he replied in an aggrieved and frightened tone. 'No one has shown himself more earnest in the cause than I have; there is no one who would make greater sacrifices for it than I would.'

Desperate to exonerate himself, Barry proceeded to enumerate the shillings and pence he had spent that very day pursuing recruits. Even before they had met with him, he insisted, he had been at yet another public house attempting to drum up support for the night's attack. He was *fully* committed to the cause.

Eugene backed off. For better or for worse, they were in it together now. Softening his tone, he affected an air of amiability, and a truce of sorts evolved. Mullen attempted to lighten the mood by expressing his regret at not having seen a priest before setting out. Barry, a man to whom the impression of piety mattered almost as much as that of importance, nervously congratulated himself for having remembered to do so.

It was only now that Luby noticed that he was the only one without a rifle and ammunition. Eugene, it was true, had supplied him with a new pike head, but not a staff to place it on and no prospect of finding one until they reached Dunshaughlin. Not one of them carried a sword or a bayonet. They were, it occurred to

Luby, worryingly ill-equipped for close-order fighting.²¹

Uphill and down, through clear and wooded landscapes, they drove in nervous silence until, at length, Eugene drew Luby's attention to a distant copse, the scene 'of the flirtations alluded to by him earlier in the day.' ²² Approaching Blanchardstown Wood, they were joined by another two carriages so that, as they closed in on their destination, there were, in total, just three cabs, each filled with armed men. At one point, as the lead car paused to allow the slowest to catch up, Eugene and Barry got out to scan the horizon for others who might yet be approaching. There were none to be seen.

At the rendezvous point, sixteen men alighted from the cabs and stood silently in little knots at a remote crossroads. Their numbers were far fewer than expected, and the Clontarf men conspicuous by their absence. It was a pleasantly warm night. The sky was clear, and the moon was shining so brightly that it was hard not to feel exposed. And it was quiet: the kind of quiet in which small sounds travel for miles. Every emotion now expanded, and the collective anxiety grew. Only the hackney drivers appeared to be calm. As for Eugene, he was busy and preoccupied, the responsibility of command weighing heavily on his shoulders.

> Eugene O'Reilly – who, to anyone glancing at his light, graceful, and active form, must have seemed in his smart, well-fitting shooting jacket, the *beau ideal* of military alertness – dashed eagerly about the roads all around us, looking carefully into the joining fields, to discover whether other bodies of our expected comrades might not be close by, awaiting our arrival. No doubt, he peered anxiously through the hedges, looked over the walls, and scrutinised every clump of trees that could give cover to friend or foe.²³

---

[21] N.L.I., Thomas Clarke Luby letters, MS 332, p.6.
[22] Ibid., p.7.
[23] Ibid.

The Blanchardstown Affair

As Eugene disappeared into the woods to search for stragglers, the anxiety of inaction rapidly gripped his colleagues, and the collective silence gave way to a murmured polyphony of disillusion. Luby began to worry:

> I began to wish that O'Reilly was back with us. Indeed I, or someone else, said something to this effect; upon which the man who had spoken to me already, or another, observed somewhat sneeringly "Oh, I suppose he's amusing himself." Luckily, however, at this point, before the restlessness and vexatious complaints grew any worse, Eugene and the others, who had been running all around, hurried up to us at full speed.

No one else had come. Not even the Clontarf men had shown themselves. Before setting out from Clontarf, they had been unwittingly forced to suffer O'Rorke's 'devotional exercises', which proved so long-winded and protracted that young McKenna, at one point, had threatened to shoot him. And then there was the small matter of P.J. Barry's involvement. The suspicion that he might be an informer had inhibited the participation of many others. The few that *had* ventured out from Dublin had gotten lost and were wandering the banks of the Royal Canal when they were discovered and arrested.[24] Others, having been told by Barry the previous day that the South had already risen and found no such reports in the papers, had deemed the call to arms to be bogus.[25]

With the hours flying by, the threat of sunrise pierced the haze of indecision. It was time to speak frankly. 'Eugene,' said Luby, 'I fear this affair has miscarried. We have apparently no chance of the two hundred club men you expected or even of anything approaching fifty. You and I have brought these men out here. It seems to me that the only course left to us

---

[24] Ibid., pp.4,8,18,19.
[25] *Advocate,* Melbourne, Letter from G. H. Supple: 12 January 1884, p.19.

to pursue under the circumstances, is to try and, if possible, get them back again safely into Dublin. This seems to me our duty. Then the events of a day or two may furnish us with a better chance of doing something.'

'I'm inclined to think you're in the right,' said Eugene, 'but let us wait a few minutes longer. I'll course around once more and see whether I may not find some stragglers. Perhaps some of our men may have missed the police in the night.'

Eugene made a final sortie down one of the side roads, but the news was no better than before. Reluctantly, he ordered everyone to get back in their hackneys and return to Dublin.[26] As the cabs began to pull away, Luby felt a sudden qualm of conscience. The Navan men would be waiting. Potential victories, lives even, could be lost for the want of their support. But before Luby could articulate his doubts, Barry excitedly gave voice to his.

'We're going back into the lion's den,' he cried out, shaking his fist indignantly.

'Then,' demanded Luby, 'if you think so, in God's name, stop the car. STOP THE CAR!'

'STOP THE CAR,' the entire ensemble chorused. Thirty seconds later, all three hackneys came to a standstill, and everyone spilt onto the road.

> The scene was a stirring and even a joyful one, when O'Reilly announced (what they all seemed to have already divined) that, few as our numbers were, instead of going back we should at once begin our March to Navan.
>
> There we stood; two or three, I think, with pike blades gleaming brightly in the moonlight, the rest with good, serviceable rifles. These last eagerly drew out their ramrods and began to load. I found myself shaking hands with someone I never met before. After a few minutes, however, things took another turn. Michael Barry, P.J.'s brother, came up to O'Reilly and

---

[26] N.L.I., Thomas Clarke Luby letters, MS 332, p.8.

quietly, but impressively, remarked that "it was madness to go on with so small a party".

Emboldened by Barry's caution, several men stepped forward to argue against going straight to Navan. Another promised that should they safely return to Dublin, he could get them all into a safe house on Kildare Street. In those moments of hesitation, the momentum was lost and the cabs set out for Dublin by a different route to that by which they'd come.[27] Close to Cabra Police Station, the convoy encountered a closed turnpike. Behind the gate, a thin line of metropolitan police stood waiting.[28] 'We must squelch them,' growled P.J. Barry, whose blood was up. 'We'll have to squelch them'.

To their collective astonishment, the gate was raised, and they were allowed to pass. As for why, they could only speculate. Had the police been warned only to expect groups heading out of the city?[29] Or was it simply that the outnumbered constabulary had decided that discretion was the better part of valour? The question remained unanswered until, minutes later, they were passed by a cab hurtling in the opposite direction. This, Luby surmised, was the much-delayed Clontarf men. Unable to warn them, they could only watch as their colleagues raced blindly into a constabulary trap.[30]

The five Clontarf men – described as well-dressed, middle class and aged between fifteen and twenty-five – were subsequently caught in possession of three guns, two pistols, two pikes, three pounds of gunpowder, two hundred bullets, eight hundred ball cartridges and five hundred percussion caps.[31] An

---

[27] *Irish Times*, 27 January 1862, p.3
[28] Devoy, John. *Recollections of an Irish Rebel...*, Charles P. Young & Co., New York, 1929, p.291.
[29] N.L.I., Thomas Clarke Luby letters, MS 332, p.10.
[30] *Warder and Dublin Weekly Mail*, 29 July 1848, p.7.
[31] *Morning Advertiser*, 30 October 1848, p.3; *Tablet*, 5 August 1848, p.2.

allegation that they had been betrayed by an informer would feature prominently in the following day's *Weekly Freeman's Journal*:

> It appears that private information had been conveyed to the authorities, through the medium of some of the detective force, that an armed meeting would be held on Thursday night in the neighbourhood of Blanchardstown Bridge, and intelligence was likewise obtained regarding some of the parties that were to attend it.[32]

The source of this intelligence was never revealed, but people had their suspicions. One of the Clontarf party later revealed that they had no sooner been secured in the police barracks than the local sergeant had enquired: 'Which of you gentlemen is Mr Luby?' The question suggested a leak within their own party, but it was not impossible it had come from elsewhere.

In later years, both Eugene and Luby would express confidence in P.J. Barry's innocence, believing the suspicion that clung to him to have been drawn only from his boastfulness and obsession with being seen in the company of the Confederate leaders.[33] At the time, however, the suspicion that Patrick Joseph Barry was an informer was so widespread that, on 30 September, during the trial of William Smith O'Brien, the *Freeman's Journal* would drop extensive hints that Barry was a government spy.[34]

> One thing is certain, that the government spy who pulled the wires in the council of the confederation, and who will figure to-morrow on the green table, has been connected with the body from its birth, and aided in bringing it into existence. A near relative of this person has not long since denied most indignantly, in a letter

---

[32] *Weekly Freeman's Journal*, 29 July 1848, p.5.
[33] N.L.I., Thomas Clarke Luby letters, MS 332, p.21.
[34] Mansergh, Nicholas. 'Reflections upon the Local Dimension' in William Nolan ed., *Tipperary: History and Society; Interdisciplinary Essays on the History of an Irish County*, Hodges, Dublin, 1985, pp. 4-5; *Freeman's Journal*, 15 August 1848.

published in the columns of the FREEMANS JOURNAL, that his brother was other than a "true man."

Until the spy unearths himself it would be, of course, imprudent to name his sirname or *either* of his Christian names; but there are very few constant readers of the FREEMAN'S JOURNAL, who will fail in hitting on the name of the individual who is destined to rank with the Newells and Jemmy O'Briens of other days.[35]

Having safely reached the junction of Dominick Street and Dorset Street, the three hackney cabs diverged now in different directions, one heading towards Bolton Street, another towards Parnell Square. Eugene's cab continued up Dorset Street towards his father's legal offices.[36] The O'Reillys had long since moved out of this building and into a house on Lower Gardiner Street, and so, apart from the ever-loyal clerk, Eugene knew the house would be empty.

Paying off the hackney driver with a generous tip, Eugene knocked on the door. Admitted by the clerk, the entire group headed immediately to the basement, crossed the backyard to the stable and made their way up to the loft. They had scarcely concealed their weapons when a double knock on the hall door resounded throughout the house. The clerk ran to answer it, followed closely by Eugene. The others remained in the stable.

After several minutes the clerk returned. Old Mr O'Reilly, he explained, had arrived in something of a tizzy and had contrived to lock his son in the office and to lock up the house. Why he should have done so perplexed everyone. Was the old man trying to prevent his son's escape?

Only it wasn't quite so cut and dried. As attorney to Sir William Somerville, Chief Secretary for Ireland, Matthew O'Reilly enjoyed a privileged position at the

---

[35] *Freeman's Journal*, 30 September 1848, p.2.
[36] *Westmeath Independent*, 29 July 1848, p.2; *Warder and Dublin Weekly Mail*, 29 July 1848, p.7.

heart of the establishment. Though nominally subordinate to the Lord Lieutenant, in practice, the Chief Secretary was responsible for the day-to-day governance of Ireland and, as Sommerville's attorney, any taint of suspect politics could cost Matthew his position and his livelihood. Eugene's radicalism, therefore, had put more than his own life and liberty in jeopardy.

Matthew needed time to assess his options and could ill afford to allow his son the opportunity to get up to further mischief. On the other hand, overt intervention to protect him could end up labelling Eugene a traitor. And so Matthew had played for time, locking Eugene in the office and his co-conspirators out of the house. Short of breaking down doors and drawing unwanted attention to themselves, there was little Eugene's comrades could do about it until Matthew returned the following morning.

Mullen, Barry, and Evans had already taken to their heels, but Luby, reluctant to abandon his friend, had not. He and Eugene had sworn an oath to stick together, come what may. He told the clerk he intended to remain. Making his bed in the manger, with a carpet bag donated by the clerk for a pillow, he settled down for the night.[37]

---

[37] N.L.I., Thomas Clarke Luby letters, MS 332, p.11.

ARREST AND IMPRISONMENT

LUBY WAS WOKEN the following morning by the clerk, who brought him a basin of water, a towel, and a comb. Eugene, the clerk informed him, was still locked in the office, and his father had yet to arrive.[38] Asking the clerk to arrange for him to meet with Eugene at noon, Luby left to get some breakfast.

It was still early when Luby arrived at the London Tavern, where the staff had just begun to lay the tables. Situated on D'Olier Street, the tavern was the nearest watering hole to the offices of the *Nation* and the first to receive the daily papers. If reliable intelligence were to be had, it would be there. His eyes lit upon the headline: 'Fresh Arrests'.

This was the first that Luby had heard of the fate of the Clontarf men. If even one of them broke under questioning, the police would be calling on the O'Reillys. Without waiting for his breakfast, Luby ran from the tavern. He didn't stop running until he reached Dorset Street.

He knocked urgently at the O'Reillys' door and was let into the hall, where Eugene's father and mother were attempting to hold Eugene back. Matthew O'Reilly was a stout man. His heft alone was sufficient to block his son's escape. Eugene's older brother, James, was attempting to calm the hysteria.

'Eugene,' cried Luby excitedly. 'Come along with me without delay. The Clontarf men are arrested; this is no place for you.'

Matthew O'Reilly let go of his son and, fists raised,

---

[38] Ibid., p.12.

advanced on Luby. 'You desperate villain,' he sputtered. 'You desperate villain.' His wife, Mary, fixed Luby with 'a dragon-like glare' while muttering an 'inarticulate wrath'.

Eugene stamped his foot in fury. 'Damn it, sir,' he berated his father. 'What do you mean by treating my friend in this manner.'

The old man was not to be pacified. Seeing no good could come of a confrontation, James calmly approached Luby.

'I presume you are Mr. Luby,' he said with a courteous bow. 'I hope you will kindly make allowance for my father's and mother's state of feeling. I hope you will understand.'

'Oh, yes,' said Luby, recovering his composure. 'I understand everything. I can make every allowance, but would you oblige me by stepping out into the street and having a few moments conversation with me.'

As Eugene attempted to reason with his parents, James stepped into the street, informing Luby that the family were planning to get Eugene quietly out of the country. This troubled Luby. The uprising was in its early days. One aborted confrontation would not determine the course of the campaign. To take Eugene out of the country when there was still so much to be done seemed excessive. Indeed, the proclamation of a provisional government was just days, if not hours away. To flee now might be interpreted as cowardice.

Luby insisted that, while loath to interfere in O'Reilly family matters, he and Eugene had agreed to act in concert. He was reluctant, therefore, to leave the city until he had heard his friend's final word on the matter. He would give the family time to discuss the situation and meet either Eugene or James at the corner of Dominick Street at noon. Luby walked away, convinced that his friend had erred in not leaving immediately.[39]

---

[39] Ibid., p.13.

Arrest and Imprisonment

After a flying visit to his parents to have breakfast, clean himself up, and collect some fresh clothes, Luby returned to the corner of Dominick Street and Dorset Street only to find the O'Reillys' clerk waiting for him with a note from James. Eugene, said the note, had been arrested. As it would be imprudent to return home a second time, Luby chose instead to hang around the city and await news of the wider rebellion.

The following day, Saturday, 29 July 1848, William Smith O'Brien, the leader of the Confederate movement, arrived in the vicinity of Ballingarry, Co. Tipperary, to find that the Catholic clergy had come out against him and that the support he'd been promised had failed to materialise. Of those that did turn up, many drifted away when he refused to commandeer provisions from the local population.

1. The attack on the Widow McCormack's House, 29 July 1848.

With the few who remained, O'Brien laid siege to forty-six well-armed police who had taken refuge in the Widow McCormack's cottage at Farrenory near Ballingarry. The confrontation resulted in the deaths of two of his men and the dispersal of the remainder. The failure to muster sufficient recruits would later be blamed by many on O'Brien's incompetence. Eugene, for his part, would blame the Church:

> From accounts I afterwards heard from Dan Hartnett of Newcastle, and Eugene O'Reilly, a nearly general cry of anathema and proscription echoed against the revolutionary leaders and the movement itself from the altars of South Leinster and North and East Munster. The priests of the Diocese of Ossery were particularly distinguished for the number and malignancy of their attacks.[40]

By the time Luby returned to Dublin, news of Eugene's arrest had hit the papers. Reports were being spun in favour of his father, and Eugene portrayed as a naïve dupe led astray by his elders.

> Mr Eugene O'Reilly, a rather prominent leader of the Confederates, and Mr James F. Lalor, of *Felon* notoriety, and Mr Halpin, the Secretary of the Irish Confederation, have been arrested under the Habeas Corpus Suspension Act. Mr. O'Reilly surrendered himself at the instance, or rather the compulsion, of his father, a reputable solicitor, who accompanied his son to the police office.[41]

Only Eugene hadn't allowed himself to be marched to the police station. His father, placing his faith in the influence of Sir William Somerville, had instead called the police to his house and surrendered his son under the Habeas Corpus Suspension Act.[42] Another press report of the arrest, printed in one of the Dublin journals and syndicated throughout the UK, left Luby flabbergasted.

> Very soon after it was known that Smith O'Brien and his companions had assembled in the neighbourhood of

---

[40] O'Mahony, John. *Personal narrative of my connection with the attempted rising of 1848*, National Library of Ireland, MS 868, p.14.
[41] *The Rambler,* No. 32, 5 August 1848, p.333.
[42] *Boston Pilot,* 22 April 1854, p.4.

Arrest and Imprisonment

Ballingarry, five or six young men, holding a respectable position in society, some having attained collegiate honours, went down from Dublin to join him. They reached the locality of the rencontre the evening after the affair at Widow Cormack's house; and on learning the result, and finding that the leaders were divided and dispersed, they made their way back to the county Meath, where they purposed to lie perdue for some time.

There, however, they found that the police were on their track, and they determined on returning to Dublin and taking their chance. Accordingly, they did so, and reached the city about eleven o'clock at night. Here, after consulting for a while they resolved on calling upon a young friend and asking quarters for the night until they could decide on their future location. Proceeding to the house of their friend's father, a respectable professional gentleman, whose political sentiments were greatly at variance with those of his son, they knocked at the hall-door and inquired for the person with whom they desired to communicate, who presently came down to them.

While conferring in the hall as to how he could best provide for them, his father overheard the conversation, and coming out he locked the hall-door putting the key in his pocket; and, having called for assistance, he sent a servant through the back door for the police. The son entreated, prayed, and pleaded the sacredness of a stranger seeking shelter and hospitality; but in vain. His parent was immovable; and, seeing the urgency of the case, he said to his friends, "Come, boys this shall never be."

In an instant the father was seized hold of and overpowered; he was brought into a back-parlour, and tied hand and foot in an armchair; the hall-door was opened, and the son, having seen his friends safe out of danger, returned to the house. Next day he was made a prisoner, as suspected of treasonable practices, and sent to Newgate.[43]

A couple of days after the publication of this comically inaccurate report, Luby was accosted by Matthew O'Reilly's clerk while walking down Parliament Street.

'How do you do, Mr Luby?' said the clerk. 'Old Mr

---

[43] *The Spectator,* 16 September 1848, p.4.

O'Reilly was very much obliged to you for that paragraph that appeared in the papers about Mr Eugene.'

'What paragraph?' enquired Luby. 'What do you mean?'

'Oh, that paragraph about his son and himself.'

'Why surely you don't imagine that I'd be a party to such a ridiculous fabrication as that,' snapped Luby.

'Oh, yes,' said the clerk. 'We understood it at once. Mr O'Reilly felt very grateful. It was just the sort of thing wanted...'

'I tell you,' Luby interrupted. 'I know nothing about it. I wouldn't, for any consideration, have anything to say to such a lying concoction.'

Alas, the more Luby denied authorship of the article, the more it confirmed the clerk in his assumptions. 'Oh, I know,' he muttered, nodding his head. 'Yes, yes, that's all right.'

Luby had had enough. He demanded that the clerk confirm his intention to call him a liar to his face. The clerk, with a knowing smirk, took to his heels. 'Oh, that's all right,' said he as he fled. 'It's all right; I understand.'[44]

Eugene's arrest proved fortunate for the Clontarf men. They had been facing two years in prison until news of Eugene's arrest and the leniency with which he'd been treated reached the father of one of the young men. Threatening to drag Eugene's name into his son's trial, he forced Matthew O'Reilly to deploy the same influence on behalf of his son. Matthew could hardly refuse, and the Clontarf men were allowed to plead to a lesser charge and to serve just six months in prison.

As for Eugene, remanded on a charge of 'treasonable practices and high treason', he was initially committed to Kilmainham Gaol,[45] where prison records would

---

[44] N.L.I., Thomas Clarke Luby letters, MS 332, p.18.
[45] Ibid., p.15; *Westmeath Independent*, 29 July 1848, p.2; *The Principality*, 4 August 1848, p.2; *Belfast Evening Telegraph*, 30 September 1878, p.3.

Arrest and Imprisonment

describe him as fair-skinned, with brown hair and grey eyes.⁴⁶

Matthew O'Reilly attempted to visit his son at Kilmainham, but Eugene refused to see him.⁴⁷ On 18 August, due to chronic overcrowding at Kilmainham and Newgate, Eugene and thirteen other prisoners were transferred by special train to Dun Laoghaire, where the war steamer *Reynard* awaited them. Taken aboard in chains, they were transported to Belfast.

The *Reynard* dropped anchor off Dunbar's Dock a little after midday on 19 August. Two thousand loyalist protesters awaited them on the quays.⁴⁸ Hurriedly transferred to a prison van, they were escorted to Crumlin Road Gaol by a troop of cavalry from the 6ᵗʰ Carabiniers.⁴⁹ As the prison van began to pull away, the protestors began to follow. Fearing a riot, the driver was ordered to speed up and the Carabiniers to draw their swords.⁵⁰ The gleaming steel deterred the mob and, danger averted, the prisoners were delivered safely to the gaol.

---

46 National Archives of Ireland, Registry of Prisoners Committed to Kilmainham Gaol for the Year 1848. No. 988.
47 *The Spectator*, 16 September 1848, p.4.
48 *Freeman's Journal*, 19 August 1848, p.3.
49 *Limerick Reporter*, 22 August 1848, p.2.
50 *Newry Telegraph*, 22 August 1848, p.3.

THE MAKING OF A RADICAL

HOW HAD IT come to this? How had the twenty-year-old son of a Castle official come to be leading an armed raid? Had he so little respect for his family that he was prepared to jeopardise their safety?

Born, in 1828, to Matthew and Mary O'Reilly, a middle-class couple then resident at 23 Queen Street in Dublin's north inner city,[51] Eugene O'Reilly had been named for his paternal uncle, the Rev. Eugene O'Reilly, at that time the parish priest of Navan, County Meath. His older brother, James, had been born two years previous; his younger brother, Matthew George, would be born the following year.

Journalists, apothecaries, scholars, solicitors and priests, such were the accomplishments of his immediate family. They occupied a conventional and middle-class niche in Irish society and had typically benefitted from the kind of education that lay beyond the wildest dreams of most of their fellow Catholics. Their hands had known neither callous nor blister; their bellies had never known hunger.

Back in 1786, Eugene's father, Matthew, along with his Uncle Eugene, had been sent to be educated at the Irish College in Lille, an establishment founded in 1610 to cater to the children of respectable Irish families denied a classical education by anti-Catholic legislation at home.[52] And in Lille, the O'Reilly brothers had remained until the French Revolution sent them scurrying home to Ireland, where they were promptly

---

[51] N.L.I., Irish Catholic Parish Registers; Microfilm: 08834/03.
[52] Cogan, Anthony. *The Diocese of Meath: Ancient and Modern*, J.F. Fowler, Dublin, 1862, p.245; *Freeman's Journal*, 4 Jan 1853; *The Evening Freeman*, 3 January 1853, p.3.

The Making of a Radical

enrolled in Carlow College.[53] In 1795, Eugene entered the Catholic Seminary at Maynooth, and Matthew entered the legal profession, the higher echelons of which were still closed to Catholics on account of the requirement to take the Oath of Supremacy, which recognised the King as the head of the church in Ireland.

Early in 1825, having established himself as an attorney of the Court of Exchequer,[54] Matthew married a certain Mary Smyth, of whom little is known. She would bear him three sons, James, Eugene and Matthew George. Their lives and ambitions had seemed set in stone until 1828, when Daniel O'Connell became the first Catholic to be elected to the British House of Commons in one hundred and forty years. Facing the prospect of civil war should O'Connell be denied his seat on religious grounds, the Government was forced to enact the Catholic Relief Act and consign the Oath of Supremacy to the dustbin of history. It was too late for Matthew to aspire to wig and gown, but he could be ambitious now for his sons.

For a Catholic solicitor, Matthew had done well for himself and counted amongst his clients some of the most prestigious and influential members of the British administration in Ireland.[55] His face was well known within the walls of Dublin Castle, and his name was a semi-permanent fixture on the invitation list to the Lord Lieutenant's levees.[56] Indeed, so profitable had his practice become that he was able to build a country bolthole for himself on the banks of the Boyne.

Just to the east of the town of Navan, Boyne Cottage sat on the south bank of the river, conveniently distant

---

[53] Dempsey, William. *Father Andrew Mullen 1790-1818: a study in early nineteenth century spirituality*, Theses, Durham University, 1998. http://etheses.dur.ac.uk/4742/.

[54] *Boston Pilot*, 22 April 1854, p.4.

[55] *Report from Her Majesty's Commissioners of Inquiry into the State of the Law and Practice in Respect to the Occupation of Land in Ireland: Volume 3*, HMSO, Alexander Thom, Dublin, 1845, p.859.

[56] *Southern Reporter and Cork Commercial Courier*, 16 March 1826, p.1.

from the soft gossip of the town and the shade of his celebrated brother. As the parish priest of Navan, a former president of the local Catholic seminary, a builder of schools, churches and convents, a competent violinist and a composer of religious music and poetry, the Rev. Eugene O'Reilly was widely recognised as a man of the people. His brother, Matthew, though widely known as a landlords' attorney, had thus become, almost by default, the attorney for the parish and Catholic schools of Navan.[57] Unlike his politics, Matthew's religious affiliation had never been open to question.

Having built his country bolthole, Matthew next turned his attention to his home and legal practice on Queen Street, Dublin. Lying adjacent to the King's Inns, but at the same time uncomfortably close to Benburb Street – a notorious red-light district that boasted no less than 11 brothels and 328 working prostitutes – the house was far from ideally located. The move, which had long been on the cards, had been further accelerated by the opening of a pungent pig market in nearby Smithfield.[58]

And so, in 1833, the O'Reillys moved to 29 Upper Dorset Street – a terraced four-storey-over-basement redbrick with tall chimneys, a back yard, and a stable that opened onto a back lane.[59] The street had become fashionable of late, and every attorney worth his salt knew the importance of accommodating the tastes and sensibilities of the gentry.[60]

Matthew, by now, had converted his oldest regrets into hopes for his sons, amongst whom the gift of academic excellence had, unfortunately, not been

---

[57] *Freeman's Journal*, 04 January 1853, p.3.
[58] Benburb St., was then called Barrack Street; National Archives of Ireland, CSO/RP/1826/447 and CSO/RP/1830/529.
[59] *Dublin Evening Post*, 17 August 1833, p.1; *The Pilot*, 16 October 1833, p.3.
[60] *Dublin Almanac and General Register of Ireland*, Pettigrew and Oulton, Dublin, 1835, pp.235-236; *Select Committee on Fictitious Votes, Ireland 1837-1838*, Dublin, 1839, p.110.

distributed evenly. As a result, his greatest hopes and a sizeable portion of his income were now invested in Eugene, who, alone amongst his progeny, appeared to possess the intellectual capacity to aspire to the bar. And so, sometime about 1837, Eugene was torn from his family and packed off to Clongowes College, a Jesuit boarding school situated in the rolling green pastures of Clane, in Co. Kildare.[61] At fifty guineas per annum, the fees were exorbitant, but O'Connell had sent his sons to Clongowes, and where O'Connell led, Matthew O'Reilly was more than content to follow.

Clongowes offered its students ample opportunity to network and make influential connections but, more importantly for an aspirant barrister, it also provided instruction in the *Eloquentia Perfecta*, a pedagogical tool employed by the Jesuits to develop the rhetorical skills of eloquence and persuasion. Delivered largely through the medium of debating competitions, the training was considered ideal preparation for a career in law, politics, and, of course, the church.[62]

With James and Matthew continuing to be privately educated at home, the burden of their father's expectations fell squarely on the shoulders of Eugene, who was taken to a gentleman's outfitter and measured for the college's iconic blue blazer with brass buttons, yellow cashmere waistcoat, corduroy trousers and rabbit-skin cap.[63] This colourful uniform, designed to make the wearer stand out from the crowd and awaken in him an awareness of his privilege and moral responsibilities, was also intended to foster the kind of patrician assurance and convivial grace that had long

---

[61] Burtchaell & Sadlier, *Alumni Dublinenses*, p. 640.
[62] Murphy, Thomas R.E. "Recusant Constitutionalist Ultramontanism: Rhetorical Practice at Clongowes Wood and Holy Cross, 1814-1920", in *Crossings and Dwellings: Restored Jesuits, Women Religious American Experience 1814-2014*, eds. Kyle B. Roberts & Stephen Schloesser J.S., Brill, Leiden & Boston, 2017, pp.256-260.
[63] Corcoran, Timothy. *The Story of Clongowes Wood 1450-1900*, Catholic Truth Society of Ireland, 1900, p.17; Cullen, Brendan. *A Short History of Clongowes College*, Clane, 2011.

been the preserve of Protestant 'squireens'.

Debating competitions were a mainstay of the educational fabric at Clongowes, but in the voicing of opposing viewpoints, they could not help but invoke visions of alternative realities, and the intellectual curiosity that this spawned could not always be contained. More than one Clongowes alumnus would go on to forsake the philosophy of service for the ideals of revolution.

One such student was Thomas Francis Meagher. Five years ahead of Eugene at Clongowes, he would, in later life, become a friend and revolutionary comrade. Wrapping the *Eloquentia Perfecta* in a green flag, Meagher would turn it towards the type of rhetorical idealism that was so often the precursor to revolution,[64] and when he did, Eugene O'Reilly would not be long in following.

Eugene's brothers, meanwhile, appear to have finished their private education in 1841, when the Jesuits opened a new school on Great Denmark Street. Less than a ten-minute walk from the O'Reilly home, the new school was the next best thing to Clongowes in terms of education, if not the social status of its students.[65] James, the more diligent and hardworking of the two, did reasonably well under the Jesuits, but Matthew George was not academically inclined.

James would be admitted to King's Inns in January of 1842 but, having served less than a year as an apprentice to his father would be allowed to leave the family practice and enter Trinity College to study engineering under Doctor Thomas Luby.[66] Why James was allowed to suspend his legal apprenticeship is unknown, but it may have had something to do with

---

[64] Murphy, "Recusant Constitutionalist Ultramontanism: Rhetorical Practice at Clongowes Wood and Holy Cross, 1814-1920", pp. 270-271.
[65] *King's Inns Admission Papers 1607-1867*, Irish Manuscripts Commission, Dublin, 1982, p.386.
[66] Burtchaell & Sadlier, *Alumni Dublinenses,* p. 640.

The Making of a Radical

Eugene having by now become the preferred heir.

Eugene had done well at Clongowes, well enough at any rate that, on 12 January 1843, he matriculated to Trinity College to study under Dr. Mountifort Longfield Q.C., Regius Professor of Feudal and English Law.[67] Freed from the supervision of the Jesuits, however, he slipped into a life of dissipation and radicalism, sloughed off the burden of parental expectations, embraced republicanism, and grew to resent his father's politics and desire to live through his children.

Disappointment would not have begun to convey Matthew O'Reilly's emotions at this time, and while it is possible that Eugene was quietly expelled from Trinity, it is equally likely that his father had discreetly removed him to spare the family the embarrassment and the unnecessary expense. Whatever the reason, Eugene would never graduate.

And so, with Eugene having scuppered his chances of ever being called to the bar, James now found himself also being withdrawn from Trinity and asked to resume his legal apprenticeship. He was joined, rather optimistically, in May 1845, by his youngest brother, Matthew George, who was similarly admitted to King's Inns as an apprentice solicitor.

Five months later, in a last-ditch attempt to turn Eugene's life around, an apprenticeship application was also made to King's Inns on his behalf.[68] But every apprentice was required to sign the Oath of Allegiance before his apprenticeship could be ratified, and Eugene stubbornly refused to do so.[69]

Eugene's radicalism appears to have been rooted as much in the question of land rights as in filial defiance. Land usage had been a pet subject of

---

[67] Ibid; Index to Admissions Records, 1829-1847, Trinity College Dublin, MUN V 24/3,O fol.77r.
[68] *King's Inns Admission Papers 1607-1867*, Irish Manuscripts Commission, Dublin, 1982, p.386.
[69] *Cork Examiner*, 12 February 1849, p.2; *Boston Pilot*, 17 March 1849, p.3.

Mountifort Longfield, his professor at Trinity – a man whose views on the subject were often more informed by economics than morality or justice. As an attorney of the Court of Exchequer, furthermore, Matthew O'Reilly's livelihood was largely dependent upon the patronage of the landed gentry. Indeed, the greater part of his working life would have been spent on the purchase and sale of land and the chasing down of unpaid rent: processes that, in times of widespread crop failures, inevitably led to evictions.

In contrast, Eugene's paternal uncle, the Rev. Eugene O'Reilly, had founded a secondary school and seven national schools in Navan and introduced the Society of St Vincent de Paul to the town to aid the poorest families. He had also created cooperative workshops to employ indigent females and had openly supported the Tenant Right League. While his father had been busy championing the rights of landlords, Eugene's homonymous uncle had been championing the rights of the poor.

Only in their abhorrence of violence and opposition to any creed that would embrace or promote it were Eugene's father and uncle on the same political page. Indeed, back in 1838, the pair had united to inform on three men who were later arrested on charges of sedition, with Matthew playing a prominent role in their prosecution.[70] Matthew O'Reilly, therefore was not the kind of man to accept his son's radical politics lying down. If Eugene was determined to sabotage his prospects and embarrass the family, then he would do so without parental support.

Eugene was now left with little option but to pursue a military career – the military being the only profession, apart from the law and the church, which was considered compatible with the status of gentleman. But without parental assistance, the purchase of a commission in the British Army was

---

[70] *The Pilot*, 31 July 1839, p.3.

The Making of a Radical

beyond his means, and pride inhibited him from enlisting in the lower ranks. He had little choice, therefore, but to head for the continent.

An Irish correspondent to an American newspaper would later report Eugene to have secured, about this time, a lieutenancy in the Austrian hussars. Austria had long been a draw for impoverished Irishmen as the Austrians viewed the selling of commissions as corruption and promotions, in theory, were based on ability alone.[71] It did not work out as planned.[72]

> ... he sought military life and adventure in Austria, where he obtained a lieutenancy in a hussar regiment. He was just the right sort of material for that branch of the service. He stood about five feet ten inches, had a lithe, active frame, red hair, sanguine temperament, bright restless blue eyes, a handsome face and a well-developed forehead.
>
> After serving for some time with distinction, his impulsive, erratic, Celtic nature and love of adventure – some said there was a lady in the case... – led him into difficulty. He quarrelled with his superior officer and challenged him to mortal combat, for which offence against discipline he was forced to leave the service.[73]

The problem with the above is that little evidence can be found to support it. His name does not appear in the official records of officers or junior officers.[74] If ever he *did* serve, it was most probably at a much junior rank.

The rest of the anonymous American's assertions about Eugene's military career, however, can be

---

[71] Harvey, Karen J. "The Wild Geese in the Service of Imperial Austria: Captain John Bellew", in *The Journal of the Royal Society of Antiquaries of Ireland*, vol. 118, 1988, pp. 6-7.

[72] *The Sun*, (N.Y.), 26 May 1869, p.3; *The Times-Picayune*, 8 Jun 1869, p.12.

[73] *The Wheeling Daily Intelligencer*, 28 May 1869, p.1.

[74] *Österreichische Militärische Zeitschrift*, Reuntes Heft, L.W. Siedel, Wien, 1846; Newerkla, Stefan Michael. "Das irische Geschlecht O'Reilly und seine Verbindungen zu Österreich und Russland Von Noahs Sohn Jafet bis zum russischen Nationaldichter Puškin" in *Diachronie – Ethnos – Tradition: Studien zur slawischen Sprachgeschichte*, Brno, Tribun EU, pp. 259–279.

verified from other sources, so perhaps there is a soupçon of truth to the story. But, however it had come to pass; the upshot of it all was that, in the early summer of 1846, still craving excitement and adventure, Eugene came home to a rapidly shifting political landscape that was waiting to offer him just that.

In June 1846, Sir Robert Peel's Tory government fell, and Lord John Russell led the Whigs into power. In return for a package of patronage that would be distributed throughout the Repeal Association – an organisation led by O'Connell and dedicated to the repeal of the Act of Union – O'Connell attempted to convince his followers to support Russell.

O'Connell's strategy was denounced by the *Nation*,[75] a newspaper staffed and run by a radical group that O'Connell had derisorily dubbed the 'Young Irelanders'.[76] Two days later, during a meeting of the Repeal Association at Conciliation Hall, Thomas Francis Meagher asserted that, were O'Connell to accept Russell's offer, the cause of Repeal would be 'purchased back into factious vassalage.'[77]

The split in the Repeal Association that was triggered by O'Connell's 'sell-out' became permanent on 29 July 1846, when William Smith O'Brien led the Young Ireland faction out of Conciliation Hall and proceeded to form a new political movement called 'The Irish Confederation', an act that triggered a slow drift towards armed insurrection.

Anathema to everything O'Connell had ever stood for, it was hardly a surprise as, the previous autumn, the potato crop had been hit by blight, and half the crop had been lost. The British prime minister, adamant that famine relief was not the responsibility of central

---

[75] *Nation*, 13 June 1846, p.1.
[76] A snide comparison with Giuseppe Mazzini's republican, anti-clerical and insurrectionist 'Young Italy' movement.
[77] Meagher, Thomas Francis. *Speeches on the Legislative Independence of Ireland. With Introductory Notes*. Redfield, New York, 1853, p.67.

The Making of a Radical

government but of local landlords and charities, insisted that only Irish resources should be used to solve what he perceived as an Irish problem. He also proceeded to dismantle the previous administration's limited efforts to provide relief.[78] The greatest famine in nineteenth-century Europe was taking place in the backyard of the wealthiest country in the world, and little was being done to stop it. Hardly a surprise, then, that even moderate liberals were now being radicalised.

And then the unthinkable happened. At the Hotel Feder in Genoa, on Saturday, 15 May 1847, O'Connell succumbed to a 'softening of the brain'. His death robbed the Repeal movement of its charismatic leader, and, in search of another, many turned to William Smith O'Brien, a forty-three-year-old Protestant landowner and the member of parliament for the county of Limerick.

Alas, O'Connell's demise, believed by many to have been hastened by the hounding of the Young Irelanders, hardened generational divisions, especially on the matters of land reform and universal suffrage, and caused such popular revulsion that, in the general election of August 1847, O'Brien would be the only Confederate to win a seat in parliament.

Enter Clongowes alumnus Thomas Francis Meagher – a fiery orator and advocate of armed insurrection. On Wednesday, 17 December, in the Pillar Room of the Rotunda Hospital, when Meagher was elected chairman of The Irish Confederation, Eugene O'Reilly was there to hear him speak.[79] He was there again on 2 February 1848, when he rose to speak in support of an amendment proposed by another eloquent firebrand, John Mitchel.[80] Three days later still, he would again

---

[78] Woodham-Smith, Cecil (1962). *The Great Hunger: Ireland 1845–1849*, Penguin, London, 1962, pp. 410–411.
[79] *Dublin Weekly Nation*, 18 December 1847, p.5.
[80] *Freeman's Journal*, 3 February 1848, p.3; Mitchel, John. *The Last Conquest of Ireland (Perhaps)*, Library Ireland, Author's Edition, 1876, p.158; Cavanagh, Michael. *Memoirs of Gen. Thomas Francis Meagher ...*, The Messenger Press, Worcester, Mass., 1892, p.84.

speak in support of Mitchel, who was calling for a campaign of civil disobedience in the form of a rent and rate strike.

In support of Mitchel, Eugene urged the people of Ireland to prepare themselves for a struggle, and warned them that 'to abstain from such preparation, lest they might offend the gentry, would cost them too dear a price, in as much as the people would perish of famine in the meantime'.[81] It was about as public an act of parental defiance as the youngster could make, as both the meeting and Eugene's contribution were reported widely in the press.

The strategic rift that now existed between Mitchel and O'Brien was slowly widening. O'Brien was anxious that the views of the landlords should be considered in the shaping of Confederate policy and that the movement be restricted to constitutional activities only. Mitchel, on the other hand, was calling for a more radical approach, so radical, in fact, that O'Brien threatened to resign if Mitchel's 'dangerous doctrines' were adopted.[82] In the end, O'Brien prevailed.

Mitchel subsequently resigned from both the council of the Confederation and his position as editor of the *Nation* and proceeded to establish his own, and significantly more radical, newspaper, *The United Irishman*,[83] the editorial goals of which he declared to be the resumption of a 'Holy War to sweep this Island clear of the English name and nation.'[84] In his public championing of Mitchel, Eugene inevitably widened the rift with his father.[85]

And then came the Paris Revolution. With political gatherings and demonstrations outlawed in France, a largely middle-class opposition began to hold a series of fund-raising banquets aimed at circumventing

---

[81] *Downpatrick Recorder*, 12 February 1848, p.2.
[82] N.L.I, O'Brien Papers, MS 449, n.d.
[83] *Dublin Weekly Nation*, 12 February 1848, p.6.
[84] *The United Irishman*, 12 February 1848, p.1.
[85] *Downpatrick Recorder*, 12 February 1848, p.2.

official restrictions on political meetings. However, on 14 January 1848, the government outlawed the next banquet, scheduled to be held on 22 February, and forced the organising committee to cancel the event.

The workers and students, who had been mobilising for several days, refused to back down. Marching boldly through the city, they overwhelmed the few municipal guards who had remained on duty and two days later overthrew both the government and King Louis Philippe I, established the Second Republic and installed the poet Alphonse de Lamartine as head of a provisional government. The revolt sent shock waves throughout Europe and raised expectations within the Irish Confederation that a bloodless coup might also be possible in Ireland.

By 15 March 1848, Eugene's profile within the Confederation had become such that, during a meeting at the Music Hall on Lower Abbey Street,[86] not only did he enter the hall in the company of William Smith O'Brien, but was also called upon to second a motion of congratulations to the French people. Addressing the assembly from the floor, he advocated the taking of inspiration from the French.[87]

'It is difficult,' he fervently declared, 'to decide which is most worthy of praise: the heroism of the French in seeking their liberty or their generous forbearance, moderation and respect for religion and the rights of property in their hour of triumph.' His contribution, received with loud cheers, was described by the *Freeman's Journal* as a 'brilliant speech'.[88]

Days later, Eugene found himself travelling to Paris as part of a Confederate delegation that included Thomas Francis Meagher, William Smith O'Brien, Richard O'Gorman, Edward Hollywood and John

---

[86] *Dublin Evening Post*, 16 March 1848, p.3.
[87] Cavanagh, Michael. *Memoirs of Gen. Thomas Francis Meagher ...*, The Messenger Press, Worcester, Mass., 1892, p.102.
[88] *Freeman's Journal*, 16 March 1848, p.3.

O'Mahony.[89] Stopping briefly in London, they were met by Meagher's father, who warned them against trusting the fortunes of their cause to the 'desperate chances of insurrection'. But it was too late. Back in Dublin, an armed revolt was already being planned.[90]

Arriving in Paris on 28 March, the Irish delegation checked into their hotels and settled down to wait their turn to address the new government. As they waited, they set about networking with the diaspora.

> Richard O'Gorman, Eugene O'Reilly, and Lord Wallscourt accompanied the deputation to the French capital, where they were received by Martin McDermott, Paris correspondent of the "Nation," and by Ledru-Rollin, who had some years previously stood on Tara by O'Connell's side, and whose sympathies for Ireland were strengthened by the fact that he had become the husband of an accomplished and patriotic Irish lady.[91]

The arrival of the Irish was observed more dismally by the British Ambassador, Lord Normanby:

> The Irish are arrived; their not presenting their address at once is not a good sign. It shows they have other business here, or that they are waiting to be better received after the overthrow of Lamartine, of which there was a vague expectation yesterday.[92]

That 'other business' was likely paramilitary training. According to the government informer, John Donnellan Balfe, the primary reason for O'Reilly and O'Gorman forming part of the delegation had been to study the guerrilla tactics that had been employed so

---

[89] Leonard, J.P. Article in *Irish World*, New York, 17 March 1877.
[90] *Boston Pilot*, 1 March 1851, p.9; Meagher, Thomas Francis. "Narrative by Thomas Francis Meagher" in Gwynn, Denis, *Young Ireland and 1848*, Cork University Press, 1949, p.275.
[91] Davis, Eugene. *Souvenirs of Irish footprints over Europe*, The Freeman's Journal Limited, Dublin, 1890, pp.109-110.
[92] Normanby, Marquis of. *A Year of Revolution from A Journal Kept in Paris in 1848*, Vol. 1, Longman, Brown, Green, Longmans, & Roberts, London, 1857, p.274.

successfully by the insurrectionists.[93] Of particular interest was the rationale behind the siting and erection of barricades, a guerrilla tactic common in continental Europe but not yet in Ireland.[94]

2. Parisian Barricades, rue Saint-Maur 1848.

As they waited impatiently for an opportunity to meet with Lamartine, a virus of disgruntlement took hold of the Irish delegation, fuelled in no small part by the superior attitude of O'Brien, who had put himself up in a separate hotel and arranged a private meeting with Lamartine to which the others were not invited.[95] Adding fuel to the fire, Meagher, O'Reilly and O'Gorman, were disheartened to discover local enthusiasm for their arrival was much less than they had been led to believe.

At 3:30 pm on Tuesday, 3 April, Eugene joined the Confederate delegation at the Hotel de Ville as they

---

[93] *Reports of John Balfe, March 1848.* Clarendon Papers, Irish Box 34, Bodleian Library, Oxford; Ibid., 17 April 1848.
[94] Kinealy, Christine. 'The springtime of the peoples?' in *Repeal and Revolution,* Manchester University Press, 2013, pp.158-182; Leonard, John Patrick. Article in *Irish World,* 17 March 1877; *The Principality,* 4 August 1848, p.2.
[95] N.L.I., Smith O'Brien Papers, MS 449, 1848, n.d.

finally queued to present their address to the new Republic.[96] The delegation was led by John Patrick Leonard, at that time Professor of English at the University of Paris, President of the local United Irish Club, and a member of the French *Gardes nationales*. Back on March 17, Leonard had led a delegation of Paris-based Irishmen to salute Lamartine, then head of the provisional government. On that occasion, Lamartine had praised Ireland's peaceful agitation as practised by O'Connell and expressed the hope that Ireland would soon achieve her constitutional independence. Anxious not to provoke the British, however, he stopped short of offering practical support.

During this earlier meeting, Lamartine had allegedly accepted from Leonard a tricolour of green, white and orange – a flag that Leonard had described as *le drapeau de l'Irlande*.[97] That flag, which had been manufactured by Leonard, had been inspired by a visit to the *Théâtre Français* during which the leading lady had sung a rousing performance of the *Marseillaise* while waving the French tricolour.[98] The French acceptance of Leonard's flag had provoked the British Foreign Minister, Lord Palmerston into threatening to close the British Embassy and forced the postponement of Lamartine's meeting with the Irish delegation, then scheduled to take place on April 1.[99]

With the encouragement of his Irish wife, the French Minister of the Interior, Alexandre Ledru-Rollin, had wanted to offer French support to the Irish.

---

[96] Cavanagh, Michael. *Memoirs of Gen. Thomas Francis Meagher ...*, The Messenger Press, Worcester, Mass., 1892, p.120.

[97] Normanby, *A Year of Revolution*, pp.243-244; Julienne, Janick. *Un Irlandais à Paris. John Patrick Leonard, au cœur des relations franco-irlandaises (1814-1889)*, Peter Lang, Oxford, 2016.

[98] Hearne, John. M. "Meagher to Leonard, July 1849. Thomas Francis Meagher 's Last Letter Written in Ireland and Some New Information Pertaining to the Origins of the Irish Tricolour" in *Decies*, No. 65, Waterford Archaeological and Historical Society, 2009, p.62.

[99] Petler, D.N. "Ireland and France" in *Irish Historical Studies*, vol. 24, no. 96, Irish Historical Society, 1985, p.499.

The Making of a Radical

But Lamartine, fingers burnt by the tricolour incident and anxious to retain good relations with Britain, no longer did, and by the time the Young Ireland delegation arrived at the Hotel de Ville on 3 April, he was singing from a very different hymn sheet.

Resplendent in his French military uniform, Leonard was again received by Lamartine, who by now had been replaced as head of the government and demoted to Minister for Foreign Affairs.[100] Lamartine listened politely to the Irish speeches but offered little in return.[101] Eugene, the most junior member of the delegation, was included amongst the signatories to the formal address but was not invited to speak.[102]

Lamartine's attitude was a setback and not what the Confederates had expected. Back in Ireland, John Blake Dillon, anticipating French support, had already begun preparing for a September insurrection. It came as a bitter disappointment then to find O'Brien and Meagher returning home with nothing more than a tricolour.[103] And yet, despite the setback, most of the Confederates continued to believe that the Repeal of the Act of Union could be achieved *only* by armed insurrection.

On Saturday, 15 April, a soiree in honour of the returning Paris delegation was held at the Music Hall on Dublin's Abbey Street. O'Reilly and O'Gorman did not attend, having remained in Paris to complete their mission. O'Brien would mention O'Gorman in his toasts that night, but not Eugene.[104]

---

[100] *Boston Pilot*, 29 April 1848, p.3; *Cork Examiner*, 10 February 1851, p.3.
[101] Duffy, Charles Gavan, *Four years of Irish history, 1845-49*, Cassell, Petter, Galpin & Co., London, 1883, pp. 561-569; Gwynn, *Young Ireland and 1848*, p.167-168; Sloan, Robert. *William Smith O'Brien and the Young Ireland Rebellion of 1848*, Dublin, 2000, pp. 214-224.
[102] *The London Journal*, 6 May 1848, p.130.
[103] Normanby *A Year of Revolution*, p.286.
[104] Duffy, Charles Gavan, *Four years of Irish History*, 1845-49, Cassell, Petter, Galpin & Co., London, 1883, pp.569-570; *Boston Pilot,* 13 May 1848, p3.

In the meantime, as Eugene busied himself in Paris, his older brother, James, was sworn in as an attorney of the Court of Exchequer and made a partner in his father's practice.[105] At roughly the same time, his younger brother, Matthew George, abandoned his legal studies and entered the Royal Irish Constabulary as a cadet.[106] Appointed, on 29 April,[107] to the rank of third sub-inspector, he could find himself on the opposite side to his brother if the Irish insurrection proceeded as planned.

Back in Paris, on 16 April, as massive gatherings of workers took place to choose nominees for the general staff of the National Guard, a rumour spread throughout Paris that they planned to march on the Hotel de Ville and overthrow the provisional government. Within the hour, 100,000 men had been placed under arms and the Hôtel de Ville occupied by the National Guard. When the workers eventually arrived to present their nominees, they found themselves face-to-face with a unit of the *Garde nationale*,[108] in which Leonard had secured places for O'Reilly and O'Gorman.[109]

Following his return to Dublin, sometime about the end of May 1848, Eugene re-engaged with a Confederation whose leaders had, since their return from Paris, become increasingly angered by the government's mismanagement of the famine and grown increasingly militant in their public pronouncements, despite O'Brien, Meagher and Mitchel being currently on

---

[105] *Dublin Weekly Register*, 19 February 1848, p.8.
[106] National Archives of Ireland, Royal Irish Constabulary Service Records 1816-1922, Officers Register, Volume 1, Archive ref. HO 184/45.
[107] N.A.I., Royal Irish Constabulary Service Records 1816-1922, Officers Register, Volume 1, Archive ref. HO 184/45; Grand Lodge of Freemasons of Ireland, Membership Registers, Volume II, 1760-1859, No.217, 5 December 1772.
[108] Julienne, Janick. "John Patrick Leonard (1814-1889), 'chargé d'affaires d'un gouvernement Irlandais en France'" in *Etudes Irlaindaises*, No. 25-2, Presses Universitaire de Rennes, 2000, p.49.
[109] Hearne, "Meagher to Leonard..." p.62; Duffy, Charles Gavan, *Four years of Irish history, 1845-49*, Cassell, Petter, Galpin & Co., London, 1883, pp.569-570.

bail and awaiting trial on charges of sedition. The possibility of an armed rebellion was now being openly discussed, though the majority were still of the opinion that, given the famine, any action should be postponed until after the harvest.[110]

A general meeting was called for the evening of 6 June at the Music Hall on Abbey Street, and the Confederate clubs requested to march to it in paramilitary style. Declaring mass processions to be illegal, the police despatched constabulary and cavalry to the streets to stop them. On the appointed day, Eugene marched alongside Thomas Francis Meagher at the head of five hundred or so members of the Grattan Club, but when the police attempted to prevent them from marching as a single body, a scuffle broke out during which a constable was injured. Meagher was arrested and charged with assault. His arraignment took place the following day.

> Mr Eugene O'Reilly was then called to give evidence for the defence. He deposed that he walked with Mr. Meagher at the head of the club when the police interfered. Mr. Meagher and he agreed before they left the club-room, that if they received any obstruction from the police they would separate, and proceed singly to the meeting.[111]

Despite the testimony of Eugene and others, Meagher was found guilty of assault and fined £5, a considerable sum in those days.[112]

As the Paris Revolution degenerated into the bloodletting of the 'June Days' revolt, O'Brien's belief in a bloodless revolution slowly dissipated. By the time the French liberals finally gained sway over the more radical Republicans, a bloodless coup in Ireland seemed naïvely unrealistic. And yet, plans for the September uprising pressed ahead. Not even the arrest

---

[110] Bodleian Library, Clarendon Papers, Irish Box 34, Report of John Balfe, March 1848.
[111] *Dublin Evening Mail*, 7 June 1848, p.3.
[112] Ibid.

and transportation of John Mitchel were allowed to derail the timetable, and plans to rescue him were shelved lest it spark a premature uprising.

With Mitchel gone, the remaining leaders of the Confederation now dispersed throughout the country to organise and recruit volunteers, with Eugene and Richard Barnewall deployed to recruit in rural Meath. It was an onerous and thankless task. The starving poor had other priorities. Described by Charles Gavan Duffy as 'a soldierly young fellow, whose frank demeanour inspired confidence and affection',[113] Eugene was also elected president of one of the Confederate clubs.[114]

On 1 July, an article in the *Dublin Weekly Nation* observed that the 'rude disorganisation of the mob' was finally being replaced by 'the strictness and discipline of an army'.[115] The British government's response to that news was to suspend the Habeas Corpus Act and empower the police to imprison their political opponents in Ireland without trial. A plan, nevertheless, soon evolved for Eugene to seize the barracks at Blanchardstown, a task that proved more difficult in practice than it had appeared in theory. It ended in failure, imprisonment, and the perilous embarrassment of his father. Whatever the future held for Eugene, it was by now obvious that it would be in some foreign field. Opportunities at home were few and far between for convicted felons.

---

[113] Duffy, *Four years of Irish history, 1845-49*, p.671.
[114] *Boston Pilot*, 17 March 1849, p.3; Ibid., 14 February 1874, p.3; Ibid., 17 March 1849, p.3; *Cork Examiner*, 21 February 1849, p.2; Gwynn, *Young Ireland and 1848*, p.212.
[115] *Dublin Weekly Nation*, 1 July 1848, p.7.

NOVARA TO KOMÁROM

IN EARLY SEPTEMBER 1848, Eugene's mother made her way to Belfast in the hope of seeing her son. Eugene, however, was no more willing to see *her* than he had been to see his father.[116] And yet, despite having been betrayed and disowned by his son, Matthew O'Reilly's efforts to secure his release never flagged and, on 30 September 1848, through the influence of Sir William Somerville, a warrant was issued authorising Eugene's transfer back to Dublin.

One week later, in an act of such blatant favouritism that it must have elicited a degree of wonder and resentment amongst his fellow prisoners, Eugene was taken from Belfast to the Richmond General Penitentiary at Grangegorman. Reports of the transfer described him as 'a young man of estimable qualities' whose case had 'excited much sympathy'. Some reporters even claimed that Matthew had had his son arrested to *prevent* him from joining 'any rash or hopeless enterprise'.[117]

Eugene, of course, had not only freely joined that 'rash and hopeless enterprise' but was widely known, in Dublin at least, to have been one of its organisers. Lewis Moore, a grocer from Merrion Street and a witness in the subsequent trial of Charles Gavin Duffy, would swear to that under oath.[118] The papers, nevertheless, remained sympathetic.

At the highest levels of government, it seemed, a blind eye was being deliberately turned to Eugene's radical activities and a propaganda campaign in his

---

[116] *The Pilot*, 15 September 1848, p.3; *The Spectator*, 16 September 1848, p.4.
[117] *The Pilot*, 9 October 1848, p.4.
[118] *Weekly Freeman's Journal*, 14 April 1849, p.4.

favour discreetly sanctioned. The first of a series of inexplicable interventions on his behalf, it would later be used to corroborate rumour and innuendo regarding his 'true' parentage, of which more later.

3. Richmond General Penitentiary, Grangegorman.

On Tuesday, 7 November 1848, just one month after his transfer from Belfast, Eugene was released.[119] He hung around Dublin for a while and, despite the conditions of his bail, remained in contact with his fellow Confederates, even daring to visit Smith O'Brien in prison.[120] But, with honourable employment almost impossible for a former rebel to find at home, he decided once more to try his luck abroad.[121]

In December 1848, he arrived in Paris, where he was briefly reunited with Richard O'Gorman. The pair had not met since Eugene's arrest when O'Gorman had fled to Constantinople to lay low for a while.[122] The

---

[119] *Boston Pilot*, 17 March 1849, p.5; *Dublin Evening Packet and Correspondent*, 12 October 1848, p.3; Parliamentary Papers, Vol. 49, Great Britain, Parliament, 1849, Habeas Corpus Suspension Act (Ireland), p.1.
[120] *Dublin Evening Mail*, 17 January 1862, p.2.
[121] *Boston Pilot*, 22 April 1854, p.4.
[122] *Freeman's Journal*, 21 December 1848, p.3; *Dublin Evening Post*, 21 December 1848, p.2; *Dublin Weekly Register*, 23 December 1848, p.8.

latter was now on his way to America.[123]

Eugene, for his part, had somehow managed to secure a letter of recommendation from the British Foreign Secretary, Lord Palmerston (to whom he would later send intelligence reports), and was currently on his way to Sardinia, then at war with Austria.[124] Exactly how Palmerston's recommendation had been procured remains a mystery, but powerful influence had obviously been employed.

In February 1849, Eugene finally arrived in Sardinia, where he enlisted in the Sardinian Cavalry as a lance corporal on a salary of 180 francs per month.[125] He was not long in seeing action. On 23 March, seventy thousand Austrian troops advanced on a Sardinian army so vastly outnumbered that they were quickly overwhelmed and routed. Eugene, wounded in battle, was reported to have 'fought so gallantly against the Austrians on the fatal field of Novara, he was made a lieutenant on the spot.'[126]

With the war over almost as soon as it started, the need for mercenaries quickly dissipated, and with little to keep him in Sardinia, Eugene returned to Dublin. He arrived in April 1849, just in time to attend the trial of Charles Gavan Duffy, in which he was identified as one of the ringleaders of the 'Blanchardstown Affair'.[127] The evidence against him, however, proved too weak to counter the influence that had so recently been employed

---

[123] *Dublin Weekly Register*, 23 December 1848, p.8; Finegan, Francis. "Daniel Doyle and Young Ireland" in *Studies: An Irish Quarterly Review*, vol. 38, no. 151, 1949, pp. 21, 352; Doheny, Michael. *The Felon's Track...*, W.H. Holbrooke, New York, 1849, p.166.

[124] Regan, Timothy J. *The Lost Civil War Diaries: The Diaries of Corporal Timothy J. Regan*, Trafford Publishing, Manchester, 2003, p.335.

[125] *Illustrated London News*, 24 February 1849, p.123; *Boston Pilot*, 30 July 1870, p.5; Ward, Thomas Humphry. *Humphry Sandwith: a memoir*, Cassel and Company, London, 1884, p.210.

[126] *Indian Statesman*, 8 April 1874, p.4; *Australian Town & Country Journal*, Sydney, 25 July 1874, p.27.

[127] For a list of others arrested and bailed in connection with this affair see *The Waterford News*, 2 February 1849, p.2.

on his behalf, and he was never re-arrested.[128]

Eugene was still in Ireland that autumn when, in response to an invitation from recently released Thomas Clarke Luby, he travelled to Templederry to pay his respects to Father John Kenyon, a clerical firebrand and vocal supporter of John Mitchel. Kenyon's suspension, and his silencing by the Catholic Church had played a major part in the failure of the rebellion in Munster.[129] Having urged his parishioners to gather arms at an assembly in Templederry on 16 April 1848, Kenyon had surprised Dillon and Meagher when they arrived in Templederry in late July by refusing to assist them or to encourage his flock to do so. Claiming that O'Brien's chivalrous approach to insurrection had been doomed to failure, Kenyon had advised Dillon and Meagher against following it and encouraged them instead towards guerilla warfare.

A tall, pale, and scholarly man, Kenyon was a fascinating and witty conversationalist unafraid to hold controversial views. He had earlier been moved from his parish in Ennis for having harassed a family that had converted to Protestantism, supporting the idea of non-denominational university education, and refusing to condemn the practice of slavery. Unlike many of his religious brethren, he was opposed to unconditional pacifism.

Despite his failure to support the rebellion, Kenyon, who had suffered surprisingly little ill will from his fellow Young Irelanders, would continue to claim that his decision to fall silent had had little to do with his being allowed to keep his parish but rather the disorganised nature of the rebellion. Had it been properly organised, he insisted, he would have been happy not only to join it, but to encourage his parishioners to follow suit.

O'Reilly made our reverend host and myself laugh heartily,

---

[128] *Dublin Weekly Register*, 14 April 1849, p.7.
[129] Duffy, *Four years of Irish History, 1845-49*, p.671.

by telling us how the Blanchardstown adventure had funnily helped to magnify, in Italy, his reputation as a desperate fighting man. In some way or other, vague rumors about the affair had got abroad among his Sardinian brother officers. He had come to be pointed out as a regular Irish fire eater, who had got up "on his own hook", in his own country, some quixotic revolutionary enterprise. This formidable reputation had so far served him, that no one had shown any great stomach for fastening a quarrel on him. In short, the "Drawcansir" tribe had given him "a wide berth".[130] Indeed he was generally too amiable to give one just grounds of quarrel.[131]

After the war, Eugene, by now a battle-hardened veteran with money in his pocket and a soldier's predilection for living for the day, returned to Dublin and proceeded to 'let himself loose in gay dissipation, as in his college days of yore'. But civilian life no longer suited him, and when the money began to run out, he took off again, this time to Hungary,[132] where, during the early months of 1849, the Hungarian army had achieved several significant victories in their fight for independence from Austria and in installing Lajos Kossuth as governor-president of Hungary. Their progress was followed closely in Ireland, where sympathy for their cause was widespread.[133]

Just before the onset of winter, like many of his former colleagues in the Sardinian Cavalry, Eugene took himself to Budapest and secured a commission as a captain in the Hungarian hussars, most likely in one of the Sardinian regiments.[134] The winter campaign was exceptionally harsh. Consisting of innumerable skirmishes rather than all-out battles, it was also

---

[130] Drawcansir – a bullying, swaggering, braggart.
[131] N.L.I., Thomas Clarke Luby letters, MS 332, p.19.
[132] *The Sun*, (New York), 26 May 1869, p.3.
[133] Zarka, Zsuzsanna. *Images and perceptions of Hungary and Austria-Hungary in Ireland, 1815-1875*, Ph.D. Thesis, Dept. of History, National University of Ireland, Maynooth, 2010.
[134] *The Sun*, (New York), 26 May 1869, p.3.

extremely costly. Scarce a day passed that didn't see an engagement of some description, and with days spent in incessant skirmishing and nights in a battle to stay warm in the clammy cold, soldiers quickly fell prey to exhaustion and disease. Friends were made and lost in a matter of weeks.

Frequently, it was only a few sword cuts that individual horsemen would exchange with one another, but occasionally, major battles would be fought, and he would have to ride in the face of cannon fire. At Gyöngiös, two squadrons of Hungarian hussars were ordered to charge no less than three times into a stubborn square of Austrian infantry, only to fall in files beneath the steady fire of the Austrians. Only on the third charge did they break the square and ply 'their sharp swords with destructive fury'.[135]

In August 1849, following the famous Second Battle of Komárom and the subsequent 'Surrender at Világos', Eugene fled with his defeated colleagues to Sardinia, where he was allowed to exchange his bloodstained Hungarian uniform for a fresh Sardinian one and, more importantly, resume his previous commission.[136] It was during this second spell with the Sardinian Army that Eugene is reported to have sent intelligence reports to Lord Palmerston concerning the make-up of the Sardinian Army. Detailing the amalgamation of its constituent parts, he even predicted the creation of a united Italy.[137] Palmerston thanked him for the intelligence and expressed a desire to meet should he ever return to England.[138]

---

[135] Baron, W. *Scenes of the Civil War in Hungary, in 1848 and 1849: With the Personal Adventures of an Austrian Officer in the Army of the Ban of Croatia*, E.H. Butler & Co., Philadelphia, 1850, pp. 112-119.

[136] *Indian Statesman*, 8 April 1874, p.4; *Australian Town and Country Journal*, Sydney NSW, 25 July 1874, p.27; *Boston Pilot*, 30 July 1870, p.5; *Empire* (Sydney), 21 July 1874, p.3.

[137] Regan, Timothy J. *The Lost Civil War Diaries: The Diaries of Corporal Timothy J. Regan*, Trafford, Manchester, 2003, p.335.

[138] *The Sun*, (New York), Wednesday, 26 May 1869, p.3; *Indian Statesman*, 8 April 1874, p.4.

That an Irish rebel should be writing to the British Foreign Secretary was unusual: that his letter could make it all the way to Palmerston's desk, even more so; let alone the fact that Palmerston would reply with an invitation to meet. It suggests that the letter had been delivered by means of a trusted third party, such as an ambassador or consul. It would not be the last time that this happened.

4. Henry Temple, Lord Palmerston.

Eugene returned to England after the war and, on 1 January 1851, attempted to enlist in the 10th Hussars, then based at Maidstone in Kent, the home of all cavalry regiments stationed in India and the place where all cavalry recruits were sent to be trained.[139] Despite his political connections and his battlefield experience, the army refused to recognise his Sardinian rank, and he was forced to enlist as a private, the lowest rank possible.[140] From 27 February to 1 March 1851, he was listed in regimental records as hospitalised. No record of the reason can be found, but it must have been serious, for by the end of March he was recorded as being on 'recruiting duties awaiting transfer or discharge'.

One newspaper report would later suggest that he was briefly been transferred to the Inniskilling Dragoons and promoted to the rank of either riding sergeant or lance-corporal before eventually buying himself out.[141] But, even if that were true, his rank upon discharge would still have been several ranks below the captaincy he had held in Sardinia. He had higher ambitions than that.

Back in Dublin, on 7 May 1853, St. Michael's Church in Dun Laoghaire, Eugene's brother, James, married Susan McDonnell, only daughter of Alexander McDonnell of Ballymore, Co. Westmeath.[142] Following the wedding, the couple moved in with James' parents

---

[139] National Archives UK, Worldwide Army Index, WO 12/12844, Form 3a, Pay &c. of Depots or Detachments of Regiments on the East India Establishment, p.11; *Maidstone Journal and Kentish Advertiser*, 6 March 1858, p.5; National Archives UK, Kew, Surrey, *Census Returns of England and Wales, 1851*, Class: HO107; Piece: 1617; Folio: 305; Page: 16; GSU roll: 193518.

[140] National Archive UK, *Census Returns of England & Wales, 1851*, Class: HO107; Piece: 1617; Folio: 305; Page: 16; GSU roll: 193518.

[141] National Archives UK, WO 12/12844 and WO 12/950; *Australian Town and Country Journal*, Sydney NSW, 25 July 1874, p..27 (cf. *Levant Herald*); *Indian Statesman*, 8 April 1874, p.4; *Empire* (Sydney), 21 July 1874, p.3; Beatson to Vivian, 21 September 1855, c.f. Beatson, W.F. *The War Department and the Bashi Bazouks*, W. Clowes & Sons, London, 1856, p.84; *South Eastern Gazette*, 9 March 1858, p.4.

[142] *Cork Examiner*, 11 May 1853, p.3; N.L.I., Roman Catholic Marriage Registers, St. Michael's, Kingstown, 7 March 1834 – 30 April 1855 (May 1853), p.40; N.L.I., Irish Catholic Parish Registers; Microfilm Number: Microfilm 09073/03.

at the family home on Lower Gardiner Street.[143] It is unknown if Eugene attended the wedding, but his brother's nuptials could not have left him untouched. James was now settled, the path of his life mapped out, a family of his own doubtlessly to follow. Eugene, on the other hand, had little to show for the passing years and could no longer even sport an officer's uniform. By summer, his patience had run out.

The Russians at this time were attempting to expand their influence over the Middle East and the eastern Mediterranean at the expense of the declining Ottoman Empire. As Britain, France, and Sardinia viewed the Russian power grab as a danger to their respective trade routes, an alliance was forged with Turkey to stop them. Commissions were now going a-begging in Turkey, with instant promotions of at least one step in rank available to European recruits. The Turks, however, had a long and decidedly mixed experience with foreign mercenaries. They would not accept just anyone.

On 13 September 1853, Eugene travelled from Maidstone to Belvedere, joined the local masonic lodge, and proceeded immediately to London to take up his long-standing invitation from Palmerston, now the British Home Secretary. Outlining his military career and reminding Palmerston of the intelligence he had provided from Sardinia, he sought a letter of recommendation for a commission in the Turkish Army. Admitting to his part in the 1848 rebellion, he expressed the hope that it would not prove to be an insurmountable impediment to service abroad.

'Not at all, my dear fellow,' Palmerston is reputed to have replied. 'On the contrary, it is one of your strongest recommendations. Anyone having the temerity to embark on an enterprise so desperate has just the sort of mettle we require in the current war.' [144]

---

[143] No. 99 Lower Gardiner Street to be exact.
[144] *The Sun*, (New York), 26 May 1869, p.3.

To understand the surprise that this must have elicited amongst his former comrades in the Irish Confederation, one needs only to note that, during the recent famine in Ireland, Palmerston had evicted some 2,000 of his tenants for non-payment of rent and claimed it vital to the Irish economy that an entire class of Irish society, namely 'Small Holders' and 'Squatting Cottiers', be eliminated.[145] In short, Palmerston was the living antithesis of everything that Eugene had once stood for, the kind of absentee landlord for whom, just four years previous, he would have nursed the deepest repulsion. And yet, despite all of that, Eugene would not have been alone in such a radical realignment of priorities, for throughout Europe, revolutionary rhetoric was slowly being replaced by hard-nosed pragmatism. People just wanted peace and stability.

Irish mercenaries and political fugitives were not uncommon in Turkey, where sympathy for the Irish cause had existed at the highest levels since the start of the potato famine.[146] Back in 1847, for example, at the behest of his Irish physician, Dr Justin McCarthy, the Sultan had sent several shiploads of wheat and maize to Ireland. The ships had arrived in May but, refused permission to land in Belfast or Dublin by the British government, they had secretly sailed to Drogheda, where they had been received as heroes. To this day, the crescent moon forms part of the city coat of arms to commemorate this event.[147]

---

[145] Anbinder, Tyler. "Lord Palmerston And The Irish Famine Emigration" in *The Historical Journal*, Vol. 44, Issue No.2, Cambridge University Press, Cambridge, 2001, pp. 441-69.

[146] The Sublime Porte was the government of the Ottoman Empire.

[147] Garland, J.L. "Reply to Query on Irish Officers in the Turkish Service, relating to Gen. Richard Guyen of Cratloe, Co. Clare" in *Irish Sword*, Vol 3, No. 11, 1957, p.132; *Sligo Champion*, 8 September 1849, p.4; *Drogheda Argus*, 15 May 1847; Dash, Mike. "Queen Victoria's £5: the strange tale of Turkish aid to Ireland during the Great Famine" in *A Blast from the Past*, 29 December 2014, online blog,

Eugene may also have been encouraged to try his hand in Turkey by Richard O'Gorman, who, in 1848, along with two other Young Irelanders, had been given shelter in the house of another of the Sultan's 'Irish' physicians, John Nassau Glascott. O'Gorman would have been well placed to advise him on the importance of impeccable references.[148] But however it came about, when Eugene eventually set out for Turkey; he did so with a letter from Palmerston recommending him to Lord Stratford de Redcliffe, the British Ambassador in Constantinople.[149] That letter would serve him well, but it would also ignite the rumours of illegitimacy that would dog him for the rest of his life: rumours, it must be said, he would never seek to disclaim.

---

https://mikedashhistory.com/2014/12/29/queen-victorias-5-the-strange-tale-of-turkish-aid-to-ireland-during-the-great-famine/, accessed 30 December 2022.

[148] John Nassau Glascott (1813-1864), youngest son of Captain Adam Glascott of New Ross; *The Gentleman's Magazine*, May 1845, p.536.

[149] *Indian Statesman*, 8 April 1874, p.4.

CONSTANTINOPLE

TOURISM CONTINUED UNABATED. This was, after all, a city of fables and childhood imaginings, a melting pot of race and religion perched on the hilly crossroads of three continents. But there came amongst the sightseers now, a new class of visitor who came, not in search of the cultural delights of lost Byzantium, but the thrill and glory of battle.

5. Constantinople, early 1850s.

As the inevitable swarm of *caiques* or water taxis descended upon the arriving ships, new arrivals could not help but notice, as they haggled for the 'best price', that the wharves from which the *caiques* had set out were teeming with a kaleidoscopic array of military uniforms and national costumes. They might even have wondered if they had not, by some queer magic, found themselves in ancient Babel, so varied were the tongues that assaulted their ears.

Pushing his way through crowds of fruit sellers, money changers and veiled beggars to engage a suitable *hamal* or porter,[150] he crossed the bay by one of three floating wooden bridges that swayed and creaked alarmingly underfoot and made his way to the Yüksek Kaldirim, a steep cosmopolitan street of wooden buildings lined with Turkish, Greek and Armenian shops. Picking his way through a midden of dead rats, dogs, cats and melon rinds, he reached, at the top, a distinctly European street lined with French shops. This was the Grande Rue de Péra, the heart of the Frankish Quarter and the European gateway to Turkey. Beyond this bustling thoroughfare, there sat a European hill station crowned with embassies and cypress trees. It was here that the British Embassy was situated.

The favoured accommodation of the well-heeled Brit was Mysseri's Hotel d'Angleterre, which overlooked the gardens of the British Embassy. Conveniently situated for balls, dinners and meetings, it was in the lobby of this hotel or at the pastry shop across the street that the wives of English officers and diplomatic officials would congregate, and the special correspondents of the London papers would forage for gossip, such as the arrival of a former Irish rebel carrying letters of recommendation from the British Home Secretary. Many a man had left his card at the embassy and never received a call, but Palmerston's letter secured Eugene an ambassadorial audience, from which he left with a recommendation to the Turkish Seraskier (War Minister), Mehmed Riza Pasha.

The breakout of military hostilities between the Tsar

---

[150] Hornby, Mrs Edmund. *In and around Stamboul*, James Challen & son, Philadelphia, 1858, p.48; Smith, Albert. *Customs and Habits of the Turks*, Higgins, Bradley and Dayton, Boston, 1857, pp. 46-48.

6. The Yüksek Kaldırım.

and the Sultan had been ignited by tensions between Catholics and Orthodox Christians over access to Jerusalem and other sacred sites. An outbreak of violence in Bethlehem had seen several Orthodox monks killed and provoked the Russians to demand equal access to religious sites and recognition of the Tsar as protector of Orthodox Christians throughout the Ottoman Empire. The Sultan had refused, and the Tsar had retaliated by invading the Ottoman principalities of Moldavia and Wallachia. Military adventurers from all over Europe, India and South America were now flocking to Constantinople to offer their swords to the Sultan.[151]

Redcliffe's recommendation saw Eugene spared the usual bureaucratic hurdles and appointed to the rank of *Bimbashi* – somewhere between major and lieutenant colonel – with a view to having him train new cavalry officers.[152] The appointment was supposedly in a consultative capacity only, battlefield command being something no Christian could normally acquire without first converting to Islam, a religious pre-requisite that would not officially be lifted until 1856. In 1853, however, desperate for experienced officers, the Turks had already begun to indulge in a degree of bureaucratic subterfuge.

At least two of the generals who had fled Hungary following the war of 1849 had been spared the necessity of conversion.[153] But, in order that the soldiers who served under them would assume them to be Muslim converts, they had been required to adopt Turkish names.[154] And so it was to be with Eugene, who was despatched that October to join the forces of Omer Pasha, the Governor of Ottoman Bosnia, under the name of Hassan Bey.[155]

At the start of the war, when the Russians positioned troops on the northern bank of the Danube, the Turks

---

[151] The Seraskeriate was the offices of the Minister of War and chief of armed forces; Ward, Thomas Humphry. *Humphry Sandwith: a memoir*, Cassel and Company, London, 1884, pp.210-211.

[152] *Indian Statesman*, 8 April 1874, p.4; The term did not actually come to signify a rank equivalent to that of major until after the restructuring of the Turkish Army in 1934.

[153] Alloul, Houssine. "Me among the Turks: Western commanders in the Late Ottoman Army and their Self-Narratives", in *European Review of History: Revue européenne d'histoire*, Vol. 27, No. 1-2, 2020, p.95.

[154] Badem, Candan. *The Ottoman Crimean War*, Brill, Leiden, 2010, p.147.

[155] *Fife Herald*, 23 March 1854, p.2.

had moved troops to the southern bank and given the Russians two weeks to withdraw. They had yet to do so. On 2 November 1853, therefore, a force of Ottoman troops crossed the Danube and entrenched themselves in front of the Russian-occupied town of Oltenitza.[156] The following day, Eugene rode out with a contingent of Ottoman cavalry on a reconnaissance mission, during which they encountered an outpost of Cossack cavalry. Five Cossacks were killed for the loss of three Turks.[157]

The following day, the Russians rode out of Oltenitza intent on attacking the Turks before they could finish entrenching themselves. They were led by a squadron of Cossacks and followed by a column of artillery. On another flank, a mass of regular Russian cavalry appeared. The Russians heavily outnumbered the Turks, and having the better artillery should have been able to overwhelm them. But they were out-thought and out-fought and by 6 pm, it was all over.[158]

During the battle, having been assigned to a cavalry division of about one hundred and fifty horsemen,[159] Eugene distinguished himself in a charge against the Russian infantry. His performance was noticed and remarked upon, not just because the fiction of his having been appointed solely in an advisory capacity had been publicly laid bare, but because his courage, horsemanship and skill with the sabre had earned him, in certain journalistic quarters, the reputation of a 'dashing sabreur'.[160]

---

[156] Engels, Frederick, "The War on the Danube", in *The Collected Works of Karl Marx and Frederick Engels: Volume 12*, International Publishers: New York, 1979, pp.516-522.

[157] Dodd, George. *Pictorial History of the Russian War 1854-5-6*, W&R Chambers, Edinburgh & London, 1856, p.37.

[158] *Empire*, Sydney (NSW), 20 February 1854, p.2.

[159] *Morning Advertiser*, 26 February 1862, p.6; *John Bull*, 1 March 1862, p.12; *Glasgow Herald*, 27 February 1862, p.2.

[160] *Morning Advertiser*, 26 February 1862, p.6

CROSSING THE BALKANS

A CHEQUERED CLUMP of white and brown patches, nestled in a horseshoe recess of wooded hills, the Bulgarian town of Shumen was approached through a landscape of wretched wattle-and-daub dwellings and packs of snarling dogs.[161] It appeared, at first, as a mass of red pantile roofs, punctuated here and there by pencil-thin white minarets or, on the eastern edge, by the tulip-like dome of the Tombul Mosque. Even from a distance, it appeared too small to be garrisoning a force of military significance.

Shumen had never been prosperous, even before the war, and many of its buildings were in no better shape than the wattle-and-daub farmhouses that had to be passed on the approach.[162] Comfortable accommodation was almost impossible to find.

> The streets and market-places, which are not wider nor more fairly paved than those of other Turkish cities, are at all times filled with soldiers, and a busy mass devoted to the satisfying of soldiers' wants ... Streams of busy people of every denomination choke the narrow spaces between the low and rickety ill-built houses; there is no passing through the bazaar where Jews and Greeks lazily loll before their wares, supremely careless whether they sell or not... In one corner, a knife grinder from the Turkish villages plies a wheel and sharpens everything from a *yataghan*[163] to a toothpick; near him sits a vendor of sweets and drinks – of these he has sorts as varied as his customers ... he is,

---

[161] At that time the town was known in English as *Shumla*.
[162] Evelyn, George Palmer. *A Diary of the Crimea*, Gerald Duckworth & Co. Ltd., London, 1954, p.35.
[163] Also called a *varsak*, the *yataghan* was a type of Ottoman knife or short sabre used extensively in Ottoman territories from the mid-16th to late 19th centuries.

accordingly, surrounded by a crowd which continuously recruits itself, and eats, and drinks, and smokes around him as if life was to be a perpetual recreation.

Another group surrounds a vendor of tobacco; a third, the maker of pancakes; whilst, in their immediate vicinity, Bashi-bozouks [164] and horse dealers are wrangling over the price of a charger not taller than twelve hands. Albanians stand by, too poor to pay but afraid to rob, and eyeing good things wistfully; whilst they scratch their dirty heads or twist themselves in their frowsy garments. Under the wooden arcades a crowd is also passing and repassing. Jews selling calico; Turkish men and women buying it. Auctions of horses and pistols and pocket handkerchiefs are held together – the prices called by hoarse but burly Turks, who deafen by their roar. Egyptians may be seen endeavouring to change a shilling banknote, whilst their cunning adversaries higgle for the discount.[165]

7. Shumen Street Scene.

---

[164] Turkish Irregular Cavalry, more commonly spelled 'Bashi Bazouks'.
[165] *Illustrated London News*, 5 April 1856, p.364.

Crossing the Balkans

This was Muslim Europe, a Europe where it was not unusual for a woman to dress so that only her eyes were visible, where the wearing of a turban or a fez never merited a second glance and where the smoking of a *nargileh* was as commonplace as in the coffee houses of Cairo. And yet, for all that, the people were still recognisably Eastern European rather than Turkish or Arabic.

It would already have been obvious to Eugene that, to advance further in Ottoman service, he would have to acquire an understanding of Islamic culture and a mastery of Ottoman Turkish, a language of complex grammar, noun-dependent articles, and verbs that changed depending on gender, mood, voice, and tense. But he had been lucky in his friendships and his new best friend, Humphry Sandwith, just happened to be a fluent Turkish speaker and a surgeon who dabbled as a foreign correspondent of *The Times*.

The widely travelled Sandwith was not a man who was easily impressed, but he liked the romantic cut of the Irishman's jib, a man he would later describe as:

> ... every inch a soldier; a splendid rider, brave as his sword, with a strong dash of the Bohemian.[166]

It was still winter. Snow blanketed the ground, and ice paralysed the streams. Camping was torturous, and scarcely a house in the town had not been asked to billet somebody. Comfortable lodgings, furthermore, could not be assigned without the personal sanction of Omer Pasha, an Austrian convert who commanded the vanguard of the Ottoman forces in eastern Wallachia.[167] Omer's bourgeois appetites and fondness for European company would often see him go out of his way to accommodate visitors of a certain social class, as one English traveller had recently had cause to celebrate:

---

[166] Ward, *Humphry Sandwith: a memoir*, pp.210-211.
[167] *Blackwood's Edinburgh Magazine*, No. 519, Vol. 85, January 1859, p.294.

As Omer was an Austrian, he had the manners of a European, but he did not disdain to exercise the ordinary rights of a Pacha. His preferred wife was an Englishwoman, but he had a harem besides, and I recollect that he was keen to find Circassian beauties as any full-blooded Turk of Constantinople. Nor was he very scrupulous even in his high position to observe the law, which forbade the purchase of female slaves... Omer was amiable and civil. He ordered a lodging to be given to me in a Turkish house which had already been surrendered, in part, to his aide-de-camps, the Prussian, Mehmet Ali Bey, and the Pole, Mahmoud Aga.[168]

Impressed by the Irishman's military bearing, Omer found Eugene a comfortable billet and, in February of 1854, entrusted him with the command of two regiments of irregular cavalry, an appointment so groundbreaking that it merited a mention in *The Times*:

The "Englishman" (Mr. O'Reilly) mentioned as having been appointed to the command of two squadrons of lancers for service on the Danube is said to be Mr. Eugene O'Reilly, the son of a respectable Dublin solicitor. If such be the case, the officer in question is "the" Mr. O'Reilly who, in 1848, and when he had scarcely attained the age of manhood, was implicated in the insurrectionary movement of that melancholy year, in consequence of which he had to fly the country on the suspension of the Habeas Corpus Act. On the strength of influential connexions at home, he subsequently obtained a commission in a Sardinian regiment of lancers and, on the breaking out of hostilities between Turkey and Russia, he volunteered his services to the army under Omar Pasha.[169]

The author of that report was most likely Sandwith's replacement for, having found himself accused by his editor of pro-Ottoman bias, Sandwith had by this time resigned his post as correspondent and enlisted with

---

[168] Crowe, Sir Joseph. *Reminiscences of Thirty-Five Years of My Life.*, John Murray, London, 1895, p.125.
[169] *The Times*, March 4, 1854, p.8.

Omer as a surgeon and interpreter. He would very soon after be deployed to Varna to serve under British general William Ferguson Beatson.[170] It would be many years before they met again.

8. Omer Pasha's audience with British visitors, Shumen, 1854.

Eugene, meanwhile, found himself celebrated in the British papers as the first Christian to have been given a battlefield command in the Ottoman Army.

> An event, which has almost the importance of a revolution, has occurred here. A young Irish officer, named O'Reilly, who fought for Italian independence at Novarra, recently offered his services to the Porte. The rank and position of *bin bachi* (major) were immediately conferred on him; but this gave him no real command – Christians being excluded, by Mussulman prejudice, from all civil and military functions.[171] Judge, then, of our surprise, when yesterday the marshal summoned Mr. O'Reilly to his presence and confided to him the command of two squadrons of lancers of the Imperial Guard. This opens a

---

[170] Ward, *Humphry Sandwith: a memoir*, pp.118-119.
[171] During the Ottoman Empire, the rank of *bimbashi* was actually closer to a British army lieutenant-colonel than a major.

breach in the old barrier of prejudices, and it is not to be feared that it will be closed up again. It will henceforth be possible for any man to render services to Turkey without being obliged to make himself a Mussulman.[172]

In Dublin, the news was met with, if not quite disbelief, then with a wry smile from John Cashel Hoey, editor of the *Dublin Weekly Nation*:

> We congratulate him [O'Reilly] on becoming the first Christian officer of the Sultan, and we hope to find him a Pasha of three tails on his next visit to Ireland.[173]

The above reports were grossly exaggerated, for while Eugene had indeed been given command of two cavalry regiments, they were about as far from 'lancers of the Imperial Guard' as it was possible to get. The cavalry regiments he had been ordered to take charge of were Bashi Bazouks, tribal mercenaries who refused to wear uniforms, looked and behaved like bandits, and were currently mustered at Calafat, a fortified town on the Danube opposite the port of Vidin.[174]

Back in October 1853, the Turks had crossed the Danube and built fortifications at the town of Calafat, provoking the Russians to march on it. The town was still under siege, and fresh attacks were believed to be imminent.[175] Getting there, however, would be no easy task in winter. Even at Shumen, a mere 184m above sea level, there was still ice in the streams.[176]

On 5 February 1854, as Eugene was preparing to leave Shumen, George Palmer Evelyn, a thirty-one-year-old English thrill-seeker, rode into town accompanied by his dragoman Constantine, a Greek.

---

[172] *Dublin Weekly Nation*, 4 March 1854, p.8; *Illustrated London News*, 4 March 1854, p.200.
[173] A Pasha's rank, distinguished by the number of horsetails on his standard was, in war, carried before him and planted in front of his tent. The highest rank was that of three tails.
[174] *Boston Pilot*, 8 April 1854, p.2.
[175] *Boston Pilot*, 22 April 1854, p.4.
[176] Evelyn, *A Diary of the Crimea*, p.36.

Evelyn's father had fought at Waterloo and he himself had served as a second lieutenant in the Rifle Brigade before taking semi-retirement and a commission in the Surrey Militia. He had not come to Shumen to enlist, or out of any sense of patriotism (Britain had yet to join the war), but, like many other 'amateurs', had travelled with dreams of martial glory and the expectation of obtaining a *firman* to join the action as an unpaid volunteer as and when it pleased him.

An impetuous and arrogant creature, Evelyn had two redeemable qualities: he was wealthy, and he spoke English. Having learned from a third party of his intention to travel to the front line, Eugene called to his lodgings the day after his arrival, accompanied by French officers, Colonel Mercier and Lieutenant-Colonel Dupuis. Ordered to proceed immediately to Calafat, they wished to invite Evelyn to make up a fourth.

Evelyn declined at first. Having suffered from headaches and diarrhoea since leaving Constantinople. The next day, however, having recovered sufficiently overnight as to be able to venture out and make some afternoon purchases at the bazaar, he called on Eugene and declared himself fit to travel.[177] And so, on Wednesday, 8 February 1854, having hired a *carvass*,[178] and a team of *surudjis*[179] to manage the pack animals, the four rode out for Calafat.

There followed a four-day mountain adventure through snow-covered passes and across raging rivers, during which they would lose a *carvass* and *surudji* to arrest following an allegation by Evelyn that they had stolen his pistol. Struggling to find fresh horses, they would regularly lodge in what another English traveller on the same route would describe as flea-ridden 'hovels.'[180] The journey was arduous and perilous, and

---

[177] Ibid.
[178] Turkish armed escort cum professional guide.
[179] A saddler cum muleteer.
[180] *Blackwood's Edinburgh Magazine*, No. DXIX, Vol. LXXXV, January 1859, p.297.

9. Balkan travellers in early 1854.

it took a heavy toll on both riders and horses.

On the fifth day, they rode out from the village of Pleven an hour after dawn. Snow had been falling through the night, covering the track so deeply in places that the horses sank to their girths. Three hours ride from the River Vit, they reached a swamp covered with wild ducks. Eugene tried to bag one with his revolver but missed. Later, for his own amusement, he fired at some vultures feeding on a carcass. His aim was no better, prompting Evelyn to regret having left his shotgun in Shumen.

At about 2 pm, they finally came within sight of the Danube and the village of Larida, where the Turks had established a garrison of 4,000 men. The following morning, the local commander promised, they would have fresh horses and a day's ride would see them in Vidin, from where they could cross to Calafat.[181] The ordeal was almost over.

---

[181] Evelyn, *A Diary of the Crimea*, pp.37-39.

THE SIEGE OF CALAFAT

A TEN-HOUR RIDE from Larida brought them to Vidin – an active port and low-lying riverside settlement on the western banks of the Danube. Surrounded and protected by flood-prone meadows and 'fever-haunted swamps,' the fortress commanded the Danube and the roads to Sofia and Ruse.[182] Approaching the town, long trains of ox carts could be seen traversing the frozen foreground. In the distance, a forest of masts rose from a brumous quayside.[183]

10. Vidin, 1854.

Beyond the quays, a pontoon bridge of boats joined Vidin to the fortress of Calafat, an isolated hamlet two miles upstream that was 'part farmhouses, part mercantile offices and shops, part residences of the proprietors'. Known as 'The Town of Roses', it was, in

---

[182] Herbert, William V. *The Chronicles of a Virgin Fortress*, Osgood, McIlvaine & Co., London, 1896, p.4.
[183] Evelyn, *A Diary of the Crimea*, p.39.

summer, a pretty place of rose bushes, centuries-old oaks and leafy chestnut trees surrounded by golden fields of wheat and barley. Even in the frosty light of winter, it had a prosperous and whitewashed look.[184]

But looks could be deceiving. Between Vidin and Calafat, there jutted into the Danube, four flat and uninhabited islands filled with bulrushes and waterfowl. Home to swarms of midges and mosquitoes, they made the district an inhospitable place. Vidin, furthermore, was subject to flooding in winter, and the streets of its old town would frequently be mired in all manner of subaqueous perils. Dysentery, smallpox and cholera were rampant.[185]

Upon their arrival, Eugene and his companions made their way to the seraglio of Abdurrahman Sami Pasha, the Greek-born governor without whose say-so comfortable accommodation would be impossible to obtain. Riding through an odoriferous warren of poorly paved streets crammed with merchants, packs of homeless dogs, and swarms of flies, they crossed the sloping bank that separated the squalid Christian quarter from the prosperous Islamic suburbs.

Sami's official residence was a two-storey building that enclosed a large courtyard and abutted the town's battlements. A wooden staircase led to a dusty lobby on the first floor, off which sat the Pasha's sitting room. Large and bright, it overlooked both the Danube and the fortress of Calafat. A plush divan ran about two of the walls. A row of high-backed chairs was set against another. It was heated by a large log fire.

Sami, a thin elderly man with a short white beard, enjoyed a small reputation as a poet. More scholar than soldier, he possessed an aristocratic countenance

---

[184] Paton, Andrew Alexander. *The Bulgarian, The Turk, and the German*, Longman Brown, Green and Longmans, London, 1855, pp.32,33; Crowe, Sir Joseph. *Reminiscences of Thirty-Five Years of My Life.*, John Murray, London, 1895, p.125.

[185] Herbert, William V. *The Chronicles of a Virgin Fortress*, Osgood, McIlvaine & Co., London, 1896, p.45.

The Siege of Calafat

and polished European manners. In his youth, he had travelled to London and Paris. He spoke French fluently and hated all things German.

As was his wont with foreigners he chose to favour, Sami furnished Eugene and his companions with a gubernatorial *firman* instructing a local bishop to find them respectable lodgings. By nightfall, they were lodged in a house outside the fortress and sharing a room with other cavalry officers. Amongst them, Eugene encountered an old friend – a Piedmontese by the name of Gardino, who had fought alongside him at Novara and earned some brief renown for having captured the Austrian standard.

A fiery Piedmontese whose duels were 'as numerous as other men's loves', Gardino currently held the rank of lieutenant.[186] At Novara, he and Eugene had been colleagues; he would now be his subordinate.[187] The inequality of rank, however, was quickly set aside in favour of old loyalties and the fellowship of mutual preservation. Eugene's arrival in a command capacity, however, did not go unnoticed beyond the doors of the dormitory, and a British journalist, lacking in first-hand information, raced to regurgitate the inaccuracies of his colleagues.

> Kalafat Feb. 18 – The first Englishman who has yet taken service in the Turkish Army arrived here a few days ago, and is now at the head of two squadrons of the Imperial Guard, a cavalry regiment. His European name is Eugene O'Reilly; the Turkish one which he has assumed, Hassan Aga. He served in the Austro-Piedmontese war in 1848-1849 as a volunteer, and afterwards in the 10th Hussars in England.
>
> On reaching Constantinople he was at first destined to aid in organising a regiment of Cossacks, but it was afterwards judged more advisable to send him off at once to the scene of war. He has since been followed by two French officers, one recently belonging to the Chasseurs d'Afrique,

---

[186] *The Cork Examiner*, 4 September 1854, p.2.
[187] Evelyn, *A Diary of the Crimea*, p.39.

the other to the Cuirassiers, and both sent here as instructors of cavalry.[188]

A walled town of some 2,000 houses, Calafat possessed a town hall, a customs house, three churches and a cavalry barracks, but little else. The town's only cafe currently housed no less than nine English volunteers, all frustrated at the lack of action.[189] As Evelyn had carried mail from Shumen for two of them, they were given a guided tour of the emplacements.[190]

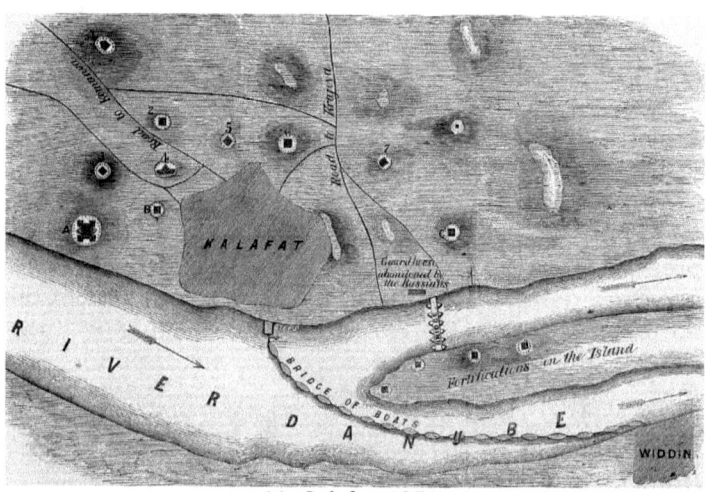

11. Calafat, 1854.

The Turkish position was strongly entrenched and surrounded on three sides by forty thousand Russians. The redoubts raised by the Turks were enormous, robust, and furnished with artillery. Two kilometres apart and raised on two hills on the plain

---

[188] *The Field Supplement.* Vol III, No. 64, London, 18 March 1854, p.259.
[189] *The Citizen, 25 March 1854, p.180.*
[190] Hart, Henry G. *The New Army List*, John Murray, London, 1863, p.p. 92, 97; *London Gazette*, 24 May 1873; *Orders, Decorations, Medals and Militaria*, catalogue for Dix, Noonan, Webb auction of 15 September 2021, London, August 2021, p.24.

The Siege of Calafat

beyond the town, they commanded the surrounding countryside. Any army daring to approach the fortress directly would suffer enormous losses.[191]

Accompanied by Evelyn, Eugene next paid a visit to his new commanding officer, a Polish nobleman by the name of Antoni Aleksander Iliński, who, since his conversion to Islam in 1844, was better known as Iskander Bey. Having broken some ribs when his horse fell on him during a skirmish with Russian Cossacks, he was currently bedridden and looked a decade older than his forty-odd years. He did not speak English.

Addressing them in French, Iskander was as welcoming to Evelyn as he was to Eugene. Unlike many of his colleagues, he actually liked adventurers. Just a few weeks earlier, in fact, he had attempted to convince twenty-two-year-old Dubliner Edwin Lawrence Godkin to join him in battle. Godkin, a trainee journalist with the *Daily News*, politely declined.[192]

Iskander confirmed Eugene's command of two regiments of *Bashi Bazouks*, a terrifying force of irregular cavalry recruited by the Turks from myriad ethnic groups across the Empire, most frequently from Albanian and Circassian tribal regions. Renowned for their bravery, horsemanship and indiscipline, the Bashis were also notorious looters, a reputation that was far from unjustified and the inevitable result of both a lack of regulation and the expectation of the Ottoman superiors that they would support themselves from the spoils of battle.[193] The Bashis regarded uniforms as a sign of slavery, and their refusal to wear them gave them the appearance of bandits. For those who would employ or command them, their instinct for self-preservation frequently

---

[191] *South Australian Register* (Adelaide S.A.), 21 June 1854, p.2.
[192] Godkin, Edwin Lawrence. *Life and Letters of Edwin Lawrence Godkin*, vol.1, McMillan, New York, 1907, p.42.
[193] Ottoman Archives of the Prime Minister's Office (BOA), HR. SYS. 1347/18 enc. 1, 2 March 1854; HR. SYS. 904/1 enc. 130–131, 14 March 1854.

12. Turkish Bashi Bazouks.

trumped the orders of their commanding officers.[194] Discipline was always a problem.

On Sunday, 19 February, while Eugene, Gardino and Evelyn were attempting to purchase some decent horses in Vidin, they heard cannon fire coming from the direction of Calafat. Procuring a boat, they crossed the river and raced to see what was up. Eugene found his new regiments saddled and ready for action. The Russian 'attack', however, proved to be little more than a reconnaissance party that had taken care to keep out of artillery range. Both sides frequently sent out such parties in the hope of drawing enemy fire and establishing enemy positions. On this particular occasion, the skirmish proved to be little more than a brief exchange of long-range artillery. Some cannon shot entered the fort, but no great damage was done.[195]

During the following week, Eugene and his bunkmates were transferred to new quarters within the fort. Eugene now lodged with Gardino: Evelyn with Mercier and Dupuis. They had barely settled in, however, when two Cossack squadrons drew up two hundred yards from the fort. Two shots from a thirty-

---

[194] Evelyn, *A Diary of the Crimea*, pp. 37-38.
[195] Ibid., pp.41-42.

The Siege of Calafat

two-pounder were fired in the direction of the Cossacks. One went wide, the other landed in front of them, forcing them to retreat. Cavalry units were sent to engage them, but by then, the Cossacks had retreated.

The following morning, five squadrons of Russians approached Calafat with two guns and four Turkish squadrons marched out to meet them, amongst them a cavalry unit under Eugene's command. He took them on a sortie behind Russian lines, where he became embroiled in a battle with Russian troops. During the encounter, a round shot passed between his bridle arm and his body and, by blessings or dumb luck, carried off his horse's head but left him unscathed.[196] The Russians did not hang around, and the Bashis did not give chase. Two men were killed in the skirmish.[197]

Back in Calafat, on hearing the canon fire, Evelyn mounted his horse and tagged onto a second party of Bashis riding out to support Eugene's.

> We here met O'Reilly, who it was plain had had a fall, but we were not prepared to learn that his horse had just been killed by a round shot, which struck it in the head – we congratulated him on his escape. We did not see the Russians at all, as they had retired before we came up.[198]

Later that night, thanks largely to Evelyn's largesse, Eugene and Gardino dined out in Vidin on the story of the Irishman's good fortune. As a European who rode with European officers, Evelyn had begun to think of himself as a fellow officer, despite not holding any official rank. The confusion that this caused amongst the Bashis would almost prove fatal.

On 8 March, Eugene, under Mercier's command, rode out with the entire Turkish cavalry to confront

---

[196] *Cork Examiner*, 24 March 1854, p.4; *Boston Pilot*, 22 April 1854, p.4; *London Illustrated News*, 25 March 1854, p.283.
[197] *The Illustrated London News*, 25 March 1854, p.283
[198] Evelyn, *A Diary of the Crimea*, p.43.

two Russian squadrons that had drawn up around the village of Ciupercenii Vechi. Six to eight hundred Cossacks were on the plain, unsupported and in danger of being cut off. Evelyn, who had once again had tagged along, attempted at one point to take command:

> As usual nothing but carabines and round shot came into play – a round shot passed between my head and Mercier's. I rode to the left front where the Bashi-Bazouk's and Cossacks were puttering away at each other with vast noise and smoke, and little execution as usual. Each side treats the other with vast respect, firing pistols and carabines at rifle ranges, so that a man placed between the hostile skirmishers and equidistant from them might smoke a chibouk in tolerable security. By dint of hurrahing and waving my sword, I got some fifty of them to close their files and to follow me towards the enemy, whose skirmishers promptly retreated on a support. I really thought that we would have accomplished something resembling a charge, a manoeuvre hitherto unknown in Bashi warfare.
>
> But though we started at a gallop, few continued that pace many yards, so that on arriving within a hundred yards of the enemy, I found on looking round, that I was entirely deserted by the whole party except four or five who were following me at a respectful distance. Not wishing to be made prisoner, I pulled up and retreated amidst Russian jeers and carabine balls. When our artillery opened fire the enemy made a precipitate retreat, moving by their right towards Payana,[199] and the Turks were fools enough to allow them to execute this flank movement, without charging them, though they could have brought twenty squadrons against the enemy's two.
>
> As we were returning to Kalafat, Achmet Pasha met us, followed as usual by his incongruous and ragged staff. He wanted, I suppose, to smoke a chibouk in the open air, so he ordered the cavalry to turn to the right, and led them a useless march of some miles. We had a few files of cavalry extended as an advance guard. They advanced very slowly, as if afraid of leaving the vicinity of the head of the column.
>
> O'Reilly and I advanced through them and found a more

---

[199] Poiana Mare, a small town 16km south-east of Calafat.

efficient advanced guard in our own persons. The plain over which we passed was undulating, and we galloped up each rise, "sabre à la main", in order to baffle by speed the aim of any Cossacks who might be lurking behind the brow, and in readiness (of course) to cut up and eat any number of them.[200]

With such skirmishes becoming increasingly regular and more serious, the Turks were forced to call up an additional ten thousand infantry and twenty-two squadrons of cavalry.[201]

> Reinforcements still continue to arrive in Widdin, and pass to Kalafat, where they live in tents, all the houses being filled to excess. The weather is still very severe, and men and horses suffer much from cold. The mortality of the sick in the hospitals is very great. Widdin lies on the edge of a great marshy plain, and so low that during rainy weather the Danube overflows its streets and lays the lower story of every house under water. All the streets are mere channels of mud, in which the passenger sinks knee deep.
>
> Almost in every part of the town all the offensive smells your imagination can conjure up, meet your unhappy senses – from the blood of the shambles to the outpouring of the cess pools. The dogs are the only scavengers! The great danger which British troops will have to encounter on the banks of the Danube is intemperance, for great facilities may be obtained for getting drunk. Laky, a liquor like whiskey, is very cheap here.[202]

On 26 March, two hours before daybreak, the Turks left Calafat with five squadrons of regular cavalry, two companies of Bashi Bazouks, and fifty Turkish Cossacks heading southeast of Calafat. They brought no cannon, it being merely a reconnaissance mission. Their task was to establish whether or not the Russians had retreated from Craiova, a Romanian city

---

[200] Evelyn, *A Diary of the Crimea*, pp.44-45.
[201] *The Courier*, Hobart (Tasmania), 26 Jun 1854, p.2; *New York Weekly Tribune*, No. 655, April 1, 1854, p.1; *Freeman's Journal*,
[202] *Waterford News*, 14 April 1854, p.3.

on the road to Bucharest.

Eugene led an advance guard of sixty horsemen composed entirely of Bashi Bazouks and European officers. Galloping towards the village of Poiana Mare they encountered some Cossack sentinels who rode away at full speed towards the Russian camp to raise the alarm. With the Bashis hard on their heels, the Russians reached the ramparts, leapt the ditches and entered the town. With the Russian infantry and artillery withdrawn in anticipation of an attack, the town had been left to the Cossacks to defend.

Believing the entire Turkish army had left Calafat and was now descending upon them, the Cossacks fled, and though outnumbered by a factor of ten to one, the Bashis took the town, killing fifty Cossacks, wounding as many more, and taking several prisoners – for the loss of just twelve of their own. Having taken the town, they left it to the infantry and returned to Calafat.[203] Following the raid, some twenty Bashis were executed or imprisoned for plundering. The performance of their commanding officers, Eugene included, was nevertheless widely praised and mentioned in despatches.[204]

Evelyn did not participate in the skirmish at Poiana Mare as he was at that time in Vidin making plans to leave. Another English war tourist, Joseph Crowe,[205] an illustrator for the *Illustrated London News* who had also ridden some sorties with the Bashis, had left two weeks earlier.[206] Between Vidin and Calafat, just a handful of British officers now remained and Evelyn, frustrated by the lack of action and the 'constant card

---

[203] Stafford, William Cooke. *History of the War in Russia and Turkey*, Peter Jackson, London, 1855, p.287.
[204] *South Australian Register* (Adelaide, SA: 1839-1900) 10 Jul 1854, p.2; *Memorial de la Loire et de la Haute-Loire*, 30 April 1854, p.1; *La Presse*, 30 April 1854, p.2.
[205] Sir Joseph Archer Crowe (1825-1896), an English journalist, consular official and art historian.
[206] Evelyn, *A Diary of the Crimea*, p.51; Crowe, Sir Joseph. *Reminiscences of Thirty-Five Years of My Life.*, John Murray, London, 1895, pp. 112, 118,119, 122, 125.

The Siege of Calafat

playing' had for some time been 'thinking of bolting'. By 29 March he was gone, his departure just coinciding with the arrival of Ottoman reinforcements from Sofia,[207] the majority of whom were obliged to live in tents. There being little accommodation to be had in the towns, it is likely that Evelyn had been asked to surrender his bed to a commissioned officer.[208]

The succeeding weeks saw the Russians deliver assault upon assault on Calafat without managing to breach the Turkish defences or tempt the Turks to advance. A major battle fought outside the fort on 19 April, saw another English 'amateur', Sam Morris, killed.[209] By 21 April, however, the siege was over and the Russians, who had suffered enormous losses to disease, privation and battle, were in retreat. Eugene's role in the victory did not go unheralded.

> On the Danube the Polish officers one and all distinguished themselves; and the heroic exploits of Count Ilinski, better known as Iskender Bey, are familiar to the European public. Major O'Reilly, and several other European officers in the Ottoman service, equally displayed undoubted gallantry in the same field of operations.[210]

---

[207] *The Advent Review, and Sabbath Herald*, 7 March 1854, p.56.
[208] *Waterford News*, 14 April 1854, p.3; Evelyn would later regularise his employment in Turkish service, achieving the rank of *bimbashi* or and adopting the Islamic name of Maksood Bey.
[209] Herbert, William V. *The Chronicles of a Virgin Fortress*, Osgood, McIlvaine & Co., London, 1896, p.4.
[210] Duncan, Charles. *A Campaign with the Turks in Asia*, Vol. 1, Smith, Elder and Co., London, 1865, p.19.

GALLANTRY AT BUZĂU

IN EARLY JULY, a Turkish detachment of two thousand men under the command of Iskander Bey marched on the Bulgarian town of Ruse, which sat on the opposite bank of the Danube to the Romanian town of Giurgiu, then under Russian occupation. Their orders were to take Giurgiu and proceed immediately to Bucharest. The Turks crossed the Danube on 5 July 1854 and engaged the Russians. Two days later, they had taken possession of the town.

In Giurgiu, Eugene found himself in a more familiar Europe, where cigars were more common than Turkish pipes and European trousers more common than the *şalvar*. The sharp contrast with Muslim Ruse,[211] not to mention the liberal availability of alcohol, made Giurgiu a popular recreational destination for mercenaries on leave.

Giurgiu – Giurgevo to English journalists – was a straggling port of multiple wharves whose buildings had largely withstood destruction in the recent battle. The Russian occupation, however, had left its mark in other ways, not least in the proliferation of spirit shops – welcomed by the lower ranks but largely eschewed by the officer class, who tended to gravitate towards the town's one good hotel, then run by an Italian emigrant and his German wife.[212] It was here, in the aftermath of the recent battle, that Eugene and Gardino met with Edwin Lawrence Godkin, special correspondent for the London *Daily News*. On 10 July 1854, Godkin joined them in making merry at the hotel and shared two bottles of champagne with them before going to dine

---

[211] Tappe, E D. *Revue de Littérature Comparée*. Vol. 39, Iss. 3, Paris, 1 July 1965, pp.439-440.
[212] *Household Words*, No. 277, 14 July 1855, pp. 467,559.

with General Cannon.[213]

The Russians may have abandoned Giurgiu, but they were still in the vicinity, and it took another battle, on 22 July, to see them off.[214] Four days later, the Russian Tsar ordered his troops out of the principalities altogether, and Iskander was finally free to march on Bucharest. He arrived on 7 August. Before entering the city, he handed command of Eugene's contingent of Bashi Bazouks to Sir Stephen Lakeman, alias Mazar Pasha, an English-born graduate of the Lycée Louis-le-Grand in Paris.

Following a spell in the French Foreign Legion, Lakeman had spent some time on the island of St Helena, where he had curated the house to which Bonaparte had been exiled. He subsequently joined the British Army and fought against the Xhosa in South Africa.[215] Knighted by Queen Victoria on 25 November 1853, he then joined the Ottoman Army, in which he had been granted the honorific of *pasha*. Of his latest command, Lakeman would later remark:

> It was a curiously officered regiment. I, the colonel, had been named through being the possessor of a certain sword; the lieutenant-colonel, Said Bey, through being the possessor of a wonderful flute (he had been chief flute-player to the Sultan); one of the majors, Mourad Bey, for being a renegade Frenchman; and the other major, an Irishman, for being the supposed son of an English Prime Minister.[216]

A 'considerable womanizer' who in his youth had danced a jig around the moral and the merry and laboured under the nickname of 'Cupid', the prime minister, Lord Palmerston, was a notorious rake who

---

[213] Godkin, *Life and Letters of Edwin Lawrence Godkin*, p.28.
[214] *The Field Supplement*. Vol IV, No. 83, London, 29 July 1854, p.716.
[215] Dod, Charles R. *The Peerage, Baronetage and Knightage of Great Britain and Ireland for 1855*, Whittaker & Co., London, 1894, p.341.
[216] Lakeman, Sir Stephen. *What I Saw in Kaffir-Land*, William Blackwood & Sons, Edinburgh, 1880, pp. 22-23.

'took mistresses from society and women from the demi-monde'. He was even reputed to have kept a diary of his sexual conquests and failures.[217] Conveniently, for the rumour mongers, he also possessed eight thousand acres in and around Dublin and estates in County Sligo. He was not known to have visited Dublin in 1827, but the movements of the O'Reillys in the year prior to Eugene's birth are also unknown. As implausible as they might have appeared, they were not easily disproved.

Palmerston, who had no legitimate heirs, was reputed to have fathered as many as six illegitimate children during his lifetime, and any young man bearing a letter of recommendation from him was always vulnerable to the suspicion of illegitimacy. And it could scarcely have been otherwise for Eugene. Acts of treason, after all, were hardly the most-trodden path to the patronage of a British prime minister.

For as long as they served his purposes, however, Eugene allowed the rumours to float uncontested. Within the hierarchy of Britain's class system, powerful connections, actual or assumed, frequently conferred upon the recipient a kind of hybrid status beyond class. As long as he conformed to the requisite tribal signatures and norms of acceptable behaviour, a man could even hobnob – as Eugene would later do – with a future king.

We have no way of knowing when these rumours began or if they ever reached his father or, indeed, Palmerston himself. All that can be said with any degree of certainty is that the rumours, privately shared for decades, would not be published for another six years, by which time both Palmerston and Eugene's parents would be dead.

On 16 August 1854, Lakeman left Bucharest on a reconnaissance mission with nine squadrons of

---

[217] Oxford Dictionary of National Biography: Tayleur-Tonneys, Oxford University Press, 2004, p.57.

Gallantry at Buzău

cavalry. Making a forced night march of forty miles, he arrived, in the early hours of the following morning, at the Focşani Road, close to the Romanian town of Buzău. Six miles beyond the town, twenty thousand Russians had been entrenched since 1853:

> On approaching the town a few Cossacks were seen outside a wood which runs at right angles to the road on the left-hand side; here the main body halted, while one party were sent to explore the wood under Major O'Reilly, an Englishman in the Turkish service, while another party, under Captain Gardoni [Gardino], went straight along the road. O'Reilly passed through the wood in skirmishing order, and on getting to the other side found about 300 Cossacks extended in a line along the plain. He formed up his men opposite to their right flank, and on perceiving this the Cossacks commenced galloping towards that point to receive him.[218]

Eugene's squadron advanced to meet the Cossacks while Lakeman took up the rear with a further six squadrons. Between them sat two squadrons under the command of Colonel Lintorn Simmons, but these were too far back to offer Eugene support.[219] As he closed the space between his squadron and the Cossacks, Eugene veered sharply to the left, bringing his squadron to the end of the line of waiting Cossacks, intending to charge along their lines rather than risk being surrounded in a frontal attack. Grasping his intention, the left wing of the Cossacks raced to the point of danger, regrouped and reformed.[220]

Eugene's order to prepare for a charge was not at first believed. Turkish cavalry had never charged during this war. They were more accustomed to riding to within half a kilometre of the enemy and exchanging pistol fire. Expecting this engagement to be no

---

[218] *The Times*, 4 September 1854, p.7.
[219] *Dublin Evening Mail*, 4 September 1854, p.2.
[220] *The Times*, 4 September 1854, p.7.

different, the Bashis had drawn their pistols. Eugene again ordered the pistols holstered and lances and sabres drawn. There would be no time to reload during a charge.

Leading his men at a trot, Eugene advanced upon the Cossacks', who remained perfectly motionless, expecting the classic exchange of pistol fire. Twenty metres short of the enemy line, however, Eugene gave the order to charge, and his men, mustering their courage, drove in their spurs and galloped directly at them. The Cossacks now received an order to charge but, finding themselves with carbines drawn rather than lances and sabres, only about half a dozen did. The remainder, having fired, fled for the shelter of a nearby village to regroup and reload. Suddenly it was no longer a fight, but a race to get control of the village. Eugene raced to cut off the Cossack retreat, but the Cossack horses were fresh and the Turkish horses exhausted from a long night march. At this point, Gardino's party joined the affray:

> At the first moment Gardino, a fiery little Piedmontese – who carried off an Austrian standard at Novara – rode straight in amongst the Cossacks, their lances tearing his clothes right and left, and in the twinkling of an eye, he knocked three or four of them out of their saddles, two being killed on the spot.[221]

Considerably in advance of their squadrons, on account of having better horses, O'Reilly and Gardino pressed bravely on the heels of the retreating Cossacks. Eugene, pursuing one with the point of his sword almost touching the man's back, struggled to get close enough to deliver the *coup de grace*. Absorbed in the chase he failed to notice a Cossack sergeant ride at him with his lance. At the last second, he saw him and wheeled his horse around. The Cossack flew past,

---

[221] Beamish, North Ludlow. *On the uses and application of Cavalry in war...*, T & W Boone, London, 1855, pp. 216-218.

Gallantry at Buzău

redirecting his lance at Eugene's ribs:

> It was luck the blow had no greater impetus than was given by the man's arm; had it had the momentum of the horse's motion, that gallant major's career would have been at an end. He was slightly stunned by the stroke, and on recovering his self-possession, saw Gardino thundering down on the unfortunate sergeant, and passing his sword through his body with a quickness and dexterity which left nothing to be desired.[222]

Both sides now entered the town. The streets were narrow, and speed was impossible. Unfamiliar with the layout, the Cossacks made a fatal error:

> ... the Cossacks found themselves caught in a trap, for they became jammed together like sheep in a pen. Horses fell every moment, stopping all that were behind them, and the Turks coming close up, plied lance and sabre with unsparing vigour. Those who fell, were transfixed on the spot; and a Turkish lieutenant snatching a lance from the hands of a Cossack, ran it into the back of another! [223]

Thanks to Eugene, the Turks had carried the day. They had even managed, as a bonus, to confiscate 'the equipment of a whole regiment of infantry that the Russians had placed upon bullock carts ready for departure'.[224] Had the Bashis fought with pistols, or had the two regiments of Russian cavalry, later discovered to have been stationed nearby, been given the time to come up, the Bashis would have been slaughtered.

Cossack losses numbered between ten and fourteen, with many more wounded. Eugene's regiment, in contrast, lost none, with just three, himself included, wounded. Having taken the town and successfully ascertained the strength and positions of the

---

[222] *Dublin Evening Mail*, 4 September 1854, p.2.
[223] Beamish, *On the uses and application of Cavalry...*, pp. 216-218.
[224] *Illustrated London News*, 7 October 1854, p.339.

Russians,[225] Lakeman returned to Bucharest, where, a few weeks later, he was appointed Chief of Police.[226]

Eugene's heroics at Buzău were widely reported in the British press.[227] His whereabouts for the next six months, however, received scant attention. It is possible that he was recuperating in a Bucharest hospital, but all that is known for certain is that, by the first thaw, he had been recruited by the notorious Major-General Beatson, with whom Humphry Sandwith had until recently served as regimental surgeon.[228]

Exactly who made the first approach is unclear, but Eugene was known to have been lobbying for such an appointment for some time. Back in November 1854, for example, he had written a lengthy memorandum on the employment of Bashi Bazouks to Lord Clarendon, the British Foreign Secretary.[229] But however it had come about, O'Reilly's acceptance of a transfer to Beatson's regiment brought his Bulgarian adventure to a close.[230]

---

[225] *The Courier*, Hobart, 2 December 1854, pp.2-3.
[226] Cernovodeanu, Paul. "Punți între două lumi. Britanici printre români" ("Bridges between Two Worlds. Britons among the Romanians"), in *Magazin Istoric*, July 1995, p.40; Nottingham University, Ne C 9861/1-4, and Ne C 9863/1-3.
[227] *Dublin Evening Post*, 2 September 1854, p.2.
[228] *Waterford News*, 16 March 1855, p.1.
[229] UK National Archives, O'Reilly to Clarendon, 16 November 1854, FO78/1058.
[230] In Franz Van Suppé's comic opera, *Fatinitza*, composed in 1876 and set during the Crimean War, the heroine, Lydia, is captured by a unit of Bashi Bazouks led by a Hassan Bey; Upton, George P. *The Standard Light Operas, Their Plots and Their Music*, A.C. McClurg & Co., Chicago, 1902, p.220.

NINE MONTHS IN ANATOLIA

BORN IN SCOTLAND in 1804, William Ferguson Beatson was a 'tough, seasoned, and imaginative soldier of fortune' who had made his name in the service of the East India Company, for whom he had raised, trained, and commanded the Bundlecund Legion and, more recently, the Hyderabad Contingent, widely celebrated as 'the finest body of irregular cavalry in India'.[231]

Having served as a Brevet Colonel in the British Army and a Major in the East India Company, Beatson had entered Ottoman service as 'Shemshi Pasha' and at a rank roughly equivalent to that of a British major general. Early in the war, he had attempted to convince Lord Raglan, commander of the British troops in Crimea, to enlist a division of Bashi Bazouks in British pay. Raglan had ignored him and, parking the idea, Beatson had left Ottoman service and rejoined the British Army as aide-de-camp to General Sir James Scarlett.

A growing shortage of British troops, however, eventually saw Beatson's idea revived, and in October 1854, the Duke of Newcastle, then Minister of War, directed him to raise four thousand irregulars under the command of British officers. Fearful that the British Army's reputation might be contaminated by the ill-discipline of the Bashis, Beatson was ordered to report directly to the British Ambassador in Constantinople, Lord Stratford de Redcliffe, rather than to the commander of the British Turkish

---

[231] Stevenson, Richard. "Highly Irregular Cavalry: Beatson's Horse 1858-60" in the *Journal of the Society for Army Historical Research*, vol. 92, no. 372, 2014, pp. 305–325.

Contingent, General Robert Vivian.

Thirsty for reputation, Beatson requested that the new corps be named the 'British Osmanli Cavalry' or, should the risk of attaching the word 'British' to the new corps prove unpalatable, that he be allowed to follow the Indian practice and name it 'Beatson's Horse'.[232] Whitehall baulked at the latter but approved the former.

Having received permission to recruit his own cavalry, Beatson next set about designing their uniforms. For himself, he designed extravagant gold-braided suits, and for his officers, a collarless green frock coat, scarlet breeches with a gold stripe, and a peakless red forage cap with gold band and braiding.[233] Indulging his fetish for bare necks, he refused to allow his officers to wear even a neck scarf.

In the spring of 1855, Eugene made his way to Beatson's camp at Çanakkale, the strongest of the many forts that dotted the headlands of the Dardanelles.[234] He arrived to find the hill behind the town already covered with the white tents and tethered horses of a Bashi Bazouk regiment. Gifted to Beatson by the Turks, the regiment was comprised largely of Circassians.[235] A line of twenty-eight windmills separated the camp from the town and, more importantly, the ill-disciplined Bashis from the civilian population.

Beatson did not camp with his troops but took a house within the town that, in summer, he shared with his wife and daughters. A rambling two-storey

---

[232] UK National Archives, Beatson to Lord Stratford de Redcliffe, 8 November 1854, DE1274/2 p.258; also 23 & 27 November 1854, FO352/40/1.

[233] The forage cap was a small cap worn by men of cavalry regiments whilst out collecting forage for the horses. Later, the term was also applied to the undress caps worn by cavalrymen when the full-dress headdress was to be preserved. It was generally round and stiffened, with or without a peak, with a cloth band in the regimental facing colour and a black leather chin strap with an adjustable buckle.

[234] Also known as *Dardanelle, Chanak-Kalessi,* Kale-I Sultaniye

[235] Woods, Laurence M. *Edward Shelley's Journal, 1856-61: A Victorian Remittance Man,* Author House, 2005, pp.14-15.

13. General Wiliam Fergus Beatson circa 1850.

building set on the shore, it was cooled by drowsy sea breezes and permanently surrounded by horses. The ground floor was forever crammed with junior officers and messengers waiting for an audience upstairs, where Beatson's office, which doubled as his bedroom, stood off a large hall on the first floor.[236]

A distinguished old campaigner, Beatson was appalled by the quality and inexperience of the pale-faced officers that were being sent out to him from

---

[236] Money, Alonzo and George Henry. *Sevastopol. Our Tent in the Crimea; and wanderings in Sevastopol. By two brothers*, Richard Bentley, London 1856, pp.396-399; Money, Edward. *Twelve Months with the Bashi Bazouks*, Newman & Co., London, 1888, pp.6,12.

London, most of whom he regarded as 'pen and paper men – not one in bodily shape'. Beatson preferred battle-hardened veterans and held no prejudice against them nor saw any problem with their having risen through the ranks to positions of command. Immediately upon Eugene's arrival, he recommended him to the Duke of Newcastle for a promotion to lieutenant colonel.[237] The *Morning Chronicle* approved of the promotion, but in other quarters it was considered controversial.

> I am glad to have to communicate news of an appointment in the British Osmanli Cavalry which augurs well for a reconsideration of what I have already had occasion to characterise as a most impolitic resolution on the part of our War Minister – namely the officering of this new corps solely by gentlemen now holding commissions in the Queen's army. The appointment to which I refer is that of Major O'Reilly to the command of this new force.
>
> This officer formerly served for a time in the 10th Hussars, whence he passed into the Piedmontese service, and under Charles Albert gave the Austrians some reason to respect Irish bravery and skill. After the conclusion of the Piedmontese war, he took service under the Sultan, and during last year's campaigns on the Danube performed more than one brilliant exploit, and showed his thorough capacity for the management of irregular cavalry. General Beatson wisely "set his eye upon" this officer.
>
> Major O'Reilly leaves for Eupatoria in a few days, to collect as many mounted Tartars as may be procurable there;[238] and these will be sent down to the Dardanelles, where the whole force (6,000 strong) is to be drilled and prepared for service in Spring.[239]

Whatever the rights or wrongs of the promotion, the bald truth of the matter was that Beatson had little choice. The majority of Bashis were unaccustomed to military discipline and expected their commanding

---

[237] *Dublin Weekly Nation*, 3 March 1855, p.8.
[238] Eupatoria or Yevpatoria, a city in Crimea.
[239] *The Waterford News*, Vol. 7, No. 338, 16 March 1855, p.1.

officer to turn a blind eye to their excesses. The imposition of discipline, therefore, required experience and tact. It was not a job for an inexperienced officer, no matter how much he had paid for his commission.

The status of a commanding officer, furthermore, hinged largely upon the numbers he commanded, and Beatson had, as of yet, only managed to muster a few hundred. Months away from combat and lacking Turkish-speaking officers, he needed a man like Eugene to remedy the situation. He ordered the Irishman to head to Anatolia and to recruit a thousand irregular cavalry. He would be assisted in the task by the British Vice-Consul, St Vincent Lloyd,[240] and the officer with whom he happened to be rooming.[241]

Three years Eugene's junior, Edward Shelley had been a soldier since the age of seventeen, when he had enlisted in the Hussars as a colour-bearer. Promoted at nineteen to lieutenant, he had since risen to the rank of Major. Following a brief service in India, he had taken a seven-year sabbatical to go lion-hunting in Africa where, in 1852, having gotten lost crossing the Kalahari Desert on horseback, he had arrived ragged and shirtless at Kuruman, so brown that a missionary's wife mistook him for a 'half-caste Grinqua'. From the moment of his arrival at camp, he had found a soulmate in O'Reilly with whom, on 16 February, he boarded a steamer bound for Sinope.

Recruiting a thousand cavalry would be no simple task in an area notoriously resistant to recruitment and from where the Turks had forcibly taken conscripts in the past.[242] Just the previous August,

---

[240] Beatson to Newcastle, 16 February 1855, c.f. Beatson, W.F. *The War Department and the Bashi Bazouks*, W. Clowes & Sons, London, 1856, p.7.
[241] Stevenson, Richard. "Beatson's Mutiny: William Beatson and the Bashi Bazouks." *Journal of the Society for Army Historical Research*, vol. 86, no. 348, 2008, p.273.
[242] UK National Archives, Havelock to Beatson, 30 April 1855, FO195/453; Beatson to Stratford de Redcliffe, 23 February 1855, FO195/453, and 17 May 1855, FO352/42A/2.

some five hundred 'recruits' had deserted the Ottoman army in the vicinity of Sivas and were now living as bandits and preying on passing caravans.[243] The province was currently rumoured to contain no less than ten thousand such men and several Turkish recruiting parties with whom they would be in direct competition.[244] The challenges that lay ahead, however, were paltry compared to the chaos they left behind.

O'Reilly and Shelley had scarcely set foot in Sinope when events in London took an unexpected turn. On 30 January 1855, the Tory government lost a vote of no confidence on their handling of the Crimean War and a new government had now taken office under the leadership of Lord Palmerston. More importantly, the Duke of Newcastle had been replaced as Secretary of State for War by Fox Maule, 2nd Lord Panmure, an abrasive politician known amongst his officials as 'The Bison'. Panmure had been given sweeping powers to reform the army.

Unimpressed by the lack of detail in Beatson's reports, Panmure had capped at two thousand the numbers that Beatson was authorised to recruit – less than half of what he had been seeking. Panmure had also refused to sanction the recruitment of any more officers until he had received a full report on the progress of the recruitment drive and the behaviour of those troops already recruited.

Beatson threatened to resign if his numbers were not restored, and Panmure was forced to back down.[245] But when Beatson's command of an independent corps was subsequently confirmed, it came at a price. He would now be reporting to the infamous Lord

---

[243] Ottoman Archives of the Prime Minister's Office, BOA A. MKT. NZD. 88/46, 30 August 1853.
[244] Sandwith, Humphry. *A Narrative of the Siege of Kars*, John Murray, London, 1856, p.229.
[245] Beatson to Stratford de Redcliffe, 4 April 1855, Panmure to Beatson, 13 April 1855, Beatson to Panmure, 25 April 1855 (FO/195/453).

Raglan, a man whose military reputation had been so thrashed by his performance in Crimea that his officers were said to run away on seeing him approach to avoid having to salute him.[246] Unlike Raglan, Beatson had few friends in Whitehall.

While this political shake-up was taking place in London, O'Reilly and Shelley continued to traverse Anatolia, threading their way along ancient paths and goat tracks as frequently as recognisable roads; passing through broken hills and scorched scrublands as often as fertile valleys; and stopping at isolated villages with names unknown to maps as frequently as towns long known to history. From the Black Sea to the Aegean, they hawked the promise of lucrative employment with steady but limited success, pausing whenever their number approached fifty and taking the batch to Sinope, from where they would be brought on to Beatson under the command of a Turkish officer.

It was a tedious and onerous task and one complicated, initially, by the lack of a *firman* from the Grand Vizier, an issue that was not resolved by the British Ambassador, Lord Stratford, until April.[247] Nor was that their only difficulty. Though offering a salary ten times the Turkish rate, they still faced competition from Turkish and Egyptian recruiters, not to mention religious opposition from the Mullahs, who objected to the notion of Muslims fighting for a Christian power.[248] On several occasions, when the Mullahs became too obstructive, Eugene was forced to make arrests. He had, after all, written permission from the Seraskier to go about his business.

Back in Çanakkale, spring arrived on the calendar to find winter overstaying its welcome. As uncommon

---

[246] Dallas, George Frederick. *Eyewitness in the Crimea – The Crimean War Letters of Lt. Col. George Frederick Dallas*, Frontline Books, Barnsley, 2015, Letter 27, 5 February 1855.

[247] UK National Archives, O'Reilly to Beatson, 7 March 1855, FO195/453.

[248] Stevenson, *Beatson's Mutiny*, p.216; National Archives U.K., FO 195/48 O'Reilly to Assistant Adjutant General, 30 August 1856.

as it was unrelenting, the frost and sleet gave the camp a pleasantly sterile appearance, but it also inhibited military activity and exacerbated the disillusion and impatience of a fighting force too long denied the prospect of action.

The British High Command had no clear vision of what they wanted to do with their Bashi Bazouks. It was even suggested in the press that antagonism between the British and Indian service had predisposed the decision-makers to deny the Osmanli regiments – led to a large degree by former Indian officers – opportunities for distinction. Discipline, as a result, had begun to collapse, and embarrassing reports from within the camp were soon leaking to a ravenous British press.

Beatson's behaviour hadn't helped. His experience in India had convinced him that native troops needed to be impressed by pageantry, and so, every morning and evening, he would take his daughters for a canter amongst the Bashis in the style of an Arab chieftain.[249] Accompanied to the crest of the high ground by an enthusiastic assembly of officers, they would be met with choruses of ululations, a cacophony of drums and erratic volleys of pistol shots.[250] Among the ranks, his behaviour was 'much discussed': within the press corps, it was derided as vulgar exhibitionism.[251]

But then, just when Beatson was most in need of an ally, a familiar face arrived at Çanakkale. Returning wounded from an ill-fated expedition to Africa, Richard Francis Burton had found the British public more interested in the progress of the war than in the sponsoring of explorers, and instead of returning to

---

[249] UK National Archives, Beatson to Newcastle, 16 February 1855, c.f. Beatson, W.F. *The War Department and the Bashi Bazouks*, W. Clowes & Sons, London, 1856, pp.8-9.
[250] Stevenson, Richard. *Beatson's Mutiny: The Turbulent Career of a Victorian Soldier*, Bloomsbury Academic, 2015, p.216.
[251] Walmsley, Hugh Mulleneux. *Journal of a Bashi Bazouk*, Groombridge and Sons, London, 1857, p.81.

Nine Months in Anatolia

14. Richard Francis Burton.

Africa, he had travelled to Balaklava to enlist in the British Turkish Contingent. A half-Irish alumnus of Trinity College Dublin, Burton was renowned for his fighting and duelling skills and laboured under the nickname of 'Ruffian Dick'. Finding himself unwelcome in London, he had gone in search of Beatson, with whom he had previously served in India, and Beatson had promptly made him his aide-de-camp.[252]

There had always been a whiff of scandal about Burton and his attitude to 'unnatural' sexual practices, largely on account of allegations of sexual misconduct during his East African expedition and the continuing fallout from his *Karachi Brothel Report*, an investigation into homosexual and pederastic activity by British soldiers that had scandalised British society and embarrassed senior members of the British Military in India.[253] Beatson, however, cared little for Burton's reputation. He simply needed allies.

One of Burton's first interventions on Beatson's behalf was to delete an undiplomatic passage from a letter Beatson had written to the British Ambassador in Constantinople, challenging him, as Burton would later put it, to 'pistols for two and coffee for one'.[254] Burton also attempted to relieve tensions amongst the Bashis by organising regular drills, with mixed success.

> At first strange scenes occurred on parade. The men would smoke, sing, and laugh; and occasionally an officer in command of a regiment would see his whole corps suddenly dash away in a headlong charge after an unfortunate hare disturbed by the noise. Away the whole

---

[252] Beatson, W.F. *The War Department and the Bashi Bazouks*, W. Clowes & Sons, London, 1856, p.75.

[253] Tredoux, G., "New Light on Richard Burton's Karachi Brothel Report", Burtoniana.org, September 2016, accessed 25 January 2023: https://burtoniana.org/biography/karachi/gtredoux-2016-burton-karachi-brothel-report.pdf.

[254] Stevenson, *Beatson's Mutiny*, p.236; Burton, Isabel, *The Life of Captain Sir Richard. F. Burton*, vol.1, Chapman and Hall, London, 1893, p.239.

line would go, shouting, yelling, and discharging their pistols, at a hard gallop; while pussy dashed away at full speed, and the European officers remained alone on their deserted parade ground. At other times, a few of the men would decline to be drilled on some particular morning; but all this was soon reduced to order...[255]

It was all too little too late. On 22 June, a pistol fight between some Irish and Albanian soldiers left four men dead and seven wounded.[256] A short while later, the wife of a Turkish interpreter was raped while walking alone in the vineyards. The rape led to a fight between Albanian and Turkish officers, during which one man received a sabre wound and another was shot in the leg. Four Albanian Bashis were subsequently arrested, one in a case of mistaken identity.

Beatson soon after found his house surrounded by eighty to a hundred Albanians demanding the release of the prisoners. After some heated discussion, he yielded to their demands but, far from placating the group, it led only to their desertion, obliging Beatson to chase after them to persuade them to return. Exaggerated reports of the chaos quickly reached Constantinople, from where they were relayed, without verification, to London. By 6 July, rumours of the ill-treatment of the wives of English officers had also become widespread.[257]

On 18 July, in response to the tsunami of adverse publicity, Burton called a meeting of senior officers at which a letter in support of Beatson was presented to all to sign. Twenty added their signatures, not all of

---

[255] Walmsley, Hugh Mulleneux. *Journal of a Bashi Bazouk*, Groombridge and Sons, London, 1857, pp. 78-79.
[256] Stevenson, *Beatson's Mutiny*, pp.226-227.
[257] Woods, Laurence M. *Edward Shelley's Journal, 1856-61: A Victorian Remittance Man*, Author House, 2005, p.22; Money *Twelve Months with the Bashi Bazouks*, pp. 78-79, 82-99; Vivian, Robert J.H. *Narrative of Circumstances which Led to Major-Gen Beatson being Relieved from the Command of the Turkish Irregular Cavalry, and the Transfer of that Force to the Turkish Contingent*, Cox & Wyman, London, 1856, pp.5-6.

whom understood what they were signing.[258] It had little effect, and a subsequent letter to *The Times*, published on 31 July 1855, would even dare to describe Beatson's forces as 'uncontrollable ruffians in British pay'.[259] Beatson, it suggested, had lost control of his regiments.

On 3 August, a report that Beatson had been murdered by his own Bashis made it into the late edition of *The Times*. The report was debunked later that same night by Lord Panmure from the floor of the House of Commons, but not before several newspapers in Britain and France had reprinted the story.[260] Despite the denials, and the evidence of those reporters who had actually travelled to his camp, Beatson's reputation was shredded.

Towards the end of August, with little to occupy them as they waited in vain for some form of battlefield deployment, a handful of Arab irregulars got into a scrape with some convalescing French troops whom they caught stealing grapes from a local vineyard.[261] Everything pointed to the French having been at fault, but Beatson's enquiry exonerated them and blamed the Arabs, creating even more ill-feeling at camp. By 22 August, Lord Panmure had had enough. He placed Beatson's cavalry under the direct command of General Robert Vivian of the British Turkish Contingent, with orders to move them to Crimea as soon as possible.

Vivian was an intelligent officer who had previously served as an Adjutant-General in the Madras Army. But he lacked combat experience and was untried under fire. Reluctant to lose command of his irregulars to a novice, Beatson wrote to Panmure on 9 September

---

[258] Beatson, W.F. *The War Department and the Bashi Bazouks*, W. Clowes & Sons, London, w1856, pp.21-22.
[259] *The Times*, 31 July 1855, p.9.
[260] Stevenson, *Beatson's Mutiny*, p.229.
[261] UK National Archives, FO78/1085, F195/488, Brett to Assistant Adjutant General, 22 August 1855.

claiming that 'the irregular cavalry would follow no other leader' than himself. In a letter to Vivian, he threatened to resign if he lost control of his regiments.[262] Accusing Beatson of insubordination,[263] Vivian sent Brigadier-General James Neill to 'assist' Beatson in bringing his troops under control and to conduct an enquiry into the state of things at Çanakkale.[264]

Angry, embarrassed, and humiliated, Beatson concealed Panmure's orders from his officers and refused to cooperate with Neill. He allowed Neill to preside over a series of courts martial to clear a backlog of disciplinary proceedings, only to then provoke him by releasing prisoners, citing 'irregularities' in the proceedings.[265]

Summer came and went, and O'Reilly and Shelley, forced to travel overland by a lack of sea transport, had yet to return to Çanakkale. On 12 September, Beatson wrote to the War Department insisting that they were expected any day, but the pair, as capable as any of reading newspaper reports of the chaos at camp, were not exactly infused with a sense of urgency and one week later they were spotted in Greece.

---

[262] Vivian, Robert J.H. *Narrative of Circumstances which Led to Major-Gen Beatson being Relieved from the Command of the Turkish Irregular Cavalry, and the Transfer of that Force to the Turkish Contingent,* Cox & Wyman, London, 1856, p.7.

[263] UK National Archives, WO6/80 Panmure to Beatson, 25 Aug. 1855; FO195 Beatson to Panmure, 9 September 1855; WO32/7295 Vivian to Panmure, 29 September 1855.

[264] Hansard, HC Debate, 22 July 1856, vol 143, cc1238-66; Vivian, Robert J.H. *Narrative of Circumstances which Led to Major-Gen Beatson being Relieved from the Command of the Turkish Irregular Cavalry* ... Cox & Wyman, London, 1856, pp.2-4, 7, 50-51.

[265] Neill to Stratford de Redcliffe, 31 July 1855 (FO78/1084); Mixed Commission 31 July 1855 (FO78/1084); Neill to Beatson, 2 August 1855 (FO78/1084); Mixed Commission, 4&6 August 1855 (FO78/1084); Hackett to Stratford de Redcliffe, 8 August 1855 (FO78/1084).

RESENTMENT IN THE RANKS

ON 19 SEPTEMBER 1855, Charles Thomas Newton, the renowned archaeologist and British Vice-Consul at Mitilini, on the Greek island of Lesbos, was sitting in his office, bored from a dearth of productive work and meaningful conversation.[266] Starved of company, he was offloading his frustrations in his diary when he heard the sound of unfamiliar voices. Two visitors had arrived: tall, haggard, saddle-sore, and unannounced. Abandoning his scribbling, he went to greet them.

> They spoke that mother tongue so welcome to my ears after long disuse; their complexions were burnt to a rich brick-red, their beards long and unkempt, their clothes worn and torn by many a hard day's ride; there was nothing smart about them but their long clanking swords and the still untarnished gold lace on their red foraging caps.
> I guessed at once whence they came, and, after the old Homeric fashion of hospitality, invited them into my house without knowing their names. They had been all over Asia Minor recruiting for General Beatson's Irregular Turkish Cavalry. Starting from Amasia, they had made a circuit by Kaisarea, Angora, Kutaya, Adramyt,[267] and thence across the Strait to Mytilene. They had been in districts where travellers were unknown, and where they were offered ancient coins in handfuls. They had met with various adventures. Sometimes they were thwarted by the fanaticism of the priests, and on those occasions carried matters with a high hand, putting refractory Mollahs in prison, and doing all sorts of unheard-of things in the name of the three allied Governments.
> Their only credential was a letter from the Seraskier; but,

---

[266] Then called Mytilene, it was then not just the name of the town, but of the entire Island.
[267] Now called Amasya, Kayseri, Ankara, Kütahya, and Edremit.

Resentment in the Ranks

being always accompanied by about fifty mounted Bashi Bozouks, they made their way like Xenophon with his ten thousand. As their recruits accumulated, they had sent them on to the Dardanelles in troops of fifty or sixty at a time, commanded by Turkish officers...

The names of my two guests were Colonel Shelley and Colonel O'Reilly. Both seemed hard as flints, and made of the right stuff for the rough work they will have to encounter. Colonel O'Reilly had been for the last two years in the Turkish service, and both had served in India. They left me for the Dardanelles last night.[268]

O'Reilly had never served in India, that experience had been Shelley's alone, and Newton is equally vague as regards the purpose of their presence on Lesbos, the third largest of the Aegean islands. The mention of rare and ancient coins, however, may not have been coincidental, for in his time at the British Museum, Newton had worked mainly in the coin collection.

Sent by the museum's Department of Antiquities to the Aegean to look after the museum's interests in Anatolia, Newton was well placed to assess, and perhaps even to purchase, rare coins. That said, their visit could equally have been related to their recruiting campaign, necessity having forced them to widen the search. Whatever the reason, the detour to Lesbos delayed their return to Çanakkale until 22 September, by which time all hell had broken loose.

O'Reilly and Shelley could not have picked a worse time to rejoin their regiments. Shortly before their arrival, incensed by the Bashi Bazouks' proclivity for helping themselves to the produce of local bazaars without paying, the Governor of Çanakkale had complained to Lord Stratford, the British Ambassador. He, in turn, had written to Beatson for an explanation, only to be told that Beatson would instigate his own enquiry and should his men be found guilty, he would hang them, but, if they were to be found innocent, he

---

[268] Newton, Charles Thomas. *Travels & Discoveries in the Levant*, Vol 2, Day & Son Ltd., London, 1865, pp. 17-19.

would hang the Turkish governor. The reply sent Stratford into goitres of rage and all but sealed Beatson's fate.[269]

James Henry Skene, the British Consul at Aleppo, was immediately dispatched to investigate. Upon his arrival at Çanakkale, he discovered that there had been yet another incident: an Albanian officer had attempted to rape the wife of an Arab officer, causing the Turkish governor to write to Beatson demanding that the Bashis leave their firearms behind when entering the town.

Acutely aware of the likely consequences of attempting to disarm the Bashis, Beatson refused, provoking the governor to call up two batteries of artillery and a contingent of Turkish cavalry and to place them between the town and Beatson's camp.[270] The French then followed suit, deploying three hundred troops to the rear. As HMS Oberon arrived and anchored off the town, HMS Redpole raced to Constantinople to inform Lord Stratford of the escalating situation, and Beatson was promptly ordered to comply with the governor's demands.

So desperate had Beaton been for competent officers that, in early August, he had been forced to 'borrow' medical officers from General Vivian and general staff from Field Marshall Paulet.[271] Any man with military experience who made even a speculative visit to the camp had found himself hired and promoted on the spot.[272] Upon their return to Çanakkale, therefore, O'Reilly and Shelley found the camp awash with raw and arrogant recruits. Struggling to find experienced officers to command them, Beatson promoted O'Reilly

---

[269] Skene, James Henry. *With Lord Stratford in the Crimean War*, Richard Bentley & Son, London, 1883, pp.48-49.

[270] Money, Alonzo and George Henry. *Sevastopol. Our Tent in the Crimea; and wanderings in Sevastopol*, by two brothers, Richard Bentley, London 1856, p.406; UK National Archives, WO32/7295, Skene to Stratford, 27 September 1855.

[271] UK National Archives, FO195/453, Beatson to Paulet, 3 August 1855.

[272] Money, *Twelve Months with the Bashi Bazouks*, p.14.

Resentment in the Ranks

and Shelley to lieutenant colonels. Their promotions were not universally welcomed.

Under the recruitment rules in force at the time, any British officer who joined the irregular cavalry would enter at one rank higher than they had enjoyed in the service of the Queen or the East India Company.[273] The last rank that Eugene had officially held in the British Army, however, was that of a lowly lance corporal. The highest rank he should have been eligible to receive was that of corporal.

Eugene, however, was an experienced and battle-hardened soldier who had risen through the ranks of the Hungarian, Piedmontese and Turkish armies to the rank of Major and who had been sending irregular intelligence briefings to both the prime minister, Lord Palmerston, and the foreign secretary, Lord Clarendon. His name, rank and reputation in the various armies in which he had served had long been accepted by the Foreign Office, and no official objection had been raised in those quarters to his promotion.[274]

The same, however, could not be said of those recently arrived recruits who had paid a small fortune for their commissions; of soldiers whose promotion upon recruitment had been limited to a single step in rank; or even of soldiers on loan from other British regiments who were prohibited from taking advantage of the kind of advancement that Beatson had offered to O'Reilly and Shelley,[275] both of whom were consequently scorned as 'Buzoukers' unworthy of their ranks.[276] Edward Money, quartermaster of the Arab Brigade, was a first-hand witness to the discontent:

> It was, that every officer should be given one grade of rank

---

[273] Woods, Laurence M. *Edward Shelley's Journal, 1856-61: A Victorian Remittance Man*, Author House, 2005, p.7.
[274] O'Reilly to Earl of Clarendon, 16 November 1854 (FO78/1058).
[275] Newcastle to Beatson, 1 February 1855 (WO6/79, FO195/453).
[276] Burton, Isabel, *The Life of Captain Sir Richard F. Burton*, Vol. 1, Asian Educational Services, New Delhi, 1999, p.238

higher than he held in the Queen or Company's service – thus a Lieutenant (as in my case) became a Captain – Captain, Major, and so on. This was all very well, but no rule existed as to men who had never been in any service, or else had served in foreign armies.

The consequence was that A, who had never seen a shot fired, nay, who had never touched a sword, but had passed his life as a clerk with the blunt end of a writing-desk screwed into the pit of his stomach for seven or eight hours a day, stood in a much better position when he applied for a commission in the force, than an officer of ten or fifteen years' standing – the former might be made anything the Chief thought best; to the latter could only be given one step in rank...

My Egyptian hero was not a bad judge of cause and effect, for he left the audience-chamber (which he had entered as Mr. Shelley, of Peninsular and Oriental fame) as Major Shelley, in command of one of the Arab regiments of Bashi-Bazouks, with pay and emoluments equivalent at least to £1,100 per annum, and priority of position, as well as rank, to many officers in the Queen's regular army of fifteen or twenty years' standing.[277]

In a camp where the lack of reading material was keenly felt, nothing was so eagerly devoured or as widely shared as a newspaper, and Eugene's career had been the source of several articles since he first arrived in Constantinople.[278] His background, both real and imagined, had been widely shared. Resentment of his promotion, in consequence, grew so swiftly that several junior officers refused to serve under him, one even going so far as to brand him a deserter from the Hussars. Beatson was quick to quash the insinuation:

> The objection to serve under Lieut. Colonel O'Reilly appears to be on the grounds of this officer having formerly held the position of a lance-corporal in one of Her Majesty's regiments; and I confess that I have still to learn that the raising of a man from the lower ranks of a profession, when

---

[277] Money, *Twelve Months with the Bashi Bazouks*, pp.6,12.
[278] *Waterford News*, 16 March 1855, p.1.

Resentment in the Ranks

all grades are honourable, can be made an excuse for not serving under him, more especially where the rank had been obtained by distinguished gallantry and merit, and at a time when these qualities are the ones sought by our government This officer was likewise approved of for this command by a letter from the Secretary for War, dated 1st July, 1855.[279]

There was also a world of difference between the resentment aimed at O'Reilly and that aimed at Shelley, under whom no British officer had refused to serve. Shelley was an English gentleman and a commissioned officer. O'Reilly, on the other hand, was an Irish rebel and a mercenary of disputed pedigree. Shelley was placed in command of the 4th Regiment, from which the majority of disciplinary issues had been emanating, and Eugene in command of the 6th, which was largely comprised of the recruits that he and Shelley had recruited in Anatolia. The pair quickly repaid Beatson's confidence by maintaining a degree of discipline that was the envy of the other Osmanli officers. One of Eugene's junior officers would later write:

> In October 1855, I was attached to the 6th Regiment (Anatolians) of this force, commanded by Lieutenant-Colonel O'Reilly, then encamped at the Dardanelles, and remained with them up to the period of their disbandment in August 1856. I cannot speak so confidently of the other regiments, though I have every reason to believe their conduct would favourably compare with regular troops, but that of my own regiment was exemplary. The men were temperate, tractable, and always quick to respond to the call of duty.[280]

---

[279] Cernovodeanu, Paul. "Punți între două lumi. Britanici printre români" ("Bridges between Two Worlds. Britons among the Romanians"), in *Magazin Istoric*, July 1995, p.40; Beatson to Vivian, 21 Sep. 1855 c.f. Beatson, W.F. *The War Department and the Bashi Buzouks*, W. Clowes & Sons, London, 1856, p. 84.

[280] *Sydney Morning Herald*, 12 July 1877, p.5; *Australian and New Zealand Gazette*, 7 May 1877, p.25.

In late September, the situation at Çanakkale deteriorated further. One of Beatson's officers, Lieutenant-Colonel Giraud, fell into an argument with the Turkish Colonel, Muheidden Bey. The Turk insulted Giraud, a Levantine of European descent whose mother kept a boarding house in the town, by calling him a 'tradesman'. In the resulting affray, both were wounded.

Exaggerated at every re-telling, the fracas provoked five of Beatson's officers to ride into town and confront the local Pasha. Prominent amongst that party were Richard Burton and George Lennox Rawdon Berkeley,[281] the latter a former captain of the 35th foot who had left the army under something of a cloud, having been named in the divorce of Dame Cécile Drummond Pellew.[282] Their extra-marital affair, begun in Paris in 1854, had famously produced an illegitimate son.[283]

Berkeley's appointment as Beatson's secretary and personal emissary had been as much a source of controversy in camp as Eugene's promotion.[284] Indeed of all Beatson's recommendations for promotion to the War Office, only those of Burton and Berkeley had to date been refused. It galled Berkeley to know that Eugene's subversive past had not been considered as great an impediment as being named in divorce proceedings. But then you didn't steal the wife of a Knight Companion of the Bath without consequences.[285]

Arriving at the Turkish picket, the British officers

---

[281] George Lennox Rawdon Berkeley, 7th Earl of Berkeley; *Berkeley Buttress*, February 2017, pp. 1-2.
[282] Cécile Drummond de Melfort.
[283] National Archives, U.K., Court for Divorce and Matrimonial Causes, later Supreme Court of Judicature: Divorce and Matrimonial Causes Files, J77; Reference Number J77/41/P24.
[284] Vivian, Robert J.H. *Narrative of Circumstances which Led to Major-Gen Beatson being Relieved from the Command of the Turkish Irregular Cavalry, and the Transfer of that Force to the Turkish Contingent*, Cox & Wyman, London, 1856, p.9; *Berkeley Buttress*, February 2017, pp. 1-2.
[285] Stevenson, *Beatson's Mutiny*, p.236.

threw down their gloves and challenged the Turkish officer to a duel. Not being familiar with the customs of European chivalry, the Turk, on the advice of the consuls, ignored them. The duels, as a result, never took place, but reports of the confrontation dealt a further blow to Beatson's reputation. He could no longer, it appeared, even control his personal staff. Upon hearing of the incident, Lord Panmure would order the retirement of Burton and Berkeley.[286]

The esteem with which Eugene was held, both by his men and his commanding officer, made what next transpired all the more surprising. Of all the officers Beatson might have expected to turn on him, O'Reilly's was a name that had never entered his mind. He had defended O'Reilly when others might have baulked at doing so, and O'Reilly had repaid his confidence with exemplary conduct. Unlike so many of his closest allies on his personal staff, O'Reilly had never once become a source of embarrassment. Then again, O'Reilly, who may have had designs on retaining his rank within the British Army at the end of the war, probably never expected Beatson to put him in a position that could so easily have led to a dishonourable discharge, or worse.

---

[286] UK National Archives, WO32/7295, Skene to Stratford, 27 September 1855; FO78/1152, Panmure to Vivian, 27 October 1855.

BEATSON'S 'MUTINY'

WITH THE SITUATION at camp becoming increasingly volatile, Beatson sent his wife and daughters, who had been spending the summer with him, to Malta. And if their departure appeared somewhat hurried, it was to prove positively lethargic compared to his own.[287]

Convinced that Beatson was losing the authority of his command, General Vivian wrote to Lord Panmure requesting Beatson's removal on the grounds that he was refusing to obey orders.[288] He also ordered Major-General Michael Smith of the British Turkish Contingent to proceed to Beatson's camp, where he was to take command and order Beatson to present himself at military headquarters in Büyükderé, to await a communication from the War Department.

Smith arrived in the Dardanelles on 28 September, at which point Beatson and several of his officers began to claim that the 1st and 2nd Regiments, which were comprised primarily of Albanian Bashis, would desert in large numbers if Beatson were to be removed. To lower the temperature, Smith agreed to postpone the announcement of his assumption of command and to allow it to be made known only that he was replacing Beatson as the senior British officer in the Dardanelles.[289]

Outside of Beatson's inner circle, none of Beatson's

---

[287] Hornby, Mrs Edmund. *In and around Stamboul*, James Challen & son, Philadelphia, 1858, p.110.

[288] UK National Archives, WO32/7295 Vivian to Panmure, 29 September 1855; WO 32/7514, WO 32/7515, 27 September 1855.

[289] Beatson, W.F. *The War Department and the Bashi Bazouks*, W. Clowes & Sons, London, 1856, pp. 90-92; UK National Archives, WO32/7295, Smith to Vivian, 4 October 1855 & Smith to Chief of Staff, 6 October 1855.

Beatson's 'Mutiny'

commanding officers, Eugene included, were made privy to this information, nor was there any urgency to their curiosity, as Beatson was currently laid up in bed following a riding accident in which his horse had fallen and kicked him in the head. On 30 September, however, Burton and Berkeley, both of whom had served under Beatson in India, convened a meeting at his bedside. Eugene was visiting Shelley at the 4th Regiment when Burton rode out to summon them.

'You know what to do,' said Burton, as if there would be a price to be paid for disloyalty.

At Beatson's headquarters Eugene encountered Wexford-born Brigadier General De Renzie Brett standing in the broad corridor that functioned as a form of anteroom to Beatson's bedchamber.[290] Smith had just asked Brett, commander of the Arab Brigade, to take over Beatson's duties until the transfer of command was complete. Brett had refused. 'Poor fellow,' he said, 'they have sent General Smith to replace him. It is a great shame. I have given in my resignation.' [291]

From his bed, Beatson outlined the current state of affairs to the six assembled officers, insisting that he answered only to Lord Panmure and questioning Smith's authority to take command.[292] What followed is clouded in controversy and dispute. From the available evidence, it appears that O'Reilly and Shelley either misinterpreted the tenor of the meeting or honestly concluded that what Beatson, Burton and Berkeley, in deliberately ambiguous language, were encouraging them to do was to tell Smith that, should he proceed to take command, they would resign en masse.

What is not in dispute is that O'Reilly and Shelley

---

[290] Later a member of the New Zealand Legislative Council.
[291] O'Reilly to Smith, 28 March 1856 (WO32/7515); *Morning Advertiser* 21 July 1856, p. 2.
[292] Smith to Beatson, 30 September 1855 (WO 32/7515); *Morning Advertiser*, 21 July 1856 (letters from Captains Berkely and Burton) cf. Vivian, p.18, 33.

left the meeting early. Under the impression they had just attended a gathering so contrary to the spirit of the Articles of War that it could easily be interpreted as incitement to mutiny,[293] they went straight to the British Consulate and requested an urgent audience with Major General Smith. Smith, who was dining with the acting British Consul, Frederic William Calvert. Smith was persuaded to leave the dinner table but, having heard what had transpired in Beatson's bedroom, he decided there was no immediate danger and returned to his guests.[294]

Neither O'Reilly nor Shelley shared the same affection for Beatson, Berkeley or Burton that many of their fellow officers did. Indeed their relationship with Burton and Berkeley, both of whom had seemingly been denied promotion on moral grounds, was especially curt.[295] It must have been obvious to Beatson when they left the meeting that they were not happy, and yet, despite the risk that they might report the matter, Beatson still proceeded to have another petition drafted, translated, and circulated among the foreign officers, asking them to refuse to serve under any general but himself.[296]

When word of this meeting reached Whitehall, Beatson, Burton and Berkeley were promptly recalled to Constantinople and ordered to report to General Vivian.[297] Relieved to be rid of the troublesome trio, Smith let the matter of mutiny drop, and Panmure ordered the removal of the Bashis, along with the rest of the British Turkish Contingent, to Kerch in eastern Crimea. Informed that there was insufficient forage in that area to sustain so many regiments of cavalry, that order was subsequently amended to send them on a

---

[293] Lieutenant-Colonel O'Reilly's Statement (WO 32/7515).
[294] Hansard, House of Commons Debate, 22 July 1856, vol 143, cc1238-66.
[295] UK National Archives, O'Reilly to Smith, 28 March 1856, WO32/7515.
[296] UK National Archives. Smith to Panmure, 5 April 1856, WO 32/7515.
[297] UK National Archives, FO78/1088, Stratford to Clarendon, 1 October 1855; Beatson, W.F. The War Department and the Bashi Bazouks, W. Clowes & Sons, London, 1856, pp.94,102.

three-hundred-mile trek to overwinter at Shumen.[298]

On 17 December 1855, Eugene's mother, Mary, died at the family home on Gardiner Street. She was sixty-one. She was buried in Glasnevin alongside her sister, Margaret, who had died in 1849.[299] High emotion was considered unseemly, if not downright offensive, in times of war. Death was part of a soldier's daily landscape. As much by habit as necessity, it was borne discreetly. Overt displays of vulnerability were believed to weaken an officer's authority. If Eugene grieved, it would have been privately.

His movements about this time are undocumented. It is possible he was given leave of absence to return to Ireland at about the same time that Shelley was given permission to travel to Péra. The pair were not popular with many of their fellow officers, and it may have been prudent to allow the dust to settle. Evidence for Eugene's return to Dublin is scant but not entirely absent. Back on 21 February 1855, his sister-in-law, Susan, had given birth to a baby girl, Mary Margaret. For some reason, the child was not baptised until 28 February 1856. On that day, the registrar recorded her godfather as one 'Eugene O'Reilly'.[300] Unlike the baptism of his godson, on this occasion he was not listed as *in absentia*.

Wherever they had spent the month of February, O'Reilly and Shelley were back in camp by March 1856, when Vivian sent Major General Arthur Shirley to Shumen to make a 'thorough inspection and special report on the irregular cavalry.'[301] At roughly the same

---

[298] *Dublin Evening Mail*, 26 November 1855, p.3; Schumla was the old name for Shumen.

[299] https://www.findagrave.com/memorial/205175085/matthew-oreilly; accessed 10 January 2023; Headstone, Plot D. 9.5, O'Connell Circle, Glasnevin Cemetery.

[300] N.L.I., Irish Catholic Parish Registers; Microfilm 09154/01.

[301] Vivian, Robert J.H. *Narrative of Circumstances which Led to Major-Gen Beatson being Relieved from the Command of the Turkish Irregular Cavalry, and the Transfer of that Force to the Turkish Contingent,* Cox & Wyman, London, 1856, p.9.

time, the British Ambassador in Constantinople despatched James Henry Skene to do the same. The latter arrived in the Dardanelles accompanied by his private secretary, Thomas Backhouse Sandwith, younger brother of Eugene's old friend, Humphry.[302]

Back on 13 February 1856, as part of his initial investigation, Shirley had spoken to Shelley at Péra, where Shelley had confirmed that both he and Eugene had left Beatson's room on the day of the alleged mutiny on account of the tenor of the discussions that were then taking place.[303] Two weeks later, on 27 February, Shirley's report was received by General Vivian, who wrote to Smith's replacement, Brigadier General Watt, claiming the reports concerning the mutinous behaviour of Beatson and Burton to be authentic and verifiable.[304] The scandal that followed the publication of that report would make household names of O'Reilly and Shelley in Britain.

Upon their arrival in Shumen, Shirley ordered the pair to provide written reports of the incident in order to confirm the charges of attempted mutiny. Eugene replied directly to General Smith:

Shumla, March 28, 1856.

Sir,
In obedience to your request to furnish you with a statement of what I can recollect of certain circumstances which occurred the day of your arrival at the Dardanelles, I present what follows, being, to the best of my belief, all of importance that occurred.

Being in the camp of the 4th Regiment, I was called aside by Captain Burton, at that time chief of staff to Major-General Beatson. He told me that you had been sent to

---

[302] Heartlet, Edward. *The Foreign Office List*, Harrison, London, January 1877, p.179.
[303] Vivian, Major-General Robert J. *Narrative of Circumstances Which Led to Major-General Beatson being Relived from Command of the Turkish Irregular Cavalry and the Transfer of that force to the Turkish Contingent,* Cox & Wyman, London, 1856, p.66.
[304] Ibid., pp. 21-22.

replace General Beatson, and that the presence of all officers commanding regiments was required at headquarters. I said that I would be down immediately. When riding away he said, "Of course you know what to do." ... When I entered General Beatson's room, he called all the officers present round his bed. He said, "That he had called us together to let us know that the Ambassador had caused General Vivian to send General Smith to replace him, which he conceived he had no right to do, as he was under the orders of no one but Lord Panmure"

Captain Burton then read the letter ordering General Beatson to give over the command to you. Captain Burton and Captain Berkeley both spoke for a long time, about intriguing on the part of the Embassy to depose General Beatson of his position, which had produced the illegal order from General Vivian which had just been read. I asked whether we had not some time previously been placed under General Vivian's orders. General Beatson said that he had been ordered to correspond through the officer commanding the Contingent. Captain Burton said that that order had been virtually cancelled by Lord Panmure himself, who corresponded directly with General Beatson.

He then produced an envelope addressed, 'To the Officer Commanding Her Majesty's Forces, Dardanelles,' and argued upon that, that General Beatson was recognised as a commander-in-chief. I then insisted on seeing all the letters from Lord Panmure, relating to the connexion of the Irregular Horse and Contingent.

While Captain Burton was looking for them, the officers present, with the exception of Major Copely, of the Osmanli Horse Artillery, and myself entered into conversation at the other end of the room. Captain Burton having produced a letter, I called Major Shelley to hear it read. The letter placed us directly under the command of General Vivian, and made the Irregular Horse part of the Contingent.

Captain Burton said that Lord Panmure had broken faith with us and the Bashi-Bazouks; that we had joined, and they had enlisted into the force as Beatson's Horse, and no one had a right to give the command to anyone else. Captain Burton said, "That it was our duty to inform General Smith that it was impossible for him to take command at present, that we should wait upon him in a body, and tell him that we could not answer for the fidelity of our regiment, and that if he persisted in taking the command, we should resign."

I argued against the preceding reasons which he was then giving for our required resignations but, perceiving that General Beatson (who was suffering from a recent fall from his horse) did not appear to notice what was going on, nor say anything to terminate the discussion, Major Shelley and myself left the room.

I have, &c.
(Signed) Eugene O'Reilly.
Lieut-Colonel Osmanli Irregular Cavalry.[305]

Shelley was not so courageous. His elder sister, Jane, had recently become engaged to the Under Secretary of War, Frederick Peel and, anxious to spare his family further embarrassment, Shelley rowed back on the statement he had given to Shirley:

Shumla, 28th March 1856.

My dear General,

To the best of my remembrance, shortly after your arrival at the Dardanelles, I found myself with the other commanding officers, at the quarters of General Beatson, when some conversation ensued, in the course of which a letter was produced, through which it appeared that the force was attached to the Turkish Contingent. Immediately upon hearing this, both Lieut.-Colonel O'Reilly and myself proceeded to report and place ourselves under your command. Beyond this, I really cannot make any distinct statement.

Believe me, &c.
Edward Shelley.
Major-General Smith, &c., &.c, &c.[306]

That was to be the end of the matter for now. Other

---

[305] *Morning Advertiser* 21 July 1856, p.2; UK National Archives, WO32/7515, O'Reilly to Smith, 28 March 1856.
[306] Vivian, *Narrative of Circumstances*, p.38.

developments had taken precedence. The signing of the Treaty of Paris on 30 March 1856 had made the Black Sea neutral territory, closing it to warships and prohibiting all fortifications and siting of armaments. Orders quickly followed to disband the British Osmanli Cavalry.[307]

Rather than simply paying off the Bashis and letting them loose in the countryside to loot and pillage, it was decided to march them to the places of their recruitment and then, and only then, to pay them.[308] And so, in the summer of 1856, Eugene found himself marching his regiment across Turkey to the town of Tarsus, where it was fully and forever disbanded.[309]

Back in London, Burton finally provided written testimony regarding his conduct in the alleged attempted mutiny. Furnished on 28 May 1856, it turned out to be as much an exercise in character assassination as a justification for his actions.

> The evidence supporting the charge of mutiny, forwarded by Major-General Smith in his letter, of the 5th of April, 1856, is that of Abdullah Tabid, M. Mallouf and Lieutenant Colonel Eugene O'Reilly. Permit me to consider the value of their testimony.
>
> Interpreter Abdullah Tabid is asserted positively, and without qualification, by Major-General Smith, to have written a 'round-robin,' inducing the native officers and men to refuse service under any General but yourself. The interpreter was then no longer with the force; yet, immediately upon this assertion, of whose perfect accuracy no doubt is entertained, follows this postscript: 'I have seen the interpreter, Abdullah Tabid, who has just returned from leave. He states that he is aware a paper of the description mentioned was signed by some of the native officers, but states that it was not prepared by him, and that he does not

---

[307] Walmsley, Hugh Mulleneux. *Journal of a Bashi Bazouk*, Groombridge and Sons, London, 1857, pp.128-129.
[308] UK National Archives, WO33/2A, Panmure to Smith, 26 May 1855; FO195/488, Smith General Orders, 12 June 1856; FO195/488, Commanding Officer's Reports, 8 July 1856.
[309] *Sydney Morning Herald*, 12 July 1877, p.5.

know by whom it was originally written.' It is evident that but for the fortunate, and possibly the unexpected return of Abdullah Tabid, the senseless assertion originally made, would have remained on the Minutes of the Inquiry.

M. Mallouf, a half-witted Syrian, educated at some Jesuit college, strong at languages, uncommonly weak in intellect, and provided with a mouth open for anything which may be put into it, is permitted to state that he does not think the preparation of the paper (marked C) to be the spontaneous act of the men, but believe that they were induced to sign it. M. Mallouf, not understanding at that time a word of English, heard me tell Lieutenant-Colonel Morgan, in English, I presume, 'to get the men of his regiment to sign a copy of the paper,' Why, may I ask, was Lieutenant-Colonel Morgan not examined? Why was this Mallouf taken as a sole authority? Why do our accusers report that the round-robin was prepared after Major-General Smith's arrival at the Dardanelles, and forward as a proof an irrelevant document (letter C) a respectful petition, dated fifteen days before his arrival?

With a sincere expression of regret, I feel it my duty to observe, that Generals Vivian and Smith, knowing, as from their long service in India they must have known, how prone are Orientals to frame statements in accordance with the bias of the requiring authority; I repeat that, fully aware of this, the blind and partial adoption on the part of these officers, of the assertion made by the abject creature under consideration, has painfully impressed me with this conviction.

Generals Vivian and Smith have either allowed private feeling to influence them, or, if that be not the case, they have failed in justice, by not subjecting their informant to an examination, which would have prevented the false and ridiculous statements appearing in a grave official form, palpably believed by and endorsed with the weighty names of two British General Officers. I need scarcely remind you that you received from M. Mallouf a letter dated Shumla, 5th February, 1856, in which he states that the men regret you much, and often ask when they are again to see their old General. The miserable answer 'soon, if Allah pleases!' Such is the character of the principal witness of the round-robin.

The Chief Interpreter, M. Giraud, asserted broadly to have prepared the paper, denies that he did it; so does M.

Mallouf; so does Abdullah Tabid. The round-robin, I need scarcely say, is purely a vision; but it is on this sort of evidence that our informant asserts of a charge of mutiny – "This is authentic, and can be fully proved and substantiated."

It is strange that while Lieut.-Colonel Eugene O'Reilly, an individual, still, I believe, holding local and temporary rank as an officer and gentleman in Turkey, furnishes minute details of occurrences, or (what comes to the same thing for the object in view), of what he imagines to have occurred, Major Shelley, when applied to, cannot really make any distinct statement. The Lieutenant-Colonel asserts that he called the Major to hear me read a letter, attaching us to the Contingent; and again, that he and Major Shelley left the room together. They acted then in union throughout the affair. The dates of their communication prove that both wrote on the same day, and from the same place, Shumla. I can state that they were intimate, had lived together for some time, and I have no reason to suppose that the same peculiar tie does not continue to bind them.

How comes, then, this glaring inconsistency of Lieutenant-Colonel Eugene O'Reilly recollecting every minute detail, and of Major Shelley, with full opportunity of refreshing his memory from his intimate's ample, I may say unlimited, store of information, forgetting every detail? Above all things, how does it happen that this glaring, and for one of these officers, this highly discreditable excess or deficiency of information did not strike Generals Vivian and Smith, and caused the latter to institute such inquiries as would have elicited the truth? Again, I am impressed with the conviction, and have deeply to regret that Generals Vivian and Smith have either allowed private feeling to influence them, or they have failed in justice by not subjecting their informants to an examination which would have prevented the false and ridiculous statement appearing in a grave official form, endorsed with the weighty name of two British General Officers.

My answer to Lieutenant-Colonel Eugene O'Reilly, the sole evidence of the second attempt to mutiny emanating, it is said, from me, is simply this:– He falsely states that he and Major Shelley left the room, saying they were soldiers, and could not listen to language which they thought most improper and mutinous. Neither you, nor Major Berkeley, nor I, are in the habit of allowing such expressions to pass unchastised; and had words so pregnant with meaning been really used, could Major Shelley, in whose honour I have the fullest confidence, have failed to remember them?

Lieutenant-Colonel Eugene O'Reilly will understand that, when saying 'of course you know what to do,' I meant nothing beyond our advising Major-General Smith to withhold publication of the order placing him in command of Beatson's Horse, a proceeding which the Major-General thought proper to adopt. I distinctly deny our questioning the fidelity of your regiments. And, briefly, to dispose of the mass of falsehood and inconsistencies of which Lieutenant-Colonel O'Reilly has made himself the mouthpiece, I assert that the matter discussed around your bedside was this:–

Did Major-General Smith bring an authority sufficient to warrant your resigning command on the spot, considering the danger attending so sudden and violent a change. I do not hesitate to own that, whilst you confined yourself to producing the orders of which Major-General Smith was bearer, I at once tendered my resignation. Brigadier-General Brett did the same. Colonel Crofton, your Commandant of Artillery, wrote from Scutari on the 27th of September, 1855, offering, in case of an amalgamation with the Turkish Contingent, to do the same. But I affirm upon my Honour that both Major Berkeley and I did all in our power to prevent a mutiny.[310]

Burton alleged Eugene to have been the mouthpiece of a 'mass of falsehoods and inconsistencies' – an attack that was not believed by Vivian, or, for that matter, by the prime minister, Lord Palmerston:

> One officer whose name has been mentioned in connection with this matter is Colonel O'Reilly – a man of perfect honour and the highest integrity, who was distinguished for his ardent desire to improve himself in his profession, and who with that view served as a volunteer in the Sardinian army, and also in the armies of other countries … As far as anything communicated by General Shirley originated with Colonel O'Reilly, I am confident, therefore, that the latter

---

[310] *Morning Advertiser* 21 July 1856, p.2; *Notes and Queries*, Volume 55, Issue 4, 1 December 2008, Pages 476–480.

stated only what he believed to be strictly correct.[311]

Having received little support in Constantinople, Beatson returned to England, where he would spend the next four years attempting to clear his name. A secret military tribunal, though finding no grounds for a court-martial, would fail to fully absolve him,[312] but he would partially clear his name by means of a successful libel action against James Henry Skene.[313]

Burton would never fully recover his reputation. Amongst his friends, he was generally believed,[314] but beyond his inner circle, Palmerston's support for Eugene held far greater weight. Burton would never forgive O'Reilly and would later publish as fact the endlessly recycled and re-embroidered lies that Eugene had deserted the British Army and converted to Islam.[315]

As for Berkeley, he would slip into the life of a compulsive gambler and playboy, gaining a reputation on the roulette tables of Paris, Liège and Hamburg as a man incapable of leaving the wheel until he had lost everything. Shelley would take himself off to Hawaii and China, where he would remain permanently 'unavailable' to testify. Eugene and he would never meet again.

Following the disbandment of the British Osmanli Cavalry, every British officer was given a gratuity of two months full pay, an allowance of thirty pounds for each horse he had to sell, and twenty-five pounds for his passage home. And so, in October 1856, his funds newly replenished, Eugene arrived in Dublin and put himself up in style at the Gresham Hotel, registering

---

[311] Hansard, Viscount Palmerston, House of Commons Debate, 29 July 1856, vol. 143, pp.1497-9.
[312] *The Times*, 21 April 1857, p.7.
[313] *The Times*, 14 January 1860, p.10.
[314] Royal Geographical Society, Speke Collection. JHS/1/20. J.H. Speke to Norton Shaw, 16 January 1860.
[315] Burton, Isabel. *The Life of Captain Sir Richard F. Burton*, Vol.1, Chapman & Hall, London, 1893, p.237.

as Lieutenant-Colonel O'Reilly. Part ostentation, part self-indulgence, the taking of a suite at the Gresham was never less than a public statement, as all arrivals at the hotel, established in 1817 to cater to the burgeoning middle class and visiting aristocracy, were routinely reported in the press.

But it was not Eugene's arrival at the Gresham that was to attract the greatest attention, rather his absence from the Crimean Banquet, a celebratory feast held at a warehouse on Custom House Docks to honour soldiers returning from the war.[316] 'Why,' a letter writer to the *Dublin Weekly Nation* asked, 'did our gallant countryman, Eugene O'Reilly' not attend the banquet, given that he was known to have been in Dublin at the time?[317]

On 1 November, Eugene checked out of the Gresham and headed to London.[318] He would return to Dublin for the Christmas holidays, but by early January he was back in Turkey,[319] and newly appointed to a command in the Turkish Cavalry,[320] an appointment reportedly facilitated by yet another letter of recommendation from the British prime minister, Lord Palmerston.[321]

---

[316] Now the EPIC Irish Immigration Museum.
[317] *Dublin Weekly Nation*, 15 November 1856, p.8; *The Union Democrat*, Sonora, California, 3 July 1869, p.1.
[318] *Dublin Daily Express*, 1 November 1856, p.2; *Dublin Evening Packet and Correspondent*, 1 November 1856, p.2.
[319] *Dublin Evening Post*, 6 January 1857, p.3.
[320] Hansard, Viscount Palmerston, House of Commons Debate, 29 July 1856, vol 143, cc1497-9.
[321] Ottoman Archives (BOA/Başbakanlik Osmanlı Arşivi), Istanbul, HR.SFR.3 33/2 April 1857

TURNING TURK

THE STORKS STILL sat upon the roofs of the tallest buildings and the cupolas of the mausoleums. Old men still sat with splayed haunches outside the coffee shops puffing on their nargiles. Knots of black eunuchs still followed the ladies of the harems through the slipper bazaar, and flocks of pigeons still burbled beneath the arches of the bazaars. Even the slave markets still operated with discretion and impunity.

On the surface, Constantinople had changed little since Eugene's first visit, perhaps even since the days of Byzantium, though the recent fashion for planting linden trees was slowly giving the city a more European look. And yet it felt very different. The war was over. The foreign mercenaries, if not their military leaders, had left and an autumnal zephyr of hope was wafting through the streets. After two and a half years of enormous casualties and military and logistical incompetence, men of fighting age could finally imagine a long-term future.

By October 1856, Eugene had settled into a life utterly different to any he had previously known, even while fighting in the Balkans. His daily routine began now, not with the sound of reveille, the peal of church bells, or the beat of an orthodox semantron, but with a discharge of musketry and a roll of drums from the Sultan's palace – a wake-up call that was regularly followed by the plangent chant of the muezzin from the local minaret. No longer a European officer who could confidently order his life by the clock, he now scheduled his day around the thrice-daily calls to prayer, the rise and fall of the sun, and the vicissitudes of markets that opened and closed according to prayer cycles and where nothing had a fixed price and every item its optimum moment of availability. Even time was measured differently, the hours being counted as hours after sunrise rather than hours after midnight.

Eugene did not want for anglophone company at this time. The city was still full of British officers, especially at the Hotel d'Angleterre, where the English-born wife of the proprietor would go to great lengths to create a British atmosphere, especially at Christmas, when exiles were most prone to regret, imagining roads untaken and lives unlived, falling prey to what the French would call the *vin triste*.[322]

For these exiles, nothing provoked regret quite so much as news from home, news that, as the years slipped by, was more frequently found in newsprint than in letters from friends and family. In the early days of 1858, however, even that tenuous tether was cut, for the new year began as the old one had ended – with a spell of severe weather. Wintry storms, sweeping down from the Black Sea, had caused part of the Golden Horn to freeze to such a depth that people could cross the strait on foot.[323] With nautical travel hindered, the post from London was significantly delayed. But, when, at length, it arrived, it brought an odd sense of satisfaction.

In direct contradiction to the rumours being spread by Burton and others, Eugene's name was prominently listed in the English papers amongst the British officers to whom the Sultan had awarded the Imperial Order of Medjidie.[324] It was, in a sense, a public vindication. Medals were not awarded to deserters. He must have wondered, however, why the only member of Beatson's regiment not to receive the medal was his

---

[322] Alcohol-induced misery.
[323] Hornby, Mrs Edmund. *In and around Stamboul*, James Challen & son, Philadelphia, 1858, pp.495-497.
[324] *Morning Post*, 03 March 1858, p.2. *Saint James's Chronicle*, 25 October 1860, p.7; *Glasgow Courier*, 1 November 1860, p.3; *West London Times*, 3 November 1860, p.3.

friend, Edward Shelley. The reasons are unclear, but it may well have been related to his volte-face during the investigation of the Beatson Mutiny.

Meanwhile, on 8 April, at St Thomas' Church in Dublin, Eugene's younger brother, Matthew, married Sophie Fenton, youngest daughter of the late Thomas Fenton, Chief Examiner of the Court of Chancery.[325] Eight days later, his father died.[326] It is unlikely Eugene attended either the wedding or his father's funeral, for he was known to be still in Constantinople at the end of the month, serving as a lieutenant-colonel in the 7th Syrian Division under the command of György Kmety (Ismail Pasha), who had entrusted Eugene with the task of communicating on his behalf with the Glasgow publisher, Richard Griffin, to whom he had offered his military biography.[327]

By the spring of 1859, Eugene had been promoted to colonel and appointed to the staff of the Seraskier, Mehmed Riza Pasha, for whom he now worked as an intermediary with the British Embassy and as a translator of diplomatic communiqués.[328] Thanks largely to his linguistic skills, he was slowly moving up in the diplomatic world, and mixing in elevated circles.

This most recent promotion was likely the result of the relationship he had been forging with an up-and-coming administrator by the name of Mehmed Fuad Pasha, son of the famous poet Kececizade Izzet Mola. If a European officer had to hitch his fortune to a rising star, he could hardly do better than Fuad, a man destined to become one of the most brilliant statesmen of his age.

Tall, witty, and handsome, Fuad had started out as

---

[325] *Saunders's News-Letter*, 14 April 1858, p.3.
[326] Matthew O'Reilly was buried alongside his wife in Glasnevin Cemetery, Plot D. 9.5, O'Connell Circle.
[327] British Library, Add MS 28510, f. 325 Eugene O'Reilly, lieut. col. in the Ottoman Army: Letter to R. Griffin and Co., 1860.
[328] Accounts and Papers of the House and Commons, State Papers: China, Japan, Syria, Vol. 69, No. 91, Consul James Brant, to Sir Henry Bulwer, 27 April 1859, p.71, London, 1860.

a *littérateur*. But when his father fell out with Sultan Mahmud II, the family's property was confiscated, and the family exiled to Sivas. After that, Fuad foreswore poetry for medicine and French, and served briefly as a surgeon in the Turkish Navy. At the completion of his military service, he joined the translation bureau of the Sublime Porte, where he devoted himself to the study of modern languages, economics and international law. Rising slowly through the ranks, he went on to serve in various diplomatic missions to London, Paris, Madrid, St Petersburg, Bucharest and Cairo.

In 1852 Fuad was appointed Foreign Minister of the Ottoman Empire and, in 1856, made chairman of the Council of the Tanzimat, a body charged with overseeing the modernisation and reform of the Ottoman Empire. His appointment marked a shift in Turkish foreign policy from a preferred alignment with Great Britain to building closer ties with France.

Through his work for the Seraskier, his fluency in French and Italian, and his command of vernacular Turkish, Eugene came to Fuad's attention, not just as a loyal, courageous and innovative military strategist but as a talented linguist. Most foreign officers in Ottoman service employed personal translators, but not Eugene, and by early 1860, his linguistic skills had led to him to a position as Fuad's aide-de-camp, where he had slowly, and largely anonymously, perfected the art of making himself indispensable.[329]

That anonymity, however, was to prove short-lived. An outbreak of sectarian violence in Mount Lebanon in May of 1860 would draw his name back into the columns of the London newspapers and O'Reilly into an extraordinary stew of diplomatic, civil and military service that not even he could have seen coming.

---

[329] Fawaz, Leila Tarazi. *An Occasion for War – Civil Conflict in Lebanon and Damascus in 1860.* University of California Press, Berkeley, 1994, p.106.

THE DAMASCUS MASSACRE

IT WAS, ALLEGEDLY, the oldest continuously inhabited city in the world – a religious, racial, and cultural melting pot that hosted within its honey-coloured walls myriad mosques, synagogues and Christian churches and accommodated all manner of religious and political beliefs, not to mention a host of historical resentments.

This was nineteenth-century Damascus, a pilgrimage destination for the world's major monotheistic religions and a strategic international crossroads that several world powers were scheming to control. Tension here was nothing new. Centuries of sieges, occupations and massacres were fossilised in the structural fabric of the city, each new generation having unsentimentally and unrepentantly repurposed the remnants of the old. Nor where these architectural tokens the only shrines to conflict, for the city sat in the shade of Mount Qasioun, where Cain was said to have murdered Abel. The latter's tomb, although outside of the city walls, had long been emblematic of the kind of internecine squabbles that had bedevilled the city's history. This was the city where Paul had had his Epiphany, and Stephen, the first Christian martyr, had been stoned to death.

Exacerbating the city's vulnerability to racial and religious violence was the influence of the many-speckled pilgrims and proselytisers that daily strolled its busy streets, each myopically cradling the texts of their conflicting religious 'truths', tolerant but never fully accepting of the presence of the other. In Damascus, one never needed to look far to find a cause for anxiety, and beyond the geniality of the coffee houses, the vibrancy of the souks, and the desert traditions of hospitality, a powder keg of political, ethnic and religious tensions had long awaited the careless or strategically engineered spark.

In 1860 that spark was provided by an outbreak of violence in nearby Mount Lebanon, an area notorious for the diversity of its population, where race and religion could change between one valley and the next. Sectarian tensions between the Maronite and Druze communities, in particular, had been escalating of late,[330] and prospects for a peaceful resolution frequently frustrated by the activities of Britain and France, each seeking to influence affairs in the region through their respective support for the Druze and Maronite factions.

A unique, tightly knit and secretive religious sect, the Druze, though technically Shi'ite Muslims, had a belief system that incorporated an eclectic mix of Islam, Judaism, Christianity, Hinduism, Gnosticism and classical Greek philosophy. Reincarnation was a central tenet of their beliefs and amongst those believed to have been incarnations of the Divine, they counted Adam and Jesus, but not Mohammed. A highly conservative society, their women still wore the *tantour*, a cone-shaped headdress that had once been popular throughout the Levant.

The Druze faith was intended to be impenetrable to all but a closed circle of initiates called the *uqqāl*, or enlightened ones. All others were classed as *juhhāl* or uninitiated. Any Druze man or woman over the age of forty who was deemed worthy, was eligible for initiation, after which they were required to adopt the distinctive dress and white turbans of the *uqqāl* and to pursue a life of religious piety, sobriety, and virtue.

---

[330] Fawaz, Leila. "The Druze-British Connection in 1840-1860", in *The Druze – Realities & Perceptions*, Druze Heritage Foundation, London, 2005, pp.105-113; Schlicht, Alfred. "The Role of Foreign Powers in the History of Lebanon and Syria from 1799 to 1861", in *Journal of Asian History*, Vol. 14, No.2, Wiesbaden, 1980, pp. 97-126.

The Damascus Massacre

The Maronites, on the other hand, were the dominant Christian sect in Lebanon. A dark-haired and sturdy mountain people, their religion had been formed in the seventh century when the Byzantine emperor, Heraclius, attempted to unite the two main factions of his Empire, the Monophysites of Egypt and Syria, who believed in the singular nature of Christ, and the Orthodox Church, who believed in a dual Christ that was both God and man. Hearing that the monks of St Maron held a compromise view, in that they believed in a dual Christ whose will was single, Heraclius had declared the Maronite view to be the official faith and in the process, created a new sect of Christianity that was initially declared heretical by Rome but later welcomed back into the fold.

The Maronite church, in accepting the leadership of the pope, had been permitted to retain its liturgy in Syriac – an Aramaic language related to the language of Christ – as well as its own saints and customs. From the time of Louis IX, furthermore, they had claimed friendship with France. Their closeness to Rome had similarly afforded them special status amongst many European nations, a status bitterly resented by their Druze neighbours, who were being courted by the British.

The Maronites and Druze had lived in relative peace since the early 17th century, but back in 1840, a Druze and a Maronite fell into an argument over the rights of the Maronites to hunt partridge on land owned by the Druze near Deir el Qamar. The argument triggered a conflict between the two communities that had continued intermittently for almost twenty years. In the summer of 1859, it began to spiral out of control.

It all started with a simple dispute over a game of marbles between Druze and Maronite children in the town of Beit Meri, in the hills above Beirut. When the parents became involved the dispute escalated into a bloody quarrel involving all the villages of the Matn District. Then, on 22 May 1860, when a small group of

Maronites fired on a group of Druze at the entrance to Beirut, killing one and wounding two,[331] it triggered a tide of violence that saw hundreds of Maronite Christians massacred at Hasbaya on 3 June, and at Rashaya on 11 June. Before any real measures could be taken to restore the peace, a Druze attack on the Christian city of Deir al Qamar on 19 June 1860 saw widespread looting and arson, thousands of Christians massacred, and Beirut overflowing with Maronite and Greek Catholic refugees.[332]

Alarmed at the reports he was receiving, Fuad sent Eugene to investigate the causes and determine what needed to be done to restore order in a challenging landscape of scattered villages, undulating ridges and vast ravines. The Irishman found the situation to be out of control and, fearing European military intervention, the local governor was encouraged to negotiate a truce. Before he could even begin, events in Damascus overtook him.[333]

On the afternoon of 9 July, a group of Muslim youths were arrested for having drawn crosses on the ground in the Christian quarter of Damascus. Arrested and forced to clean the streets they had defaced – an outrage to Islamic sensibilities – their punishment provoked a riot that rapidly descended into the largest Muslim massacre of non-Muslims in the city since the time of Nero.[334] A mob of anything from twenty to fifty thousand Muslims from the Maidan and Salihya districts stormed the Christian Quarter. The Greek Orthodox, Greek Catholic and Armenian churches were burned to the ground, as were several foreign consulates. Rather than fight, many of the Christians opted to hide, which proved a poor strategy against

---

[331] Lutsky, Vladimir Borisovich. *Modern History of the Arab Countries*, Progress Publishers, Moscow, 1969, pp.135-136.
[332] Fawaz, *An Occasion for War*, pp. 63–74; *Daily News*, London, 9 July 1860, p.5; *Sheffield Daily Telegraph*, 28 June 1860, p.2.
[333] Harris, William. *Lebanon: A History 600-2011*, OUP, 2012, p.158.
[334] *New York Times*, 13 August 1860, p.1.

fire. In the subsequent conflagration, hundreds were burned to death. Even the local Chief of Police was alleged to have lured Christians from their homes with promises of safety and then shot them.

15. The Massacre of Christians at Damascus.

Amongst the Muslim population, the Algerian separatist Abd el Kader was the most prominent figure in attempting to staunch the bloodshed. Roaming the Christian quarter with a private band of armed men, he rescued many European consuls and merchants and escorted them, and many thousands of others, to the citadel, where he forced the governor, Ahmed Pasha, to protect them.[335]

---

[335] Emerit Marcel. "La crise syrienne et l'expansion économique francaise en 1860" in *Revue Historique*, vol 207, Presses universitaires de France1952, pp.213-216; Aouli S., Redjala R., Zoummeroff P., *Abd El Kader*, Fayard, Paris, 1994, p.460.

Charles Henry Churchill, the British Consul in Syria, reported the resulting casualties to be 11,000 murdered, 100,000 refugees, 20,000 widows and orphans, 3,000 habitations burnt to the ground, and 4,000 perishing from destitution. The actual figures were probably much less, but his report created such outrage across Europe that France, Great Britain, Prussia, Russia and Austria, all despatched troops to the region. [336]

Though the cause of the violence on Mount Lebanon was fundamentally different to that in Damascus, they became conflated in the universal outrage, and when the British despatched Lord Dufferin to investigate the Sultan responded by sending Fuad Pasha to the region in the role of Extraordinary Commissioner. He left on the steam frigate *Taif* on 12 July 1860, charged with maintaining the dignity of the Sultan and with permission to act as he saw fit to ensure that neither the French nor the British were afforded an opportunity to use the protection of minorities as a pretext for intervention in Ottoman affairs.

Before he left, Fuad received a letter from the British Ambassador, Sir Henry Bulwer, urging him to consider Eugene O'Reilly for a command position.[337] As a Christian with military experience in Ottoman service, Eugene was always more likely to be accepted by both the British and the Maronite community than a Muslim Turk.[338] Upon his arrival in Beirut, therefore, Eugene found himself pressed into service as Fuad's intermediary, most frequently with Bulwer himself.

My dear Sir,

Fuad Pasha has requested me to write to you and to give

---

[336] Churchill, Charles Henry. *The Druzes and the Maronites Under Turkish Rule from 1840 to 1860*, London, Bernard Quartich, 1862, p.219.
[337] Farley, James Lewis. *The Massacres in Syria*, Bradbury & Evans, London, 1861, pp. 6-7, 86, 163.
[338] National Archives UK, Norfolk Record Office, O'Reilly to Bulwer, 7 March 1861, BUL1/277/259.

you an account of what he has found to be the state of the country, and of the subjects contained in his official despatches, which he thinks you would desire to have information of. He desires me at the same time to present his compliments and to say that were it not owing to the great press of affairs, he would write to your Excellency himself.

He finds, and I myself believe, the state of the country round Beyrout to be perfectly tranquil, as a kind of truce between the Druses and Maronites has been made, and the former have returned to their villages. He is endeavouring to restore the public confidence in the authorities, which has been shaken by the conduct of the Turkish Commanders in some places: for this purpose he has ordered Khoorshid Pasha to visit in a corvette the towns on the coast as far as Latakia, and the Vice-Admiral Mustapha Pasha to proceed for the same purpose as far as Acre, sending along with him one of the Catholic members of the Commission to distribute money to be used for the relief of the wounded Maronites along the coast; he has already given money to the Sisters of Charity (French) here, for the additional expenses of their hospital incurred by the reception of the wounded...

In a few days more we will advance into the interior, when His Excellency intends to inflict a most severe punishment on the guilty parties at Damascus.

I have, &c.
E. O'Reilly.[339]

And I myself believe! On the face of it, the phrase appears presumptuous, but Eugene, if not actually a British spy, was at the very least being employed as a diplomatic back channel. And not just with the British. Fuad was also using the Irishman as a conduit to

---

[339] Destani, Bejtullah. *Minorities in the Middle East, Christian minorities 1838-1967 – Christian Communities in the Levant, Part II, 1860-1861*, Archive Editions, Anthony Rowe, Chippenham, 2007, pp.130-131; F.O. 78/1509, Bulwer-Russel, no.464, 30 July 1860; *Great Britain Parliamentary Papers*, vol.68, 1860, State Papers Syria, p.56, O'Reilly-Bulwer, 18 July 1860, encl. in no.73, Bulwer-Russell, 1 August 1860; Bulwer to Russell (FO195/659).

Stanislas D'Aragon, the Count of Bentivoglio and French Consul General in Beirut, with whom Eugene was also on friendly terms. Tasked with convincing Bentivoglio to make efforts to forestall a French peacekeeping mission, Eugene enjoyed limited success.[340] Bentivoglio *would* write to his superiors on the matter, but the French government was not about to pass up an opportunity to gain a foothold in Syria.

By 29 July 1860, Eugene had moved with Fuad to Damascus, where for several days, they camped outside the gates, rejecting all efforts by local notables to establish communication.[341] By the time Fuad allowed them to visit, anxious tongues were easily loosened in the hope that cooperation might lead to leniency.[342] It did not. By 10 August, 700-1000 suspects had been imprisoned.

By this time, the Porte had been forced to assent to a French 'humanitarian' mission, which placed enormous pressure on Fuad to restore order before they arrived. Though the French mission was limited by agreement to six months, a general mistrust of Napoleon III meant that fears were rife that it could yet escalate into occupation, or even annexation, as had happened in Nice and Savoy earlier in the year.

During the second week of August, Cyril Graham, an Arabic-speaking Englishman who had travelled to Hasbaya and Rasheya as Lord Dufferin's investigator, returned to Damascus. Accompanied by the English consul, James Brand, he called on Fuad. To forestall the deployment of French troops, he suggested, Fuad should send Turkish troops to Hasbaya and Rasheya to protect the surviving Christians. Fuad agreed only to send Eugene to Sidon with a battalion and two pieces of artillery to secure the evacuation of two thousand Christians before the French could do so

---

[340] Fawaz, *An Occasion for War*, p.120.
[341] *Morning Chronicle*, 24 August 1860, p.5.
[342] Testa, Le Baron Ignaz von. *Recueil des traités de la Porte ottomane avec les puissances étrangères.* Vol. 6, Muzard, Paris, 1884, pp.91–92.

and claim the credit. On 5 August,[343] stopping in Beirut to brief the British Consul General, Niven Moore,[344] Eugene presented the following letter from Fuad:

> Knowing beforehand that all that I may communicate to you will cause you an especial pleasure, and that an exact relation of facts may prevent those complications which may arise from a movement of troops which I have been informed has been combined, I have thought it my duty to bring to your knowledge all that has passed here, and I send to Beyrout my Aide-de-Camp, Colonel Hassan Bey, in order that he may give you, as well as the Admiral Commanding the Naval Forces or Her Britannic Majesty before Beyrout, details concerning our operations here, and in order that he may make to you, *vivá voce*, certain observations which I have thought fitting to cause to be addressed to you.[345]

Moore's reply was drafted two days later:

> ... With respect to the verbal observations which Colonel Hassan Bey was charged by Your Excellency to make to Admiral Martin and myself, I beg to state that I sought a special interview with the Admiral in order to confer with him thereon. The result of our deliberations I have verbally confided to Hassan Bey, to be by him communicated to your Excellency.[346]

Fuad's subsequent instructions to Eugene were promptly leaked to the press, conveniently providing advanced warning of his intentions to the Druze:

> The instructions are most precise and emphatic for the

---

[343] *Liverpool Albion*, 13 August 1860, p.9.
[344] *Journal des Debats*, 9 September 1860, p.1.
[345] Destani, Bejtullah. *Minorities in the Middle East, Christian minorities 1838-1967 – Christian Communities in the Levant, Part II, 1860-1861*, Archive Editions, Anthony Rowe, Chippenham, 2007, pp.148-149; Moore to Russel (FO195/659).
[346] Accounts and Papers (35), State Papers – Syria, 5 February – 6 August 1861, Vol. LXVII *Correspondence Relating to the Affairs of Syria 1860-61*, Harrison & Sons, London, 1861, p.75.

safety of the Christians, in whose defence the Turkish soldiers are told they ought not to hesitate to shed their last drop of blood. When the Christians are in safety it is probable that Hassan Bey will unite under his command the Turkish garrisons and tribes willing to fight against the Druses, and establish himself in force either in Rashaya or in Hasbaya, with a view to maintaining communications between Sidon and Damascus, and at the same time intercept the Druses who may seek to retire from hereabout into the Hauran.[347]

While Eugene was preparing for his expedition into the mountains, Fuad arrived in Beirut and met in person with Moore, and with Martin, the Commander in Chief of the British Mediterranean Fleet. The British were extremely exercised regarding the liberty of Khurshid Pasha, the Governor of Sidon, whose decision to garrison his troops on 20 June had resulted in the massacre of twelve hundred Christians at Deir el Qamar.[348] At Moore's insistence, Fuad had Khurshid arrested and transported to Constantinople.

On 14 August, a Turkish liner left Beirut with 800 Turkish troops bound for Sidon. It was followed the next morning by a Turkish gunboat carrying Fuad's chief-of-staff, Ismail Pasha (György Kmety) and his aide-de-camp, Hassan Bey (Eugene O'Reilly).[349]

> Hassan Bey (Colonel O'Reilly) started for Sidon on Wednesday, to make a night attack on the Druses in the vicinity of Hasbaya and Rasheya, and bring away some 2,000 Christians, chiefly women and children, who are still in that district. One of the Druse Sheiks has declared that if a French soldier sets foot in their territory he will massacre every Christian he can lay his hand on, and make for the Hauran. O'Reilly is to take 1,200 Turks from Sidon, and the result of the expedition is to be looked for with great anxiety.[350]

---

[347] *The Times*, 31 August 1860, p.7.
[348] *New York Times*, 28 July 1860, p.1.
[349] *The Scotsman*, 8 October 1860, p.3; *The Times*, 31 August 1860, p.7.
[350] *John Bull*, 8 Sept. 1860, p.4; *The Montreal Witness*, 3 October 1860, p.2.

The Damascus Massacre

By 16 August, Moore was writing to the British prime minister, Lord John Russell, that:

> ... proper measures have been at last taken by the Turkish Authorities; the Governor of Sidon is to be recalled, the Commanders of troops at Sidon, and of those despatched to Hasbaya and at Rasheya under Hassan Bey (Colonel O'Reilly), as well as the battalion stationed on the limits of the Christian and Druse districts in Lebanon, have received orders to check the Druses, and if necessary to fire upon them.[351]

Eugene's orders were to proceed to Hasbaya and Rasheya to supervise the evacuation of Christians to Sidon and then unite, under his command, those Turkish garrisons and tribes that were willing to fight against the Druze and to garrison them in Hasbaya, a site of considerable strategical importance which, if occupied in force, would effectively divide the Druze and cut off their line of retreat into the Hauran.[352]

Sidon, however, was an odd choice of rendezvous for Christian refugees. A small, mediaeval town of sandstone buildings and narrow shady streets, it was situated on a headland joined by a short causeway to the ruins of an old Crusader castle, remnants of a Christian past that had long since been abandoned. When the Druze attacked the mountain village of Jezzine, the entire Christian population had raced to the steep ravine that stretched downhill from the waterfall – the fifth highest in the world – in an attempt to escape the sword-wielding Druze. More than twelve hundred were slaughtered in the space of just two miles. A large number of women and children did, nevertheless, manage to stay far enough ahead of their pursuers to make it, terrified and exhausted, to the gates of Sidon, only to find themselves refused

---

[351] Accounts and Papers (35), State Papers – Syria, 5 February – 6 August 1861, Vol. LXVII *Correspondence Relating to the Affairs of Syria 1860-61*, Harrison & Sons, London, 1861, p.89.
[352] *The Times*, 31 August 1860, p.7.

entry by the town's Sunni population, who joined in the slaughter. Three hundred bodies were later recovered from the beach and gardens. Many had been raped.

Sidon did, however, possess the advantage of being a seaport and of offering the shortest and quickest route into and out of the mountains. Any rescue mission involving predominantly Muslim soldiers, however, would require strong leadership and would have first to gain the trust of the terrified and mistrustful Christian survivors. It would not be an easy task.

The plan was for Eugene to gather his troops in Sidon and then proceed to the Druze stronghold of Hasbaya, where he would be assisted by a certain Ali Bey, chieftain of the Metuali,[353] a community of dissenting Shia Muslims noted by generations of travellers for their toughness, treachery and inhospitality. A Metuali, it was said, would not eat with a stranger, and should he allow a Christian to drink from one of his vessels, he would feel compelled to smash it afterwards. No less than the Druze, the Metuali had their own reasons for assisting in the evacuation of Christians.

> Fuad Pasha is taking vigorous steps to prevent a retreat to the mountains, and, if the force which has just left Damascus under the command of Hasan Bey [Eugene O'Reilly] executes its object, these savages will not only be intercepted, but divided, and one half prevented from communicating with the other. This manoeuvre, if it is accomplished, will bring the savages to terms, and the loss of so many heads will follow.[354]

---

[353] Accounts and Papers (35), State Papers – Syria, 5 February – 6 August 1861, Vol. LXVII *Correspondence Relating to the Affairs of Syria 1860-61*, Harrison & Sons, London, 1861, pp.88-89; *Liverpool Albion*, 13 August 1860, p.9; Shannon-Chastain, Joshua. *For Queen and Sultan: Anglo-Ottoman Advisors, Soldiers, Mercenaries and Imperial Agents in War and State (1853-1878)*, M.A. Hist., thesis, İstanbul Bilgi University - Institute Of Social Sciences, Istanbul, 2016, p.80.

[354] *Evening Mail*, 3 September 1860, p.2.

The Damascus Massacre

The day after Eugene's departure for Sidon, six thousand French troops landed in Beirut. Time was now of the essence, and upon his arrival in Sidon, Eugene immediately set out for Hasbaya, marching his troops through the lemon and orange groves of the coast and oak stands of the lower hills into a rocky landscape of goat-strewn hills and olive trees that in its vernal splendour would be carpeted in blood red anemones. It currently offered a parched appearance broken only by the odd red clump of corn poppies.

A solitary man might walk this route in half a day, but an army took at least twice that, and by the time they arrived among the olive groves of the Wadi el Taym, their presence had long been expected, not least because of the frequency with which Fuad's intentions were being reported in the press. Militarily unwise but politically astute, the leaks alerted the Druze and gave them time to escape. Whether or not these leaks were a ploy by Fuad to avert further bloodshed, the effect was the same.

> ...on arriving at Hasbaya, Hassan Bey found that the Druses had decamped and that instead of there being 2,000 Christians to bring in there were only a few hundreds.[355]

There may have been just a few hundred Christians remaining at Hasbaya, but there were others at Meri Ayume and in the surrounding villages, all of whom Eugene took under his protection. By the end of August, they numbered almost three thousand. All were transported to Sidon, a town too small, corrupt, and woefully ill-equipped to cope with the sudden influx.[356]

Though European journalists welcomed the rescue mission, they were less enamoured with Fuad's tardiness in organising public executions.[357] And so,

---

[355] *Lancaster Guardian*, 8 September 1860, p.7.
[356] *New York Times*, 25 October 1860, p.2.
[357] *The Times*, 31 August 1860, p.7.

between 20 and 21 August, in response to the burgeoning international pressure, up to 172 Muslim prisoners were executed in Damascus.[358] And it didn't end there. As residents of a holy city, the youth of Damascus had long been exempted from military service. Following the massacre, however, 20,000 young men were suddenly conscripted and marched over the mountains to Beirut. To pacify European anger, there was even talk of making Christian Lebanon a separately ruled state.

Having deposited the refugees in Sidon, Eugene returned briefly to Hasbaya to oversee the execution of local civic and military leaders.[359] Recalled to Damascus soon after, Fuad next charged him with another important mission, this time neither diplomatic nor military – though it certainly had elements of both – but judicial!

---

[358] Salibi, Kamal S. "The 1860 upheaval in Damascus as seen by al-Sayyid Muhammad Abu'l-Su'ud al-Hasibi, Notable and later Naqib al-Ashraf of the City" in *Beginnings of Modernisation in the Middle East: The Nineteenth Century*, ed. William R. Polk and Richard L. Chambers, Univ. of Chicago Press, Chicago, 1968, p.200; Skene, James Henry. *Rambles in The Deserts of Syria and Among The Bedaweens*, John Murray, London, 1864, p.258.

[359] Abkarius, Iskander Ibn Yaqub. *The Lebanon in Turmoil - Syria and the Powers in 1860 - Book of the Marvels of the Time Concerning the Massacres in the Arab Country*, vol. 7, Yale University Press, 2010, pp.152-154.

TRIBUNAL JUDGE

On 9 September 1860, at Beirut, Fuad convened an extraordinary tribunal – much like the one he had already established in Damascus – to try a small number of Turkish officials charged with abetting the massacres. The tribunal was to be held concurrent with the international commission of inquiry despatched by the European powers to Damascus to investigate the causes of the violence. Unlike the international commission, the Beirut tribunal would have the power to apportion guilt and carry out punishments, up to and including execution.

Five men were appointed to sit as judges at Beirut, amongst them two Christians: Abro Sahak Efendi, the Armenian director of French correspondence at the Ottoman foreign ministry, and Colonel Eugene O'Reilly, Fuad's aide-de-camp. These Christian appointments were intended to reassure the British and French, who had serious concerns regarding transparency.[360] James Lewis Farley, the Irish Accountant-General of the State Bank of Turkey, observed at the time that:

> If there were anything to be concealed, it is not probable that Fuad Pasha would have placed a man like Hassan Bey (Colonel O'Reilly) on the commission at Damascus.[361]

---

[360] Accounts and Papers (35), State Papers – Syria, 5 February – 6 August 1861, Vol. LXVII, *Correspondence Relating to the Affairs of Syria 1860-61*, Harrison & Sons, London, 1861, p137; Destani, Bejtullah. *Minorities in the Middle East, Christian minorities 1838-1967 – Christian Communities in the Levant, Part II, 1860-1861*, Archive Editions, Anthony Rowe, Chippenham, 2007, p.221; *Morning Post*, 3 September 1860, p.5.

[361] Farley, James Lewis. *The Massacres in Syria*, Bradbury & Evans, London, 1861, pp.99-100.

One of the prime targets of the Beirut tribunal was Khurshid Pasha, the Ottoman general who was alleged to have garrisoned his troops and allowed three thousand Druze to launch an unimpeded assault on Deir el Qamar on 2 June. His trial was scheduled to be held in public and under the presidency of Ahmed Pasha, the former Governor of Izmir. When the tribunal began its work on 19 September, however, it did so in secret,[362] prompting the British plenipotentiary, Lord Dufferin, to write to the British Ambassador, Sir Henry Bulwer:

> This is a better tribunal than the one erected at Damascus. Although not entitled, perhaps, to very much confidence, it might have been impossible to find among the subjects of the Porte the elements of a better one.[363]

As a sitting member of the tribunal, Eugene's reputation could not have been higher in Syria or at home. A month into the deliberations, however, in October 1860, reports began to appear in the British and Irish papers alleging that Eugene had re-joined the Sardinian Army and led a successful cavalry charge against a regiment of his fellow countrymen at Castelfidardo. The news was not well received in Ireland as the Irishmen he was alleged to have defeated had been fighting in the Papal Army of Pius IX.[364]

Though a unification movement, under the leadership of Giuseppe Garibaldi and Giuseppe Mazzini, had been growing in popularity since the mid-1850s, Italy still consisted of a patchwork of small independent states. Key to their dreams of unification was the annexation of the Papal States, which occupied the middle of the Italian peninsula. Ill-

---

[362] *The Times*, 6 October 1860, p.10.
[363] Accounts and Papers (35), State Papers – Syria, 5 February – 6 August 1861, Vol. LXVII *Correspondence Relating to the Affairs of Syria 1860-61*, Harrison & Sons, London, 1861, p137.
[364] *Globe*, 24 October 1860, p.4; *Morning Post*, 24 October 1860, p.2; *Dublin Evening Mail*, 29 October 1860, p.2.

equipped to defend them, Pius IX had called on the Catholics of Europe to help him raise an army and, in March 1860, papal emissaries had arrived in Dublin to recruit an Irish battalion. Within weeks they had collected over £80,000 in donations and 1,400 volunteers. Motivated as much by anti-British sentiment as by religious fervour, the volunteers had journeyed to Italy and formed an Irish battalion under the command of a Major Myles O'Reilly (no relation).

16. Italian States in the 19th Century.

When the Sardinian forces crossed into the Papal States, on 11 September, they had faced minimal resistance except in those areas protected by Irish regiments. During the largest battle, which took place on 18 September at Castelfidardo, one hundred and five Irishmen under the command of Captain Martin Kirwan were routed in a cavalry charge led, allegedly, by Eugene O'Reilly:

> The colonel who led on the charge was an Irishman – Eugene O'Reilly of '48. This is an extraordinary, and perhaps a melancholy fact... After the Crimean War he entered the Sardinian Army as a sub-lieutenant, and, during the late campaign in Italy, rose to the rank of colonel in the lancers. This accounts for his appearance the other day at Castelfidardo.
>
> There is something awfully sad in seeing Irishman against Irishman, and especially so in this case. I am quite sure Eugene O'Reilly has as warm a love of country as ever, and even though from circumstances obliged to draw his sword in an unholy cause, is still as much a man of honour and principle as when he left Ireland in '48. He has the character of being a first-rate officer, possessed of the most wondrous pluck and energy – a fact, by the way, which our poor fellows felt bitterly at Castelfidardo. I wonder how he felt when he saw his countrymen cut down? [365]

The source of the above report was a letter written by a Lieutenant Crean, a member of the Irish Papal Brigade. Dated 16 October 1860, it was written almost a month after the battle and possibly by the same Michael Theobald Crean who had been wounded during the Siege of Spoleto and subsequently decorated by Pius IX for bravery.[366] The letter, widely reprinted, unleashed a torrent of indignation.

Crean would almost certainly have trained with many of those who had fought at Castelfidardo and would have known some of them personally. He may even have received reports of the battle as he recovered from the wounds he had received at Spoleto. But he had not been there, and neither had Eugene. The

---

[365] *Globe*, 24 October 1860, p.4.
[366] *New Zealand Tablet*, 3 September 1914, p.41.

Tribunal Judge

continuous reprinting of Crean's letter, nevertheless, forced James O'Reilly to write letters to all of the Irish newspapers refuting the reports and asserting that Eugene had not been in Italy at the time but commanding a cavalry regiment in Syria.[367] Not every paper published a retraction.

While the Castelfidardo scandal raged at home, Eugene continued to languish in Beirut, sitting for days on end in a crowded, airless courtroom, listening to testimony after repetitive testimony. It was neither a pleasant nor an easy task, but his presence was deemed essential to public confidence. On 22 October, the Beirut correspondent of the *Boston Traveller* observed:

> The trial of Kourshid Pasha is still in progress, and much fear is expressed lest he may be declared innocent. I have much faith, however, in the commission which will pronounce judgment upon him. It is composed of Admiral Mustapha Pasha, Ahmed Pasha, the new Governor General of Beirut, Hassan Beg (Colonel O'Reilly), Abro Effendi (an Armenian), and the Mufti of Beirut.
>
> All but Mufti have the confidence of the people generally, but the majority of the commission is Moslem. The result is awaited with great anxiety by every one of all creeds who are interested in the Syrian question, for he has already been condemned by public sentiment, and I think there is not a Frank in Beirut who would not be willing to sign his death warrant, so strong is the moral conviction of the community as to his guilt.[368]

Though the hearings had begun in private, such was the growing concern about transparency that they were soon after opened to public scrutiny. They became, as a result, something of a tourist attraction:

---

[367] *Evening News* (Dublin,) 25 October 1860, p.3; *Dublin Evening Mail*, 29 October 1860, p.2; *Cork Daily Herald*, 26 October 1860, p.3; *Wexford People*, 27 October 1860, p.5; *Dublin Weekly Nation*, 27 October 1860, p.142.

[368] *New Orleans Daily Crescent*, 29 October 1860, p.3.

> The foreheads of European assistants unwrinkle when in the presence of the indiscreet curiosity of tourists, mostly English travellers who, taking advantage of an open court, were sketching the faces of the accused and even those of the Ottoman judges, to the great displeasure thereof.[369]

Of late, many of Eugene's missions had been more diplomatic than military in nature, his letters to Bulwer at times verging on espionage. The Ottoman Empire needed British help to survive, and Britain needed the Ottoman Empire to block Russian expansion in the east and protect its trade route to India.[370] Affable, likeable, and resourceful, Eugene was trusted by both parties to walk this diplomatic tightrope, but not even *his* presence on the Beirut Tribunal could deflect criticism of the tribunal's deviations from European norms of justice:

> These persons sit at one end of a long room, which is very luxuriously furnished with divans, carpets, &c., and smoke their cigars deliberately, none of them taking notes or even possessed of writing materials. The great Mufti sits in the middle of the upper end of the room quite by himself, with his legs crossed under him in oriental style, and rocks from one side to the other, puffing his tobacco smoke, resembling not a little a steamer rolling at the anchorage in a Syrian harbor... The prisoner ... sits in a chair in the end of the room opposite the Mufti. By his side sits six or eight Maronite and Greek Christian witnesses, who appear to testify against him.
> In the middle of the room and nearly halfway between the Mufti and the prisoner, sit the clerk and the interpreter, and opposite them, in a row extending along the side of the room from the Mufti and the Pashas down towards the witnesses, are the seats of the agents of the Five Powers and spectators. The Mufti rocking to and fro, looks at the prisoner and asks the interpreter a question in Turkish. The interpreter writes it down carefully, and then repeats it

---

[369] Anonymous. *Souvenirs de Syrie (expédition française de 1860) par un témoin oculaire*, Plon-Nourrit, Paris, 1903.

[370] Temperley, Harold. *England and the Near East: The Crimea*, Vol. 1, Archon Books, 1964, pp.66, 80, 146, 272.

in Arabic to the prisoner. The prisoner replies to the questions to "what he knows about the cause of the war," that he knows absolutely nothing, that he was a private individual, knowing nothing of what was transpiring, and proceeds in a long speech to exculpate himself, and call upon God to witness that he is innocent, and that the resurrection day will reveal all hearts, etc., etc. The interpreter explains the meaning in a few words to the Mufti, who takes another cigarette, and proceeds to mediate. The other Pashas ask questions, and then the witnesses are examined.

None of the examiners take notes either of the questions or answers. The prisoner has no counsel. The witnesses and prisoner converse and dispute together, denying each other's statements, and then in a loud voice, and while the Mufti and Pashas are engaged in conversation, the Druse culprit, notoriously guilty, turns to the witnesses and says, "why do you testify this way, oh my children?"

They answer, "because it is true and you cannot deny it", and the trial drags along. The prisoner is compelled to defend himself, which he does, keeping up a running fire upon the witnesses and interpreter, abounding in assertions of innocence and pious ejaculations just about in proportion to his own iniquity and complicity in crime.[371]

When judgements were finally pronounced, in December 1860, forty-three prisoners had been sentenced to death and three to life imprisonment, while Khurshid Pasha was found guilty of nothing more than incompetence and given a lifetime ban from holding public office.[372] By that time, Eugene had already moved on as Fuad again had need of him in Lebanon.

---

[371] *Bombay Times and Standard*, 26 February 1861.
[372] UK Accounts and Papers (35), State Papers – Syria, 5 February – 6 August 1861, Vol. LXVII *Correspondence Relating to the Affairs of Syria 1860-61*, Harrison & Sons, London, 1861, pp.298, 309, 311.

MOUKHTARA

THE PROBLEM NOW was what to do about the Druze. To absolve the Porte from responsibility for the massacres, Fuad wanted to throw as many of them to the firing squads as possible. However, the British had a political interest in protecting the Druze, and the French in protecting the Maronites. To balance the needs of all concerned, Fuad brought 3,500 soldiers to the strategically located village of Moukhtara in the Chouf District of Mount Lebanon, where he convened yet another extraordinary commission under the presidency of Eugene O'Reilly.

Just 52km from Beirut, close to the confluence of the Barouk and Wadi el-Maa rivers, Moukhtara was a picturesque little village surrounded by aromatic forests and filled with flower gardens. Characterised by small streets, charming staircases and traditional stone buildings, it was particularly noted for its olive groves and vineyards.[373] Upon his arrival, Fuad ordered his chief-of-staff, General Kmety, to requisition as his headquarters the palace of Said Bey Jumblatt, the leader of a prominent Druze family imprisoned following the recent troubles. Eugene was allocated quarters within the palace.

With Jumblatt's powerful friends in London having issued orders to the British Embassy to 'save him, whatever the costs', on account of the close relationships the British had nurtured with the Druze since the 1840s, Eugene's contact with British Embassy officials increased significantly, and not always through official channels.

---

[373] Lester, Laela Ateah. *Cedars of Lebanon*, Columbia Press, Winnipeg, 1951, p.36.

Moukhtara

17. The Jumblatt Palace, Moukhtara, 1861.

On Thursday, 25 October, Charlton Whittal, a British businessman with strong ties to the Ottoman government, arrived in Moukhtara with a journalist from the London *Morning Post*. Accompanied by a unit of Turkish soldiers, Whittal had been sent into the mountains at the behest of Lord Dufferin and the Anglo-American Relief Committee to recover plunder taken during the massacres. They, too, were given rooms at the palace.[374] Whittal rose early the following morning and went to seek out Eugene, who was recovering in his quarters from a recent fever. For the journalist who accompanied Whittal, it was to prove a dramatic and memorable visit:

> I went with Mr. Whittal to pay a visit to Asam Bey (Colonel O'Reilly) and while we were sitting smoking on his divan a servant came in to him and pronounced a word or two, which had the effect – although he was only recovering from fever, and therefore not well – of making him jump up and run out of the room. But on seeing my companion, who understood what was said, rush out equally fast, I saw that something was the matter, so I followed them, and directly received the comfortable news that the powder magazine directly over which we were standing was on fire.
>
> "Well, that is some news at any rate," was my answer; for it struck me in rather a comical light at first. I had just been asking for news, but was told there was none.
>
> I along with the others, however, soon got downstairs into the court, where I saw the smoke issuing from a grated window, and wishing not to be too close when the explosion took place, I went to another part of the building, where I found Asam Bey, who at last explained the mystery.
>
> The powder magazine was below where we were, but it was underground. The smoke was issuing from a window, but it was one that belonged to a kind of stable over the magazine; a fire having been made inside was the cause of the smoke. The little stir that was caused, therefore, was from the mistake of a stupid fellow who knew nothing of the matter, and came in to say that the powder magazine, forsooth, was on fire. Had it been so of course everyone near the palace would have been killed.[375]

Come November, Fuad departed, leaving Kmety in command of the military and entrusting Eugene with

---

[374] *Morning Post* (London), 10 November 1860, p.5.
[375] Ibid.

Moukhtara

responsibility for overseeing the tribunals and controlling the conduct of the new civil governors appointed after the abolition of the Druze feudality. That appointment effectively gave Eugene civil control of the district.[376]

Shortly after this, Kmety, finding himself criticised by Fuad for his alleged partiality towards Christians, resigned his commission and retired to London.[377] His departure created a power vacuum in the military that Fuad asked Eugene to fill until such time as a permanent appointment could be made. The level of trust implicit in this decision cannot be understated, for, in addition to his civil and judicial duties, Eugene effectively now commanded the Ottoman Army in Syria. All of a sudden, the Irishman found himself holding the reins of civil *and* military power in the region and governor in everything but name.

This was exactly the type of responsibility that the Irishman had hungered for – a moment ripe with the promise of celebrity and a place at the top table. It was also the kind of posting that, in normal circumstances, should have led to greater things. But further promotion was dependent upon the pleasure of Fuad, and in December 1860, as Eugene relinquished control of the military to Omer Pasha, moves were already afoot to recall Fuad to Constantinople.[378]

At 850m above sea level, Moukhtara made for a comfortable summer posting. But it could get bitterly cold in winter when underfoot conditions would see local women strapping six-inch stilts of wood or iron to their feet to avoid sinking in the glutinous clay. And so, on 22 December, before the rains could turn the roads to mud, Fuad instigated a massive military

---

[376] *Temple Bar, A London Magazine,* Vol. VI, Ward and Lock, London, November 1862, p.321.
[377] *The Illustrated Usk Observer and Raglan Herald,* 1 December 1860, p.2; *The Spectator,* 24 November 1860, p.1115.
[378] *Morning Post,* 19 November 1860, p.5; *Morning Chronicle,* 3 October 1860, p.5; National Archives UK, Norfolk Record Office, O'Reilly to Bulwer, 7 March 1861, BUL1/277/25a.

operation on Mount Lebanon, during which almost a thousand Druze were arrested and brought to Moukhtara where, on 26 December, Fuad's other aide-de-camp, Abro Sahak Effendi, arrived to sit alongside Eugene on the extraordinary tribunal[379]

With every passing day, the radiance of the Irishman's celebrity dimmed a little more, as even with Abro's assistance, little progress was made. Frustrated by the refusal of Christian victims to give evidence, mostly from fear of retaliation, Eugene and Abro were forced to conduct the trials without them.[380] How much of a role Eugene had in the subsequent executions is difficult to ascertain, but a letter from Damascus, dated 16 December 1860, records an order for the execution of twelve Druze. The persons ordered to carry out these executions were Omer Pasha and Eugene O'Reilly.[381]

Eugene was not averse to carrying out such orders, but his military career had not entirely robbed him of morality and volition. A letter to Major A.J. Fraser, a British agent attached to Lord Dufferin, concerning the case of a certain Ishmail Quaida, suggests that Eugene was far from happy with every decision of the tribunal and quite prepared to lobby British influence if he felt a miscarriage of justice was to be perpetrated in the cause of expediency.[382] Mostly, however, he was Fuad's man and did Fuad's bidding.

In January 1861, Eugene received a letter at Moukhtara from his older brother, James, with whom he had maintained a dutiful fraternal correspondence. James detailed the various untruths that were currently being spread concerning Eugene's alleged conversion to Islam, most recently in the *Dublin*

---

[379] *Morning Post*,(London) 12 January 1861, p.5.
[380] Ibid.
[381] *Liverpool Mercury*, 1 January 1861, p.2; *Saint James's Chronicle*, 1 January 1861, p.6.
[382] British Library, Add MS 44913 A, O'Reilly to Major A.J. Fraser, ff. 216r-217r.

Moukhtara

Evening Mail of 29 October 1860. Eugene did not delay in replying:

Head Quarters, Muktarah, 24 January 1861.

My Dear James,
A letter from you, dated a long time back, has just reached me here. I am sorry for the delay, because there is one subject of which it treats, upon which I am anxious to communicate with you as soon as possible. You tell me that an Irish provincial paper, in reference to a statement that I had become a Mussulman, called upon you to contradict it, and you say you did not think it worthwhile to give a contradiction to a statement you regarded as so palpably incredible.

Now, I think that you should have done so, because if the report had been that I might have had a great advancement had I become a Mussulman, and that I had refused to do so, no one would have remembered the matter in a week after; but the statement that I had become a Mussulman, with the inference that I did so in order to hold the high post in which Fuad Pasha placed me here, will certainly be recalled by someone or other hereafter, and your not contradicting the rumour will seem to give it confirmation. Pray, therefore, have a communication with the editor of the paper containing this statement and let it have my unqualified contradiction.

To me, it is evident that it has arisen from the excitement created in Europe by what took place in these mountains last summer. The feeling against the Turkish government has, in fact, amounted to Christian fanaticism, and any calumny on the Porte or its servants has been hitherto willingly accepted without inquiry.

Owing to this state of feeling, I am not at all surprised that people, on learning that the President of the Commission which formed the Provisional Government of the Lebanon after the abolition of the Druse Feudality, and the Commander of the First Division of the Army of Syria, was one Hassan Bey, and becoming aware that Hassan Bey was Eugene O'Reilly, should take it for granted that he had changed his religion as well as his name.

But the fact is, I was left here to direct affairs precisely because I am a Christian. Hassan Bey is but the title by which I am known in the army, and I beg of you to correct the false impression which has been created on the minds of some; for although my future career will be in a distant land, I have still too many sympathies with my countrymen at home not to desire that such of them as know of me at all should know me as I am.

If any of my old friends should ask you why I am in the Turkish service, tell them that I am living by an honourable profession, exercised in the cause of humanity and civilization. Unfortunately, after the late deplorable events in this country, it requires a greater knowledge of the true state of the East than the generality of people at home possess to understand this perfectly.

The following is the truth about the Turkish Government, compressed into a few sentences:–

European statesmen, seeing the immense distance, morally speaking, which separates the Asiatic nations from the European, conceived the idea of creating in Turkey a Reformed Government, which would seek to govern the vast provinces of that empire according to wise and liberal laws, and would endeavour, by degrees, to draw its population into the habits of civilized nations.

That government they have succeeded in establishing at Constantinople; but, unfortunately, the Sublime Porte does not as yet possess a full sufficiency of agents capable of carrying out its ideas, and attending to the administration of its provinces. Those provinces are vast and distant from the capital; their populations are rude and ignorant; and, as the Porte cannot always find men capable of understanding its system, and having all the qualities necessary for the administration of affairs, foreign intrigue takes advantage of this weakness to increase its difficulties.

In contributing such services as my sword or my brain can render to this government, I may, in some degree, lessen the difficulties with which it has to struggle, and help it to sustain the just application of the laws which it has promulgated. If I see I may be of use in this way, I will not easily abandon what, in this case, becomes my duty; and I shall be happy if I can contribute, no matter how distantly, to the maintenance of the authority of the Porte, and thereby help to avert the evils which would follow the overthrow of the Sultan's government.

The existence of a Reforming Government, such as that

Moukhtara

of Constantinople, produces an effect throughout the Mussulman world. It is an intermediary between Christianity and Islam. Destroy it, and you remove from Islamism all that it has of promise and of hope; and Europe, having no means of persuading or enlightening the Mussulman world, must meet it as an enemy.

But Europe will do well to be patient with the weakness of a government endeavouring to do its best. For, if a struggle come, although Islam will fall, it is after its submission that the great torrent of blood will flow. Who will possess Egypt? Who will rule at Constantinople? A Sheik once said to me – 'If the Franks choose to do so, they can force us to abandon the shores of the White and Black Seas. We will return to the Steppes, beyond the Caspian, from which our fathers came; and the Franks will then destroy each other, fighting for the possession of the countries which we have abandoned. When they are again weak and barbarous, as they were before our Arabs gave them the light of science, our sons will return and repossess what we have lost.'

I do not believe that the Turks, if they abandon the conquests of the sons of Seljeik, and of Osman, would ever return; but I think, as the Sheik did, that the greatest misfortune for Europe and mankind would follow the overthrow of their dominion. Therefore I willingly serve the Porte, and have been grieved to see that Europe, owing to an excitement, which looked very like the fanaticism which itself condemns, has been ready, for some time past, to misinterpret the acts of that government, and to doubt, without reason, the upright principles of those who serve it.

Your affectionate brother,
Eugene O'Reilly.[383]

At James' request, the *Dublin Evening Mail* agreed to publish Eugene's letter and to precede it with the following half-hearted retraction:

COLONEL EUGENE O'REILLY. We willingly comply with

---

[383] *Dublin Evening Mail*, 15 March 1861, p.2; *Dublin Evening News*, 15 March 1861, p.3; *Dublin Weekly Nation*, 23 March 1861, p.478; *Dublin Weekly News*, 23 March 1861, pp.6-7.

the request in the following note, and publish Colonel O'Reilly's letter, not less influenced by its own intrinsic interest than by our desire to do justice to that gallant soldier. We may observe, however, that the article which Mr. J. W. O'Reilly refers as having appeared in the *Mail* of the 29th of October was by no means intended, or we think, calculated to support the injurious rumour then in circulation respecting Colonel O'Reilly's religious profession. Our paragraph – for it was nothing more – was merely playful allusion to another allegation, that he had charged the Irish Brigade at Castelfidardo.

It is no more discredit to Colonel O'Reilly to "turn Turk" – that is to serve the Sultan— than it was to Sir Baldwin Walker (Pasha), Sir W. F. Williams (Pasha) of Kara, or to Admiral Slade, whose Turkish synonym has escaped our memory. We should greatly prefer to see the task of restoring peace in the Lebanon intrusted to Hassan Bey rather than to a French Marshal.[384]

The *Kilkenny Journal* was similarly cooperative and sympathetic:

Our readers will probably remember the question which has elicited this interesting letter. Eugene O'Reilly, a prominent member of the Irish Confederation in '48, was obliged to become an exile save himself from prosecution. Like many of his ancestors, possessed a proud military spirit; and after a few campaigns in the service of Sardinia, in '49, he joined the army of the Sultan, in which he was quickly promoted to the rank of Colonel. In the commencement of the Crimean war, some of the most daring and successful exploits were achieved under the command of Eugene O'Reilly, the Irish Refugee of '48.

Thenceforward lose sight of him, till a letter from our friend, Lieutenant Crean, of the Irish Brigade, stated that, at Castelfidardo, the Irish Company suffered severely from a charge of the Sardinian Lancers, commanded by Colonel Eugene O'Reilly! Everyone was surprised that a brave Irishman, and devoted adherent to creed and country, should fight against his own countrymen, on such an occasion; but a letter from the Colonel's brother, Mr.

---

[384] *Dublin Evening Mail*, 15 March 1861, p.2.

Moukhtara

O'Reilly, of Gardiner-street, Dublin, soon set the matter right, by stating that Colonel O'Reilly was still in the Turkish service.

The *Evening Mail*, in its usual sneering tone, commented on this, and said – "Colonel O'Reilly has not fought against the Pope he has only turned Turk!" Here, in Kilkenny, we found this impression to prevail, also, to a certain extent; and we called upon Colonel O'Reilly's brother to contradict this statement, as well the former; and for the sake of Eugene O'Reilly, are delighted that we did so...[385]

March was perhaps the best time of year to be in Moukhtara. The heavy rains of January and February had refreshed the countryside, and the last of the snow had melted. The brown grass had turned green again, and the groves of orange and lemon trees had begun to put forth their annual blossoms. With temperatures averaging between 14 and 17°C, the climate was about as pleasant as a northern European could find anywhere in the Middle East. In May 1861, however, just as the valley brightened into the kind of place to which an old soldier might dream of retiring, Eugene found himself recalled to Beirut.[386] During his absence, Druze militia attacked two Maronite Christian villages inciting Fuad to personally lead another 'inspection tour'.

The Druze chief who had led the attacking party was soon arrested, and his subsequent execution temporarily inhibited the Druze from taking further action.[387] Having reassured the Christian community and European diplomats of his seriousness, Fuad returned to Beirut, where he had no sooner settled behind his desk than he was recalled to Constantinople.[388] The

---

[385] *Kilkenny Journal*, 13 March 1861, p.2.
[386] Destani, Bejtullah. *Minorities in the Middle East, Christian minorities 1838-1967 – Christian Communities in the Levant, Part II, 1860-1861*, Archive Editions, Anthony Rowe, Chippenham, 2007, p.526.
[387] *Hull Packet*, 21 June 1861, p.7; *London Evening Standard* 19 June 1861, p.5; *York Herald*, 22 June 1861, p.2.
[388] *Whitehaven News*, 27 June 1861, p.3; *Lancaster Gazette*, 29 June 1861, p.7.

new Sultan, Abdulaziz, impressed by Fuad's decisiveness, had decided to raise him to the post of Grand Vizier, the Ottoman equivalent of prime minister. The promotion removed Fuad from Damascus and stripped Eugene of his fleeting authority in the region.

Eugene did not return to Mount Lebanon where, in June 1861, a *mutasarrifiyya*, was established, with the aim of providing a more regular form of government under local control. Nor did he accompany Fuad to Constantinople. There was a world of difference between being aide-de-camp to the Foreign Minister and aide-de-camp to the Grand Vizier, not least in the type and scope of influence that could be wielded.

There was only so high that a foreigner, and most especially a non-Muslim, could be allowed to rise in Ottoman service, and Eugene now found himself cut adrift from Fuad and appointed instead as aide-de-camp to the new Governor of Damascus, Halim Pasha, the former president of the Council of War. After all that he had done at Moukhtara, Eugene felt cheated.

Early in 1861, when the possibility of creating an independent mounted police force in Lebanon and Syria began to be mooted, Eugene immediately set his sights on command. On 3 July 1861, he wrote to the British Ambassador, Sir Henry Bulwer:

> My Dear Sir,
>
> If I thought that I could not rely upon a continuation of the favor which Your Excellency has already shown to me, I would point to the services which I rendered last autumn and winter to, I may say, the government which you represent as giving me some right to make the request which I am about to take the liberty of pressing on you.
>
> According to the new arrangement for the government of Mount Lebanon a new force is to be created to the duties of the police of the districts comprised in the Pashalic. This force will of course be commanded by a Christian, and I ask Your Excellency to use your influence to procure me this position.
>
> If the nature of my experiences and my conduct since I

have been in Syria has been fairly represented, I have no doubt that Your Excellency will perceive that no one can have the same claims to be appointed to this important post. The fact of my being a British subject is the only obstacle I know to my obtaining it, and this I feel will prevent Fuad Pasha from giving me the assistance which he ought. He seems to forget that a few months ago (in more difficult times it is true) I held civil and military power in the greater part of this district.

I suppose that the appointment rests with Fuad Pasha and hope that Your Excellency will dispose His Excellency to look favourably upon the claims which I really possess. By doing so you will add greatly to the many favors rendered by,

Your obliged and faithful servant,
Eugene O'Reilly.[389]

Eugene's entreaties fell on deaf ears until such time as the Druze began to intensify their raids on the roads to and from Damascus, so disrupting the trade of the region where Eugene's name was once again mentioned at the highest levels.[390] Summoned to Constantinople on 4 January 1862, he was promised his desired appointment. He could do little now but wait for it to be ratified.[391]

---

[389] National Archives UK, Norfolk Record Office, O'Reilly to Bulwer, 2 July 1861, BUL1/277/26.
[390] Archives de Ministere des Affaires Étrangères, Correspondence Politique et Consulaire, Damas, Lanusse a Thouvenel, Vol.7, I, 10 February 1862.
[391] *The Times*, 18 March 1862, p.26; Archives du Ministere des Affaires Etrangeres, Correspondance Politique du Consulat de Damas, Hecquard, Vol. 7, I, Jan. 4, 1863, pp.3-7.

THE LETTER TO WILLIAM SMITH O'BRIEN

GIVEN ALL THAT had occurred in Syria, it was perhaps inevitable that the 'Dashing *Sabreur* of Kalafat and Oltenitza' should be feeling disillusioned and weighed down by the drudgery of waiting for an appointment, the ratification of which appeared to be slipping further away with every passing day. He had experienced war at a visceral level, and his body still bore the scars. He had been just nineteen when the course of his life had been irretrievably altered by the '48 rebellion. And for what? incompetently led rebellion that had never stood any realistic chance of success?

It was perhaps unfortunate that, at the very time his natural optimism began to desert him, he should come across an open letter from William Smith O'Brien to Abraham Lincoln's Secretary of State, William Seward,[392] for it provoked him into making one of the most ill-judged decisions of his life. As he waited in Constantinople for his official appointment to Damascus, Eugene decided to write an open letter of rebuke to O'Brien, who, in his letter to Seward, had offered to mediate between the warring parties of the American Civil War and help unite them against the common enemy, Britain. O'Brien's offer would be politely rebuffed by Seward, but not before Eugene had had his say.

Eugene had had his fill of inflammatory rhetoric, the realities of war having long since cured him of the implacable certainties of youth. He denounced O'Brien for inciting his young disciples to engage in what

---

[392] *The Times*, 7 December 1861, p.9.

The Letter to William Smith O'Brien

Eugene believed would be yet another disorganised debacle. There had been much to provoke public anger in 1848, and yet the rebellion had failed to harvest popular support. What chance did another stand now that the circumstances had improved? He also refused to believe that professional Irish soldiers would ever desert the armies they had committed to serve.

Constantinople, 2nd January 1862.

Sir,

When the probability of a war between England and the Northern States of America became apparent to me, I determined to write to you and ask you to join with Mr. Dillon and some other respectable men of your former party, in endeavouring to impress upon our countrymen at home that they should not allow themselves to be led away by any hot-headed and wrong-minded men who might attempt to get up a political movement amongst them. I had even begun a letter to you on this subject when I saw that which you had addressed to Mr. Seward. I see little chance now of altering your opinion, but for many reasons I cannot allow that letter to pass in silence.

It is now thirteen years since I pressed your hand; you were then in a jail, condemned to pass the rest of your life as a prisoner and an exile. I had just been set at liberty, and was going to Italy to serve in an army fighting in a cause similar to that for which we had both been willing to sacrifice our lives. On my quitting you, you told me to endeavour to do honour to the party of which I had been one. I have endeavoured to do so, and have at least succeeded in gaining a position in an honourable profession which gives me a right to hope that my word will have some weight with many of my former friends, and, perhaps justifies me in coming forward publicly to express my opinion of your conduct in the present crisis.

I tell you plainly, then, that you should not have written that letter to Mr. Seward, in the first instance, because you owe your life, your liberty, and the possession of independent means to the clemency of that government against which you sought to excite people; and, secondly, because with the experience you have had of the nature of the stuff of which the revolutionary element in Ireland is made, you should have avoided writing anything which might have the effect of inducing even one young man to turn away from his profession or his trade, and give his time to political conspiracy, which, you must know well, will, in Ireland, never produce a movement even worthy of being called a rebellion. Therefore, in publishing the letter the letter to Mr. Seward, you committed a crime, because you uselessly induce young men, of a certain class, to expose themselves to dangers, and become involved in difficulties which will affect them all their lives. I cannot see what good you expected to do by that letter.

If the difficulties which are about to come upon England are so great that she may have apprehension for the continuance of her dominion in Ireland, then that letter was quite unnecessary to call people's attention to them. But, if the coming difficulties are not of that magnitude, your letter shall only have contributed to turn some young men from tradesmen into conspirators, to ruin them, and to inflict an injury on Ireland by disturbing its tranquillity, and lowering the character of the nation in the eyes of the world.

It is to protest against this that I take up my pen. Living amongst foreigners, I have been frequently asked by them how it happens that the Irish nation, having the power that it has, undoubtedly, to return a large majority of Liberals to Parliament, never is able to secure its honest action to obtain redress of those grievances, about which there is such a constant will.

They say, "If there be any public virtue in the country its representatives would be forced to unite and have a common action in the House of Commons, to secure the redress of those grievances, if they really exist. We all know what a united party can do in the English Chambers; and, when we see that there is no common action of the Irish members, we conclude that either there is no public virtue in the nation, or that there are no real grievances of any magnitude." The respectable portion of the French Press, the *Revue des Deux Mondes*, and other periodicals of that class, have long since disposed of present Irish grievances in this way.

In the year '48 the deaths of nearly two millions of our fellow-countrymen justified you and me in adopting what we considered to be the quickest remedy for such a state of things. Yet, after such an affliction as that famine was, and after every man and child had been led to believe that it was the result of English rule, how many men did you find ready to join you in arms against the government? Reflect on this, and then tell me whether any good can come now of talking about taking advantage of England's difficulty, now, when Ireland is, comparatively speaking, prosperous.

But I see that others have as little reflected on this subject as you have done, for the same paper which contained your letter had a report of a meeting assembled at Dublin to devise means for taking advantage of the difficulties which the American quarrel would create for England. Now, I think that you, and the speakers at that meeting, over-rate these difficulties, at least in thinking that they can give an opening for a revolutionary movement in Ireland.

None of you can believe that the Americans could succeed in transporting an army across the Atlantic, and you know well that Ireland, by herself, will make no move. You must know this to be fact, and, explain it as you may, I believe it to be so, because the present grievances of Ireland are not such as drive nations into revolt. The results, then, of your letter, and of the meeting in the Rotunda (which I was glad to see was attended by no person of important position), will simply be that for some time a few more copies of the papers which write in a rabid manner about England will be sold weekly, and probably some clerks and tradesmen will get into mischief, by starting a secret society.

I will not here enter into a discussion of the many dangers which you foresee for England if she goes to war, but there is one about your right to speak of which I protest against. Why do you assert that one half of the army which may be sent to Canada will desert? Because that half will be Irish of course! How can you, an Irish gentleman, rejoice in the prospect of soldiers, your countrymen, deserting their flag? How dare you assert that our countrymen are perjurers, ready to break the oath which they took when they entered the ranks? What gives you the right to speak thus of the Irish soldier, and to endeavour to cast a stain upon our military honour, and remove the prestige of the only merit which the nation still possesses in the eyes of Europe? And, moreover, you are ignorant of the subject you are treating. Now, I am not so. I have served in the ranks of the British army, and I can tell you how Irish soldiers feel.

While they serve, their corps is their country, is their family; and its honour, its fortune, its weal, and its woe, is their own: they have proved this on a hundred fields of battle, and will yet prove it again and again, please God.

If it surprises you that I should speak in this way, I can tell you that it is simply the result of the experience of the world which I have had since I last saw you. During that time, I have been in many countries, and in Italy and Germany I lived much with the classes of men amongst whom the great thoughts which move nations to revolution germinate and take root, and the German philosopher and student, and the Polish, Hungarian, and Italian patriot soldier, repeated to me the same thing, "England is the Ark of the liberty of the world," and by degrees I came to believe in this creed, and I believe it still.

Do not miscalculate. Many of the educated men who were with you in '48 now think as I do. Do not imagine either that the Irish in the Southern army will desert to fight against the British. You speak of their gratitude, feel resentment for the ruffianism of the "know nothings," the tarring of priests, the burning of convents, and sacking of chapels. Do you imagine that their officers have not recalled these outrages to the minds of the Irish soldiers, who fight under the Southern flag, against the fanaticism of the North? But I will not enter on this subject now. I have made my protest against your saying those things which it did not become you to say, and conclude –

Yours obediently,
Eugene O'Reilly.[393]

Eugene's reference to 'the fanaticism of the North' was very much reflective of the opinions of John Mitchel, who had recently drawn parallels between Ireland and the southern states of America, both of which he saw as agricultural economies tied to an unjust union. But it was not Eugene's echoing of Mitchel that most outraged public opinion, but his attack on his former and highly-esteemed comrade.

Prominent amongst Eugene's supporters was a

---

[393] *Dublin Evening Mail*, 17 January 1862, p.2; *Dublin Evening Packet and Correspondence*, 17 January 1862, p.2.

certain Walter Thomas Meyler,[394] a fellow prisoner at Kilmainham and Belfast.[395] He hadn't seen Eugene since 1848. His letter to the *Irish Times* in support of Eugene was rife with inaccuracies and carried little weight. The Rev. George Bomford Wheeler, on the other hand, was editor of the *Irish Times* and unofficial chaplain to the British military forces at the Curragh. Support from that particular quarter Eugene could well have done without, but Wheeler was anxious to capitalise on Eugene's letter to O'Brien:

> This letter coming from so well-known a soldier as Colonel O'Reilly must do good. It tears away the flimsy drapery which weak or designing men fold round their own paltry discontent while they dignify it by the name of treason. It is cheering to find that they who were foremost in rebellion once are also foremost in condemning agitation now, and fear not to tell their countrymen that they have learned by experience to believe that England is the Ark of the liberty of the world.[396]

Eugene was not alone amongst the more radical wing of the defunct Young Ireland movement in his belief that an unsupported rising was doomed to failure from the start. Kenyon had already dismissed the futility of any insurrection without the intervention and support of foreign powers. Mitchel would likewise admit to having nurtured similar doubts.[397] Eugene's opinions, nevertheless, were widely pilloried, most notably in the *Freeman's Journal*, which even went so far as to suggest that he was now a disciple of Allah with multiple wives and slaves, and too much time on

---

[394] Dawson, T. "Some Echoes of 'St. Catherine's Bells.'" *Dublin Historical Record*, vol. 31, no. 3, 1978, pp. 82–93.
[395] Meyler, Thomas Francis. *Saint Catherine's Bells*, Vol I, Robert S. Magee, Dublin, 1868, p.267; *Irish Times*, 18 & 20 January 1862, p.3.
[396] *Irish Times*, 17 January 1862, p.2; *The Times*, 20 January 1862, p.6 and 22 January 1862, p.9.
[397] Catholic University of America, Fenian Brotherhood Collection, Mitchel to Moynahan 17 November 1866.

his hands.[398]

Perhaps the most vehement of Eugene's detractors, however, would prove to be Michael Francis Barry, brother of P.J., the alleged informer of 1848. In his letters to the press, Barry accused Eugene of treachery and cowardice, and of having stigmatised 'in the most offensive and insolent language' the conduct of Smith O'Brien in his dealings with Seward. He further alleged that, in 1848, Eugene could easily have escaped but had instead chosen to be a willing party to his own arrest in order to ensure a more lenient sentence.[399] In refuting the smear, Meyler again took up his pen:

> I remember there was a person, named Barry, rather celebrated in '48, in reference to the Blanchardstown affair, and I am not surprised that O'Reilly and his young companions, on seeing the party who had joined them, saw the prudence of a retreat ... On referring to a return of State prisoners, printed by order of the House of Commons, 8th February 1849, and sent to me by the late Henry Grattan, I extract the names of the gallant young fellows who were arrested, in which list Mr. Barry is not included.[400]

Ottoman bureaucracy moved slowly and despite having appointed Eugene the post of commander in January 1862, it was to be late February before Fuad publicly ratified the creation of the Damascus Gendarmerie. This new force, he then declared, would consist of two thousand irregular cavalry armed with rifle carbines and their primary function would be the protection of the countryside from Bedouin incursions. They would be recruited and commanded by Colonel O'Reilly.[401] The news was favourably received in the

---

[398] *The Freeman's Journal*, Sydney, NSW, 3 May 1862, p.2.
[399] *Cork Examiner*, 27 January 1862, p.4; *Dublin Weekly Nation*, 25 January 1862, p.12.
[400] *Irish Times*, 27 January 1862, p.3.
[401] Çiçek, Talha. *Negotiating Empire in the Middle East*, Cambridge University Press, Cambridge, 2021, p.89; Archives du ministère des Affaires étrangères (La Courneuve), CPC, Turquie, Damascus-7, 4 January 1863.

international press.

> The Porte has at length determined to organise a regular corps of gendarmerie for the district and appointed Hassan Bey (Colonel Eugene O'Reilly) to the command. A better appointment could not have been made. This officer is well acquainted with the country, and possesses all the qualities which will ensure his success. Although a Roman Catholic, he is not likely to be biased by any one-sided view in dealing with either Maronite or Druse, Turk or Christian.[402]

The *Levant Herald* insisted that 'no better selection of a chief for these new police could be made' and, describing Eugene as 'the dashing *sabreur* of Kalafat and Oltenitza', echoed the widely-held hope that 'with such a force under such a commander, the peace of the Mountain may be safely looked on as secure'.[403] The editor did, however, also recognise that the new force would be more easily announced than established.[404]

The question of how the force was to be financed, for example, had yet to be fully determined, as had the question of whether it would be subject to the control of an elected police board or a commission. In the short term, it was felt prudent to allow Eugene a free rein, the Irishman having made it known he preferred 'to be his own administrator for a time'.[405] And so, on 2 March, Eugene departed Constantinople for Beirut, carrying confirmation of his appointment and, most likely, news of a looming security headache.[406]

---

[402] *Morning Chronicle*, 25 February 1862, p.6.
[403] *Morning Advertiser*, 26 February 1862, p.6.
[404] *The Times*, 18 March 1862, p.26.
[405] *Glasgow Morning Journal*, 28 February 1862, p.2.
[406] *The Times*, 18 March 1862, p.10.

THE PRINCE AND THE MATRIARCH

IN AN EFFORT to broaden the education of her eldest son, Edward (later King Edward VII), the British monarch, Queen Victoria, sent him on an extended tour of Egypt and the Middle East to learn about ancient cultures, history, and religions, while also gaining valuable experience in interacting with foreign rulers and diplomats. He arrived at a hill on the outskirts of Damascus on April 28, where he was met by Halim Pasha, the governor of Damascus; a welcoming party of local officials; and a cavalry escort led by Eugene O'Reilly.

Acting as Halim's aide-de-camp and unofficial translator, Eugene rode into Damascus with the royal party, as indeed did Thomas Backhouse Sandwith, brother of Humphry and, at that time, Acting Consul at the British embassy in Damascus. Thomas knew Eugene of old, having been part of the team sent by Lord Stratford to investigate General Beatson's command of the Osmanli Cavalry during the Crimean War. Between his friendship with Sandwith and his position as aide-de-camp to the Governor, Eugene found himself riding alongside the prince, who even noted the encounter in his diary:

> We rode to the English Consulate with Mr. Sandwith,[407] the acting Consul, and Colonel O'Reilly (Hassan Bey), who is an Irishman in the Turkish service, and is a pleasant and conversable fellow.[408]

---

[407] Thomas Backhouse Sandwith, the British Vice-Consul in Syria.
[408] Royal Collection Trust. *The Prince of Wales's Journal: 6 February to 14 June 1862*, p.120.

The Prince and the Matriarch

That afternoon, the royal party pitched their tents, Arab style, on a piece of land adjacent to the house of one of the most notorious women of the age, Jane Digby el Mezrab, the former Lady Ellenborough.[409] Amongst her lovers and previous husbands, Jane could count the Governor-General of India, Lord Ellenborough; King Ludwig I of Bavaria; King Otto of Greece; Prince Felix zu Schwarzenberg; and the Greek general Christodoulos Hatzipetros. Currently married to the Arab sheikh, Medjuel el Mezrab, a man twenty years her junior, her numerous divorce settlements had left her so comfortably well off that she wielded enormous influence amongst the Bedouin. According to Sir Edwin Pears:

> He [Medjuel] was devoted to her service and the two got on very well together. I was told that no European woman knew more of harem life than did she. Her husband's Bedouins were devoted to her, and she exercised remarkable influence over her husband and his men.[410]

Pears, if anything, understated the case. Jane's wealth had not only brought prestige to the Mezrabs in terms of camels, sheep, horses and black slave boys, but it had also allowed them to purchase arms. At the time of her marriage, the use of guns had been uncommon among the Bedouin but, through Jane, the Mezrab had managed to acquire the advantage of modern European weapons and ammunition.

Amongst her tribe, Jane Digby had become something of a matriarch.[411] She adjudicated in squabbles, counselled the sick, comforted divorced wives, and enjoyed a tribal reputation as a doctor and a vet. She was trusted and respected, generous to the

---

[409] Lovell, Mary S. *A Scandalous Life – The Biography of Jane Digby*, e-book, Richard Cohen Books, London, 1995, p.212.
[410] Pears, Sir Edwin. *Forty Years in Constantinople. The Recollections of Sir Edwin Pears 1873-1915*, Herbert Jenkins Limited, London 1916, pp.72-73.
[411] Variously translated as 'Mother of Milk' or 'our gracious lady'.

poor, and never affected airs and graces. She milked the camels and sheep and walked with the other women behind the caravan collecting camel droppings to be dried for fuel.[412] On first-name terms with everyone from the British Consul to the Emir Abd el Kader, she was arguably the most influential European in Syria.[413]

Because of the many scandals that had surrounded Jane and the fact that her husband had fallen out of favour with the Turkish government, an invitation to official functions could not be issued. Nevertheless, unable to stifle his curiosity and, through the intercession of Edward Buxton, recently married to Jane's niece, Emmie, with whom he was currently honeymooning in Damascus, the young prince requested a private meeting.

The following morning, Eugene accompanied Edward on a tour of the city, guiding him through the bazaars, showing him the mosaics of the Umayyad Mosque and taking him to the mausoleum of Saladin, the first Sultan of Egypt and Syria. They also visited a shrine, said to have contained the head of John the Baptist, and climbed to the top of the highest minaret in the city. Returning to the royal encampment, the prince even received a visit from Abd el Kader, whose private security had saved many Christians during the 1860 massacre. In the years to come, there would be much speculation about the nature of his relationship with O'Reilly, but for the time being, it appears they were just fleeting acquaintances on friendly but hardly intimate terms.

After lunch, the royal party spent the afternoon visiting the Christian quarter and viewing the ruins of the buildings and churches destroyed during the massacre, hearing first-hand accounts from survivors, and visiting the 'Tomb of Judas'. The obligatory

---

[412] Lovell, Mary S. A Scandalous Life – The Biography of Jane Digby, e-book, Richard Cohen Books, London, 1995, pp.208-210.
[413] Oddie, E.M. *A Portrait of Ianthe*, Jonathan Cape, London, 1935, p.234.

sightseeing concluded; the prince then repaired to the house of Jane Digby for a private visit.

Having been given a tour of the house and gardens, a private viewing of Jane's paintings of Palmyra, and an introduction to her menagerie of animals, birds and thoroughbred horses, the prince apologised for the intrusion, thanked her and left. It would not be the last that Eugene saw of Jane Digby. In fact, their names would very soon become inextricably linked to one of the most curious episodes in the history of the region.

That evening, as a military band played in a nearby garden, Eugene sat down to dine with the prince at the Embassy banquet.[414] It was to be the last Eugene would see of Edward until the morning of his departure, when he would escort him to the outskirts of the city. Here the governor would wish the prince a safe journey onwards and return with Eugene to Damascus, where the royal visit had done little to improve Ottoman relations with the Druze. The prince's meetings with Digby and Abd el Kader, however, might just have planted the germ of an idea in Eugene's brain, an idea not so very different to that imagined by Lord Dufferin in 1861.

---

[414] Royal Collection Trust. *The Prince of Wales's Journal: 6 February to 14 June 1862*, p.122, 125.

THE DAMASCUS GENDARMERIE

CHARACTERISED BY EXTINCT volcanoes, ancient lava flows and mineral-rich basalt, the Hauran is a dry-farming region of fertile hills and plains that spans parts of southern Syria and northern Jordan. To its northwest lies Mount Lebanon; to its south, the Jordanian Highlands. Between both sits the Golan Heights, through which the moist Mediterranean air is funnelled inland, providing the rainfall that sustains this improbable island of green in the Syrian Desert.

For centuries the Hauran had occupied the attention of the Sultan only during the Hajj, when aspirant hajjis, passing through the region on their way to Mecca, would depend on the hospitality of local villages for food and shelter. Once the Hajj was over, it would revert to being a quasi-autonomous state ruled by a body of local chieftains or Aghawat.[415]

In return for providing policing, security and provisions during the Hajj, local chieftains had up to now been permitted to exercise economic and political power in the Hauran. Of late, however, the Ottoman government, desperate for increased revenue and military conscripts, had begun to regret the degree of autonomy they had ceded to the Aghawat and to make plans to replace their private bands of irregular troops with civil functionaries and a modern gendarmerie under the command of Colonel Eugene O'Reilly.

Fuad was anxious to bring the Hauran under tighter Ottoman control as both Britain and France had begun to show an economic interest in the crops of the region. Were these crops to be directed to an

---

[415] Plural of *Agha*, a civilian honorific, roughly translated as 'Chief', 'Master' or 'Lord'.

export market, the pilgrimage supply would dry up. The Aghawat, however, were never going to to surrender their privileges lightly.

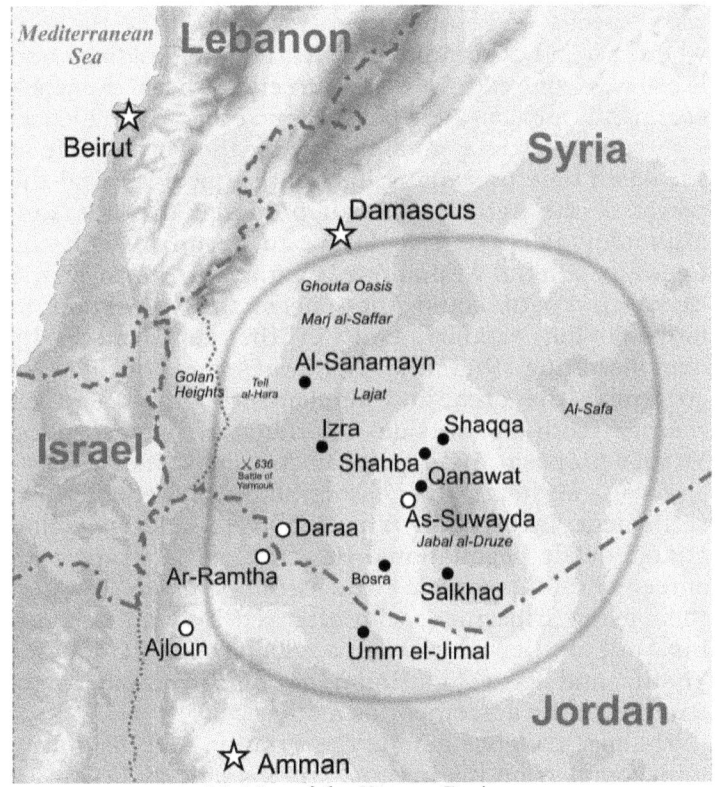
18. Map of the Hauran Region.

Back in December 1861, when Fuad left Damascus to return to Constantinople, he gave Halim Pasha command of Ottoman troops in the region and appointed him governor of the city. At the time, Halim's sympathy for the Aghawat had not been a problem, but when Fuad ordered him to collect military conscripts from the Druze, the Druze formed an alliance with the Bedouin, and together they declared their intention to resist conscription and taxation in the

Hauran. Suddenly, Halim's sympathies mattered.

Enter Ahmad Agha al-Yusuf, the sexagenarian head of a prominent Kurdish family. Yusuf had recently been named commander of the pilgrimage relief caravan and was expected to be appointed Governor of the Hauran, where he had accumulated extensive landholdings and livestock. An effective gendarmerie under Eugene's command threatened his political and economic influence.

Anxious to win a small victory for the Porte, while at the same time preserving his political position and the power of the Aghawat, Yusuf proposed that his son, Muhammad, be sent to Bosra to negotiate with the Bedouin. Should Muhammed manage to win over the Bedouin, Yusuf could then negotiate with Fuad to forestall the establishment of the gendarmerie by demonstrating that the Aghawat were capable of governing the area and implementing the required reforms without outside interference. In accepting Yusuf's proposal, Halim tied his fortune to its success.

Alas, Muhammad's attempts to negotiate a settlement failed, and Yusuf had to take personal charge of the negotiations. He managed to wrangle an agreement that satisfied the Bedouin chiefs but not their fellow tribesmen, who attacked his tent and ran him out of Bosra. It was a galling humiliation for Yusuf, and also for Halim, who had prematurely trumpeted the agreement as a success.

Halim's intrigues among the Bedouin and his failure to decommission his irregular troops quickly became a source of intense political irritation within the Porte and, according to the French consul, Yusuf had also been discovered to be claiming funds for three times as many conscripts as he had actually recruited. The creation of the Damascus Gendarmerie, therefore, had resulted not just in a loss of prestige to Yusuf but a loss of income.[416]

---

[416] Archives du ministère des Affaires étrangères (La Courneuve), CPC, Turquie, Damascus-7, 4 January 1863.

Against all the odds, Eugene had managed to establish a disciplined gendarmerie and shine an unflattering light on the incompetence and indiscipline of the Aghawat irregulars.[417] To rub further salt in the wounds, he had done so with a mix of Christian *and* Muslim recruits.

> At Damascus, after the Syrian Massacre, a certain Colonel O'Reilly was entrusted with the task of organising an efficient police. And the Colonel – Hassan Bey, as he was called in Turkish – succeeded very well considering the materials he had to work upon. His rural police comprised Mussulmans, Koords, and men of other communities – and many of them were of far lower character than is the ordinary Turkish zaptieh in Bulgaria. But by strict discipline and regular pay, Colonel O'Reilly was able to organise a very creditable and orderly body of men.[418]

Strict discipline and regular pay! The first was within his control, the second, alas, was not, and when Yusuf, as sub-governor of the Hauran, began to make political mischief, the funds for the gendarmerie dried up, forcing Eugene to pay his men from his own pocket,[419] and to borrow £1400 from a certain Mr. Levi, a British moneylender in Damascus, on the mistaken understanding that Fuad would settle the debt.[420]

Writing to the Hon. E.M. Erskine, British Chargé d'affaires in Constantinople, the British Consul at Damascus, Edward Thomas Rogers, described the Irishman's predicament:

---

[417] *Allgemeine Zeitung München,* 8 May 1862, p.2124; Schilcher, L. Schatkowski. "The Hauran Conflicts of the 1860s: A Chapter in the Rural History of Modern Syria", in *International Journal of Middle East Studies,* Vol. 13, No. 2, Cambridge University Press, May 1981, p.160; Sessional Papers, Vol 9, Great Britain, Parliament, H.M. Stationery Office, 1880, p. 92.
[418] *Sheffield Daily Telegraph,* 10 April 1877, p.2.
[419] National Archives UK, FO195/760, E.T. Rogers, 15 January 1863; June 24, 1863.
[420] Ottoman Archives of the Prime Minister's Office (BOA), HR. SYS. 244/29 (Ministry of Foreign Translation Room), Kazolani to Ottoman Foreign Ministry, 8 December 1867.

The establishment of a new corps of mounted and foot police under the command of Col. O'Reilly is one of the wise and beneficial results of the Syrian policy of his highness Fuad Pasha, according to whose first arrangement, discipline and effectiveness were to have been ensured in this force by good and regular pay, distributed by the cashier into the hands of every individual soldier; but unfortunately this corps is already in more than six months arrear, and the commanding officer cannot enforce that amount of discipline which he would otherwise do; and he feels himself obliged to pass over in silence those derelictions of duty which he knows the men resort to for their sustenance and that of their horses.

Were this force maintained on its original principles it would be of infinite service, and the villagers would be protected from the incursions of the Arab tribes and relieved from the expense of maintaining those armed forces sent out for the collection of the revenue; but under present circumstances the new force is no better than the old and pernicious system of irregular cavalry.[421]

Thus began the years of resentment, the Irishman's feelings becoming so public that, by October 1862, rumours were flying about Damascus that he was conspiring with a group intent on forcing the Turks out of Syria and, with the aid of a united Bedouin army and support from the French, installing Abd el Kader as the leader of an Arab Kingdom in Syria. In a letter to his French counterpart, the British Consul, Edward Rogers, described the rumours as 'stupid'.[422]

Only they weren't. Abd el Kader, an Islamic and Sufi scholar had, back in 1830, led the Algerian military resistance to the French invasion of Algiers and, with an army composed largely of Algerian tribesmen, had managed to hold out against the French for many

---

[421] National Archives UK, FO195/760, Rogers to Erskine, 15 January 1863.
[422] Centre des Archives Diplomatiques de Nantes, Rogers to French Consulate, Damas/Consulat/66, 16-10-1862; Centre des Archives Diplomatiques de Nantes, Register no. 22, correspondence received from the department and the French embassy.

19. Abd el Kader.

years, winning widespread admiration for his humane treatment of prisoners. Following his surrender in December 1847, he was taken to France and imprisoned in conditions which adversely affected his health and contrasted sharply with his own treatment of enemy prisoners during the French invasion. His plight became something of a *cause célèbre* and excited the outrage of such figures as Émile de Girardin, Victor Hugo and Lord Londonderry, all of whom campaigned for his release.

On 16 October 1852, when Abd el Kader was finally set free, he was given an annual pension of 100,000 francs, subject to his taking an oath never again to disturb the peace of Algeria. He briefly took up residence at Bursa in Turkey before moving in 1855 to the Amara District of Damascus, where he devoted himself to theology and philosophy, became an active Freemason, and developed close ties to several French intellectuals. His intervention to save many of the Christian community during the massacres of 1860 had brought honours and awards from around the world. The French government had even awarded him the *Légion d'honneur* and increased his pension to 150,000 francs, in the process raising his profile to a level he had not enjoyed since his surrender in 1847.

Abd el Kader, then, was a credible leader under whose leadership the notion of an Arab state was far from inconceivable. In November 1862, furthermore, Napoleon III had invited five Arab chiefs to a hunting party at Compiègne, where a policy for an Arab kingdom had been formulated. Given Eugene's predicament, a certain amount of loose talk and disaffected musing may well have given substance to the rumour of a plot, but while his thoughts on the subject appear to have never gone further than wishful thinking, the rumour grew legs.

Shortly after his appointment as the new Governor of Damascus, Rushdi Shirwani Pasha now proposed that both the current gendarmerie *and* the disparate bands of irregulars still under Aghawat control should be disbanded and incorporated into a new corps under the command of O'Reilly, who was still considered the quintessence of probity by the European population of Damascus.[423] Under this compromise, Shirwani believed, a new and modern police force might still be formed,

---

[423] Ottoman Archives of the Prime Minister's Office, TR-BOA/A-MKT-NZD/419-82, Dosya 419, Gömlek 82, May 19, 1862.

drawing on the personnel of the Aghawat and with the Aghawat themselves serving as Eugene's captains.[424] The plan was implemented and, for a short time, appeared to be running smoothly. By 22 March, the *Levant Herald* was trumpeting it as an unqualified success.

> It is hardly to be believed the great change that has been wrought in the police throughout Syria since Hassan Bey was put in charge of this corps, and in place of the vile vagabonds, under chiefs more vagabond still, who until now have robbed under the guise of guarding travellers on the public roads, there is now a police organisation throughout Syria which would not discredit any country in Europe. Hassan Bey has the entire control of all the police in Syria, from Aleppo to the confines of Egypt, excepting only those belonging to the confines of Mount Lebanon.[425]

That article was no sooner published, however, than Eugene found two of his best squadrons transferred to the command of Ali Bey, a man he considered 'an incompetent Turk'.[426] By 24 June, the British Chargé d'affaires, Edward M. Erskine, was reporting to Sir Henry Bulwer, the British Ambassador, that Eugene's patience had finally snapped.

> I have had the honor in several of my despatches to Your Excellency, to advert to the opposition evinced by the local authorities to the position till now held by Colonel O'Reilly at the head of the mounted police force. After having experienced a great deal of difficulty, being in a year's arrear of pay, his men being 9 months in arrear, and having contracted debts in his own name for the payment of some of the men on account, he has at last resigned his arduous post;- in consequence of which he has been summoned to

---

[424] Rogers, Jan. 15, 1863, FO195/760; Archives du ministère des Affaires étrangères (La Courneuve), CPC, Turquie, Damascus-7, 4 January 1863.

[425] *Morning Post*, 14 April 1863, p.6.

[426] Schilcher, L. Schatkowski. "The Hauran Conflicts of the 1860s: A Chapter in the Rural History of Modern Syria" in *International Journal of Middle East Studies*, Vol 13, No. 2, May 1981, p. 171.

Constantinople, and I believe he starts tomorrow.⁴²⁷

In September 1863, the Porte received another telegram from Damascus suggesting that Eugene, with the encouragement of the French, was conspiring with Abd el Kader to overthrow Turkish rule in Syria. How real this alleged plot was, is hard to tell, but a letter sent from the French Embassy on 23 December 1863, suggests that it was being treated seriously.⁴²⁸

> Colonel O'Reilly, who was responsible for forming a modern gendarmerie corps in Damascus, was called to Constantinople ... he is said to have engaged in schemes aimed at the expulsion of the Turks by means of an agreement between the Bedouins and Algerians to have Abdelkader proclaimed King of Syria. The authors of this project would have contacted the French consulate in Damascus, which would have given them encouragement [...] and a certain amount of support.⁴²⁹

As the Aghawat conspired to prevent Eugene from regaining control of the gendarmerie, they began to allege frequent trips by Eugene to Egypt and to spread rumours of his involvement in a failed attempt to provoke an insurrection at Şanliurfa, a town in south-eastern Turkey close to the Syrian border.⁴³⁰ In a further attempt to pressurise Fuad into dropping the idea of a gendarmerie, Yusuf then resigned from his post as sub-governor of the Hauran, claiming that without the irregulars under his *sole* command, he

---

⁴²⁷ UK National archives, FO195/760, Rogers to Bulwer, Jan. 15, 1863.
⁴²⁸ Archives du Ministere des Affaires Etrangeres, Consulat de Damas, Correspondance Politique/8, Hecquard, 14, 4 September 1863; Archives des Affaires Étrangères à Nantes: registre n°?22, correspondance reçue du département et de l'ambassade de France, 23-10-1863; Geoffroy, Eric. *Abd el Kader, un spirituel dans la modernite*, Dar Albouraq, Paris, 2010, p.85; *Australian Town and Country Journal*, Sydney NSW, 25 July 1874, p.27; *Boston Pilot*, 22-April-1854, p.4; *York Herald*, 2 April 1874, p.3.
⁴²⁹ Etienne, Bruno, *Le choc colonial et Islam*, La Découverte, Paris, 2006, pp.469-483.
⁴³⁰ *The Times*, 19 October 1868, p.8; The town was then called Urfa.

could no longer maintain order or control in the area. With the irregulars withdrawn from the gendarmerie, the much-diminished force was unable to prevent the Bedouin from disrupting the Hajj. On 8 October the following report appeared in *The Bombay Gazette*:

> Syria, Beyrout, Oct. 8
>
> I stated quite recently that, among the hopeful signs with regard to the peace of Syria, was the fact that Col. O'Reilly, known as Hassan Beg in the Turkish Service, had been raised to the rank of Pasha or General, and was about to return to Damascus with authority to pacify that province. It is true that he left Damascus and repaired to Constantinople where he was honourably received by Fuad Pasha, and at once raised to the rank of Pasha; but just at that time there arrived a telegram from Damascus asserting that evidence had come to light that Hassan Beg had conspired to overthrow the Turkish Rule in Syria.
>
> It was a foul Turkish lie. The Pasha of Damascus is afraid to have an honest man in power in his district, especially with a rank equal to his own, and raised this false accusation to prevent his return to Damascus. Mr. Rodgers, English Consul in Damascus, wrote at once to the Porte refuting this assertion, and it is not, nor was it, credited in high quarters; but for some reason General O'Reilly has not returned, and it is feared that he will not.
>
> There may be more than is generally imagined in this matter. Not a few suppose that Fuad Pasha himself has his eye on Syria, and that he intends yet to become Viceroy, as Lord Dufferin proposed in 1861. In that case he will demonstrate that Syria cannot be kept at peace under its present regime, and persuade the Sultan that the French can only be kept away by making him Viceroy. If so, we shall have another outbreak when it suits Fuad Pasha...
>
> Meantime affairs in the Houran are getting serious. The various Arab tribes under Mohammed-ed-Duchy and Faisol have united with the Mizrab Arabs and others to resist the government... If O'Reilly does not soon return, they may even threaten Damascus itself.[431]

---

[431] *The Bombay Gazette*, 25 November 1863, p.2.

As a public show of confidence in the loyalty of his former aide-de-camp, Fuad raised Eugene to the rank of Pasha, a title evocative of nobility but so rarely a guarantee of it. The Irishman was not slow in flaunting it.[432] A curious account of his elevation, published just three years after the fact, asserted that:

> ... the gallant Bim-Bashi O'Reilly, who, on being presented with three beautiful Circassian damsels for his services, duly informed his friends in Ireland that he had been created a Bashaw of Three Tails.[433]

Female slaves of Circassian or Georgian origin were still being sold behind closed doors, but foreigners and Christians were not normally permitted to purchase them, let alone possess them.[434] That said, it was not unknown, and at a later date it would be reported that Eugene had travelled with a Circassian woman to whom he entrusted the care of his private papers.

In Eugene's absence the relationship between the Sultan and his Arabic-speaking Bedouin subjects came into perilous play and led Eugene to an epiphany of sorts. If he was going to be accused of fomenting a rebellion in the desert, then *Cur Non?* The Hauran was no Valley Forge, and he was certainly no Lafayette, but the union of the Hauran tribes against the Turks had demonstrated what might one day be possible, with the right leadership. The bones of a plan began to emerge, only to be shelved as impracticable.[435]

---

[432] Meagher, Thomas Francis. *Meagher of the Sword*, M.H. Gill, Dublin, 1916, p.347; British Library, Diaries of Lady Ann Blunt, Mss. BL 54146, Wentworth Bequest; *European Review of History: Revue européenne d'histoire*, Vol. 27, No. 1-2, 2020, pp. 88-110; Jalabert, Henri, ed. *Un Montagnard contre le pouvoir. Liban 1866. Document publié avec une introduction des notes, une postface et une chronologie.* Dar El-Machreq, Beirut, 1975, p.152.

[433] Grant, James. *The Constable of France and Other Military Historiettes*, George Routledge and Sons, New York, 1866, p.87.

[434] Andersen, Hans Christian. "A ramble through Constantinople" in *A Poet's Bazaar*, Hurd and Houghton, New York, 1871, pp. 231-232.

[435] *New York Herald*, 4 July 1870, p.11.

With the situation in Syria shrouded in confusion, rumour and innuendo, Eugene was not permitted to return. Instead, by way of compensation, he was appointed as Commissar of Public Works. It wasn't a military posting, nor did it come with an impressive uniform, but a new realm was opening before him and what he was losing in terms of status and glamour, he would now gain in opportunities for profiteering.

One of Eugene's first acts as Commissar was to find a position for his friend, E. W. Ward. Little is known of Ward's background other than he had come to Turkey as a farming settler, had been employed in multiple occupations, and had recently designed a 'peculiar kind of wheeled conveyance specially adapted to the narrow and uneven streets of Stamboul'.[436] Eugene appointed Ward Superintendent of Bridges, a post he assumed under the name of Ismail Bey.[437] Curiously, Humphry Sandwith's mother was a Ward, and so too was his brother-in-law.

Allowed to retain the title of Pasha, and his rank in the Turkish military, Eugene disappeared from public view. Trading his passion for horseflesh for a passion for steam, he began to aim at something more lucrative than the lofty military ranks and public offices that were effectively closed to him.

One of the busiest departments of his ministry was the Office of Roads and Passages,[438] which had responsibility for railways. Steam was now king and even the mobilisation of modern armies bowed to the imperative of the railway timetable. This was where the future lay, and where real money was made.

The latest railway concession, granted in 1863 to one Edward Price, was for a line from Izmir to Kasaba. This concession granted the applicant gratuitous access to all government-owned land, coal mines and

---

[436] Ibid.
[437] Crane, Augustin. *From South Britain to Bagdad – Incidents in the Career of Henry M. Canfield*, Davis & Nye, Waterbury, Conn., 1920, p.22.
[438] *Turuk u Maabir Idaresi*.

forests along the route and promised government arbitration of any conflicts that might arise during the acquisition of privately owned lands or mines necessary for the construction and operation of the railway. Also guaranteed was a six per cent return on his investment, not to exceed £1,200,000 in total. Price, effectively, had been given a licence to print money.[439]

Eugene proved a quick study and set his sights on procuring a concession of his own to build a railway line from Homs to the copper mines at Ergani.[440] If palms had to be greased, he knew which were susceptible. He was, it seemed, determined to become a railway entrepreneur. Or at least that was what he *appeared* to be up to.

---

[439] Cobb, Elvan. *Railway Crossings: Encounters In Ottoman Lands*, Dissertation, Doctor of Philosophy, Cornel University, August 2018.
[440] Formerly known as Arghana or Arghni.

THE LAING CONVERSION SCHEME

THE OTTOMAN EMPIRE was slowly disintegrating. Mounting trade deficits; the cost of the Crimean War; internal and external debts; and the global financial crisis of 1857 had all been serious enough in their own right, but now the treasury also had to deal with reparations to victims of the civil war in Syria and a sybaritic Sultan whose profligacy was as boundless as the desert.

The state accounts were awash with red ink – the debt believed to be in the region of 774 million francs – and the Porte was having to face down a ravenous pack of European financial predators. Back in November 1860, having failed to contract loans with several European syndicates, the Porte had secured a deal with the French financier Jules Mirès, a deal that collapsed when Mirès was arrested in Paris and charged with fraud. The resulting scandal triggered a financial crisis and bankrupted several major commercial houses in Britain and France. It also caused the value of the Ottoman currency to drop by two-thirds, forcing the Porte to appeal to the British and French governments for 'moral support'.[441]

In 1863, shortly after his recall to Constantinople, Eugene became involved with an international group of capitalists who had created the General Credit & Finance Company in order to bid for the contract to consolidate and convert the Turkish debt. Led by Samuel Laing, the group was acting in concert with an

---

[441] Osavci, Ozan. *Dangerous Gifts - Imperialism, Security, and Civil Wars in the Levant, 1798-1864*, OUP, Oxford, 2021, pp.330-332.

American Confederate agent by the name of Louis Merton, a banker with offices in London and Paris.[442] Provided with funds to bribe officials, Merton (a.k.a. Louis Moses) sought Eugene's help.[443]

> Some time before this date, 1867, he had been made use of by a clique of English financiers in some rather questionable financial affair connected with the consolidation of the Turkish Debt; an affair out of which the financiers made £20,000 apiece, and O'Reilly got for his share £5,000, which effectually whetted his appetite for this kind of spoil. O'Reilly told me that one of the jobs he was charged with was to bribe the editor of a Constantinople newspaper who was strongly denouncing what he called the nefarious scheme of these financiers. The editor accepted £500 and then changed his opinions.[444]

Almost all of the newspapers in Constantinople at that time accepted bribes to carry opinion or propaganda pieces, including the *Levant Herald*, the *Levant Times* and *La Turquie*.[445] But the editor most likely to have been bribed by Eugene was his friend and fellow freemason, Alfred Black Churchill.

The end of the Crimean War had seen a sudden proliferation of Freemasonry in the Ottoman Empire. It was becoming especially popular amongst supporters of modernisation like Fuad Pasha. Inaugurated at the British Embassy on 24 June 1862, the Bulwer Lodge was formed to recruit not just European expatriates but high-ranking officials of the Ottoman state. Back in April 1866, Eugene had been initiated alongside Alfred Black Churchill, editor of the *Ceride-i Havadis*

---

[442] The group also included M. Erlanger, a French Banker; Sir Henry Drummond Wolfe; and three other English capitalists.
[443] *The Scotsman*, 25 February 1868, p.2; *Indian Statesman*, 08 April 1874, p.4.
[444] Ward, *Humphry Sandwith: A Memoir*, p.211.
[445] Douin, Georges. *Histoire du regne du Khedive Ismail*, Vol. II, Istituto Poligrafico della Stato, Rome, 1933-1934, p.595; preussische Geheime Archiv, Dahlem, 12 Chiffre, Bressier to Bismarck, 22 January 1867.

The Laing Conversion Scheme

(Journal of News).

Influential but not universally read, this privately owned paper survived only with the support of the Sultan, who used it as a vehicle for modernisation. Its journalists, as a result, were drawn largely from the translation bureau of the Sublime Porte. Churchill, nevertheless, still held a degree of editorial control, and whenever the British wanted to influence Ottoman policy, a carefully worded story in the *Ceride-i Havadis* was often more effective than greasing the palms of multiple officials.[446]

By early 1865, Merton had gained such sway over Fuad Pasha that, on 31 March 1865, he succeeded in winning the contract for the conversion and consolidation of Turkish debt. A prospectus was subsequently issued inviting subscriptions to the proposed loan of approximately four million Turkish lira. This loan, known as the *Turkish Five Per-Cent Scheme*, would eventually run into difficulty, but not before the financiers had made a tidy profit.[447] Eugene's consultancy fee, roughly equivalent to three-quarters of a million pounds today, vastly exceeded his current salary as Commissar for the Construction of Roads in Ismidt, Ghevé and Sabandja.[448]

---

[446] Senior, Nassau W. *Journal kept in Turkey and Greece*, Longman, Brown, Green, Longmans and Roberts, London, 1859, p.182.

[447] Bell, K. *The Constantinople Embassy of Sir Henry Bulwer, 1858-1865*, PhD. Thesis, University of London, June 1961; Baster Albert. "The Origins of British Banking Expansion in the Near East", in *The Economic History Review*, Vol.5, No.1, 1934, p.80; *The Economist*, Volume 24, Part 2, 24 July 1866, p.848; *Morning Post*, 11 May 1865, p.3.

[448] *Indian Statesman*, 08 April 1874, p.4; Ward, *Humphry Sandwith: A Memoir*, p.211.

THE KARAMIST REBELLION

IN EARLY JANUARY 1866, a politically ambitious Lebanese Maronite, Yūsuf Bey Karam, led a rebellion against Davud Pasha, head of the newly created Lebanese *mutassarifiya,* a semi-autonomous region established on Mount Lebanon in 1861, following the recommendations of the International Commission of Enquiry into the massacres of 1860.[449]

Born in 1823 at Idhin, where the Maronites had first established themselves in the seventh century, Karam had been raised in a tradition of separateness. At seventeen, he had fought against the Egyptian occupation of Lebanon, displaying such courage and leadership in battle that, in 1846, when his father died, it was he and not his eldest brother who was chosen to succeed as ruler of the district. His reputation was further enhanced in 1860 when he acted as the protector of both his people and the patriarch of the Maronite Church. His dream of Lebanese self-rule was viewed in much the same way by the Ottoman Empire as Irish demands for independence were viewed by the British.

Following the massacres of 1860, when two provisional Governors were appointed to rule Lebanon – one to rule Christians and the other to rule the Druze and Muslims – it was Karam who had been appointed to the Christian *Kaymakamate,* which for a time he had led with distinction, restoring law and order and the honest conduct of government. Following the introduction of the 1861 *Reglement*

---

[449] Spagnolo, John P. "Mount Lebanon, France and Dâûd Pasha: A Study of Some Aspects of Political Habituation," in *International Journal of Middle East Studies,* vol. 2, no. 2, 1971, pp. 148–167.

The Karamist Rebellion

20. Yūsuf Bey Karam.

Organique and incensed at the appointment of a non-native governor, Karam began to campaign for home rule for Mount Lebanon, forcing the new *mustarrif*, Davud Pasha, to issue an order expelling him from Lebanon. Allowed to return in 1864, he promptly instigated a rebellion.

Enter Charles de Schwartzenberg, a German-born Belgian whose career had more or less paralleled Eugene's. During the Belgian Revolution of 1830, he had volunteered in a local militia in Ghent and, having distinguished himself in battle against the Dutch, had been accepted into the Belgian Army at the rank of lieutenant, only to abandon his post in search of promotion and battle experience. Having failed to secure a position in the Sardinian Army, he fought with the Hungarian rebels in 1849 as a lieutenant colonel of Hussars and, after the war, enlisted in the Ottoman cavalry. Like Eugene, he had been the subject of various intrigues, but there the similarities ended. Schwartzenberg had never enjoyed the confidence of Fuad to the same extent as the Irishman.

On 6 January 1866, while Karam was attending mass at Saint Doumit's Church in the village of Maameltein, his troops were attacked by Ottoman forces. With the assistance of local villagers, Karam routed the Turks, forcing the Mustarrif, Davud Pasha, to appeal for military assistance. Fuad despatched Schwartzenberg with orders to march on Ghazir and subdue the Karamists.

Faced with a superior force, Karam agreed to discuss a truce and met with Schwartzenberg on 27 January 1866 at the village of Karamsaddeh, where he symbolically surrendered his sword. The ceasefire, however, quickly collapsed, leaving Schwartzenberg with no alternative but to order his troops to eliminate the rebels. Late the following evening, as he marched his troops up to Bnash'i, a small village in the Zgharta district of north Lebanon, he stumbled into an ambush, lost between sixty and two hundred men, and was forced to retreat.[450] Embarrassed by reports of the debacle, Fuad recalled Schwartzenberg to Constantinople.

In need of a military leader familiar with the area

---

[450] Alloul, Houssine. "Me among the Turks: Western commanders in the Late Ottoman Army and their self-narratives", in *European Review of History: Revue européenne d'histoire*, Vol. 27, No. 1-2, 2020, pp. 88-110.

The Karamist Rebellion

and with the necessary skills to suppress a rebellion, Fuad sent Eugene to replace Schwartzenberg. Several major battles later, the revolt was all but over and Karam was exiled to Algeria. Comparing Eugene's efforts to Schwartzenberg's, one French journalist declared:

> It is on a Belgian pasha that she [the Karamist rebellion] had inflicted its first and brilliant victory, and it is to an Irish pasha that she owes her defeat.[451]

Eugene was not alone in the Ottoman Army in being a nationalist rebel forced into exile for his part in a failed insurrection. But if ever he reflected on such things, it could not have been without a sense of irony, perhaps even a pang of regret that he should be reduced to assisting an imperial oppressor in the brutal subjugation of an independent-minded minority. Whether through a qualm of conscience, or a belated recognition of the fickleness of Ottoman patronage, his thoughts turned to Egypt and Prince Halim,[452] the youngest son of Muhammad Ali, the founder of modern Egypt, who had recently been deprived of his right to inherit the throne of Egypt.

In return for a promise of increased tax revenue, Sultan Abdulaziz had introduced a new law, making succession in Egypt a matter of primogeniture rather than the traditional transfer between brothers. At a stroke, all other male members of the Khedive's family were deprived of the possibility of inheriting the throne, a change the Khedive had long sought to guarantee the throne for his son, Tawfiq.

Deprived of all hope of the throne, Halim attempted a coup d'état, the failure of which had seen him exiled to Constantinople, where Eugene began to see in him

---

[451] D'Alaux, Gustave. "Le Liban et Davoud-Pacha. — La Réorganisation de la Montagne, Youssef Caram et la Réaction turque", in *Revue des deux mondes*, 1 May 1866, pp.5-49.
[452] Muhammad abd al Halim (1831-1894).

an alternative to Abd el-Kader as a possible leader of an independent Syria. The Ottoman Empire was in flux. Apart from the goings on in Egypt, revolutionary movements were currently active in Lebanon, Crete, Bulgaria and Serbia. Britain, France and Russia, furthermore, were pressuring the Porte for more extensive institutional reforms and opposition voices within the Porte were growing daily in confidence and calling for change. Given the current weakness of the Sultan, an old idea was resurrected. The acquisition of high-risk investors no longer seemed impossible.

A VISIT HOME

EUGENE ARRIVED IN Ruse in north-eastern Bulgaria at the beginning of January 1867.[453] As Commissar for the Inspection of Railways, he had been charged with inspecting the Varna to Ruse railway, a project undertaken by the Barkleys – a family of British entrepreneurs with extensive railway interests in the Balkans and coal mining interests in Turkey.

The previous October, the Barkleys had declared the line ready for use and the Porte had given the green light to start operating. The moment the Barkleys sought the interest payments guaranteed by their concession, however, local inspectors descended on Ruse and closed the line. The Barkleys complained to the Porte, and Eugene was sent to investigate. His report found the line in good condition, and believing the matter resolved, he returned to Constantinople.[454]

The governor-general of the province, however, had other ideas. No sooner had Eugene departed than he imposed new conditions on the Barkleys, requiring them to construct, at their own expense, a connecting road between the city and the railway station in Ruse. The Barkleys refused, and the project stalled again.[455]

Eugene's failure to permanently resolve the situation in Ruse would once have been felt as a professional embarrassment. But his priorities lay elsewhere.

He had already decided to resign from his post, having recently acquired a concession for the construction of a railroad to transport minerals to the

---

[453] Then called Rustchuk.
[454] *Pall Mall Gazette*, 14 March 1868, p.9.
[455] *Centralblatt Fur Eisenbahnen Und Dampfschifffahrt In Oesterreich*, Wien, 2 Mar 1867, p.66.

Mediterranean from the mines at Ergani; a concession, it would later be alleged, he had procured by means of bribes and political intrigue.[456] He had also acquired a *firman* from the Sultan directing local authorities to provide him with whatever assistance he required in the furtherance of the concession. Without investors, however, these were worthless pieces of paper; with investors, they were the keys to a treasure chest.

On his way home to Dublin, Eugene stopped briefly in Paris, where he met with Mustapha Fazil Pasha, the exiled brother of Ismail, the Khedive of Egypt. The previous year both Mustapha and his uncle, Halim, had been stripped of their right to succession by an edict of the Sultan who, at the request of the Khedive, and contrary to Islamic law, had permitted the introduction of a civil law allowing succession by primogeniture rather than a transfer between brothers. Dismissed from his official posts, Mustapha had been forced into exile,[457] and having settled in Paris, he had begun to support the Young Ottomans, an increasingly influential party of opposition to the Sultan.

In the course of Eugene's meeting with Mustapha, the ease by which an independent Syria could be achieved by a properly funded Arab insurrection was discussed. Mustapha was cautious, but indicated a willingness to discreetly fund it and, should it appear to have a reasonable chance of success, to accept the titular leadership of it. Such a scheme, however, could only proceed if Eugene could raise significantly greater financial backing than Mustapha alone could offer. He needed to find other investors, speculators with the financial clout to underwrite it.

From Paris, Eugene proceeded to Dublin, where he arrived on 8 February 1867. He put up, as usual, at the Gresham Hotel.[458] His brother, James, was now living now at 43 Lower Gloucester Street with his wife,

---

[456] *La Liberte*, 13 December 1868, p.4.
[457] *The Times*, 1 March 1866, p.12; Ibid., 6 April 1866, p.10.
[458] *Saunders's News-Letter*, 9 February 1867, p.2.

A Visit Home

Susan, and his eight children.[459] There was Matthew (12), Maria (11), Honoria (9), Susan (8), Rosa (6), Eugenia (4), James (3) and Anna (11 months).[460] All Eugene could finally put faces to the names. All he had known of them prior to this had come from letters.

In Turkey, the distant past was but a shadow that held the faintest echoes of all that had happened, all that ought to have happened, and all that had never happened. But in Dublin, such things did not silently hide within the monochrome pleats of memory. They had real bricks and mortar, flesh and blood, substance. And they had words, and smells, and sounds: small evocative things that could unfetter in a moment of inattention, a torrent of nostalgia, anger, or regret.

In this oddly liminal space, friends and family became repositories of memory, holders of cherished fragments of his past, some of which he could still remember, others long since forgotten. They had known him in the smallest of unfinished ways and would know him like that forever. But, after more than a decade of being shaped by experiences they could never share, the world in which that past still lived was no longer his. He had grown neither with it nor within it: but had created for himself a new and separate history, had put down roots in a land whose customs and culture they could never hope to understand. A degree of estrangement was to be expected. Dublin, with all its ghosts and shadows, was no longer home.

---

[459] *Limerick and Clare Examiner*, 10 June 1854, p.3; *Saunders's News-Letter*, 21 February 1856, p.3; *Dublin Evening Packet and Correspondent*, 23 February 1856, p.3; *The Evening Freeman*, 17 July 1857, p.3; *Dublin Daily Express*, 9 December 1858, p.4; *Dublin Evening Mail*, 3 September 1860, p.3; *Cork Examiner*, 3 September 1860, p.3; *Irish Times*, 16 May 1862, p.4; N.L.I., Roman Catholic Parish Baptisms, Vol. 1, St. Mary's Baptisms, May 26, 1865 to July 2, 1868, p.128

[460] N.L.I., Irish Catholic Parish Registers; Microfilm Numbers: 09152/02, 09153/01, 09153/02, 09154/01.

Little is known of Eugene's personal life or romantic entanglements prior to this date, but what *is* known is that, at the time of this visit to Dublin, and at the age of thirty-nine, he found himself suddenly and hopelessly smitten with a woman at least twenty years his junior. Her name was Mathilde Solymassy, the Turkish-born daughter of a Turkish father and a Hungarian mother.[461] An intelligent and independent spirit, she brought a welcome lightness to his life.

Eugene had not fallen placidly in love with this dark and unspoilt Aphrodite: it had been an ardent and urgent romance and, given that they would marry just a few months later, not impossible that she had accompanied him to Dublin (his reservation at the Gresham had been made in the name of 'Hassan Bey and suite').[462]

In her later years, and in her only surviving written testimony, Mathilde would claim to have been fourteen at the time she became involved with Eugene, an age that might appear abhorrent to modern sensibilities but in the Victorian era was not uncommon. The age of consent at this time was twelve, and even the Queen's eldest daughter had become engaged at fourteen. That said, European society tended to look upon exceptionally large age differences in marriage with a *moue* of disgust. They may have been legal, but beyond the making of royal alliances, they were generally viewed as unnatural – a subconscious reflection of the incest taboo and, occasionally, of paedophilia and gerontophilia. Simply put, they made people uncomfortable.

The birth certificates of Mathilde's children, however, would record her stated age at the time of delivery and those declarations would put her in her early twenties in 1867. On the other hand, her stated

---

[461] This is the spelling Eugene used on his children's birth certificates. In later life, Mathilde would spell it Solomassy. Both are probably variations of the more common spelling of Solymosi.

[462] *Saunder's News-Letter*, 09 February 1867, p.2.

age on other official documents, signed after 1880, would put her at everything between twelve and seventeen when she married.[463] Throughout her life, her year of birth would be something of a moveable feast.[464]

Eugene was still lodging at the Gresham on 5 March when seven thousand young members of the Irish Republican Brotherhood set into the hills overlooking the village of Tallaght, intent on establishing an Irish republic by force. This latest act of insurgency, later to become known as the Fenian Rising, was no better organised or equipped than that of 1848 and, just as Eugene had predicted in 1862, turned out to be yet another paramilitary debacle. By the following day, it was all but over and the rebels defeated, despondent and dispersed.

His political views may have evolved since 1848, but Eugene had not forgotten his roots and would never be less than benevolent towards those fellow countrymen who would arrive in Turkey without the advantage of an influential letter of introduction. Upon his return to Constantinople, he would procure commissions in the Turkish military for two of the Fenian rebels, James Murtagh and Pat Sullivan, the latter of whom, as Sulieman Pasha, would later achieve a certain notoriety as the leader of the 4th Syrian Army in the Montenegrin War of 1876-1877.[465]

---

[463] *U.S. Naturalization Record Index*, Soundex Index to Petitions For Naturalizations Filed in Federal, State, and Local Courts in New York City, 1792-1906 (M1674), vol.53, record no. 299-298; *New York, U.S., State and Federal Naturalization Records*, 1794-1943 for Matilda Massy, Circuit Court, Southern District Vol A, 1, 1 Sep 1845 - 27 Oct 1894, M-160; M-200 (Vito); *1871 Census, London*, St. George Hanover Square, Belgrave, 17 Ranelagh Grove, Folio 15, p. 24, Mathilde Hassan.

[464] Ibid.; *United States Federal Census 1910*, Islip, Suffolk, New York, Central Islip State Hospital, Sheet No. 33A, 9 May 1910; *United States Federal Census 1915*, Islip, Suffolk, New York, Central Islip State Hospital, 1 June 1915, p.90.

[465] *The Brisbane Courier*, 14 September 1877, p.3.

Eugene had played no active role in the Fenian rebellion, despite his old friend, Thomas Clarke Luby, being up to his eyes in it.[466] Indeed, on 18 March, he was to be found on the opposite side of the political divide, hobnobbing with the cream of Anglo-Irish society at the Saint Patrick's Day Ball hosted annually by the Lord Lieutenant at Dublin Castle.[467] Mathilde, if indeed she *had* travelled with him, was not recorded in the list of attendees.

Back in Constantinople, the Sultan, invited by Napoleon III to attend the Paris Exhibition, had decided to undertake a summer tour of European capitals to improve his relations with European states and counter improving Western relations with Russia. Leaving the Ottoman Empire, however, was no small matter for Abdulaziz as no Sultan had ever set foot outside the Empire in peacetime. To the Turks, lands under the control of the Caliph of Islam were considered *Darü'l-Islam* or the 'Abode of Peace', while those ruled by Europeans were considered *Darü'l-Harp* or the 'Abode of War'. A Sultan could only travel to the latter to wage a holy war.

The diplomatic and practical challenges were enormous and all manner of preparations had to be agreed upon months in advance. With the Grand Vizier, Mehmed Emin Ali, tied up in Crete, where he was busy putting down a revolt, the Sultan ordered Fuad to assume the dual role of Foreign Minister and acting Grand Vizier.

An increase in his workload was the last thing Fuad needed, given his already fragile health, and so, in need of a trustworthy ally, he recalled Eugene to public service. In writing to the Irishman, he referred, somewhat enigmatically, to the resumption of 'certain projects abandoned in 1860'.[468] At a later date, this

---

[466] *Mount Ida Chronicle*, Vol. 8, Issue 440, 20 September 1877, p.3.
[467] *Saunder's News-Letter*, 19 March 1867, p.2; *Dublin Evening Post*, 19 March 1867, p.4.
[468] *La Liberté*, 13 December 1868, p.4.

A Visit Home

enigmatic reference would provoke questions as to whether or not Fuad was aware of what Eugene was up to; whether he had been entertaining similar plans of his own; or whether he had been manipulating a crisis behind the scenes.

On receipt of Fuad's summons, Eugene wrote to his old friend, Humphry Sandwith, indicating that he had a matter of the utmost urgency to discuss with him. An invitation to visit was received by return, and on 26 March 1867 Eugene and his 'suite' checked out of the Gresham Hotel and headed for Llandovery, in south Wales.[469]

Sandwith had become something of a folk hero since Eugene last saw him. Lionised by the British press for his conduct during the Siege of Kars, he had been made a Companion of the Order of the Bath by Queen Victoria, awarded an honorary Doctorate in Civil Law by Oxford University, and presented with the *Légion d'Honneur* by the French government. He had also attended the coronation of the Czar and been presented with the Russian Order of St. Stanislaus in recognition of his humane treatment of Russian prisoners during the Crimean War. Eugene was anxious to discuss with him the project he had tentatively pitched to Prince Mustapha in Paris.

Meanwhile, back in Syria, the Damascus Gendarmerie had become so ineffective and the Bedouins of the Hauran so belligerent that Eugene was now convinced that he could easily rally with promises of plunder, a large enough coalition of the discontented as to mount an effective insurrection. Such numbers, of course, could never defeat the might of the Sultan should he decide to wield the full force of his armies against them. But then winning, was not the primary goal.

The plan, as Eugene explained to Sandwith, was not as preposterous as it might first appear. His intention was not to overthrow Ottoman rule in Syria but to

---

[469] *Saunders's News-Letter*, 22 March 1867, p.2.

21. Humphry Sandwith.

cause enough mischief in the Hauran by arming the warring tribes as would depress Turkish securities on the *Bourse de commerce* in Paris and force the Porte to sue for peace, the price of which would be the installation of Mustapha as Khedive of Syria.

Under cover of a railway engineering survey, he intended to purchase and distribute modern weapons amongst the Bedouin and encourage them to unite against their Ottoman overlords. But even if they simply turned on each other, the proliferation of modern weapons amongst them would create chaos in the region, and on the financial markets, allowing his investors to make significant political and financial gains. Stunned by the magnitude of the Irishman's ambition, but neither unnerved nor unsettled by it,

A Visit Home

Sandwith agreed to fire off some letters on his behalf.

> His present business was to arrange an interview with me, and accordingly he visited me in Wales, and detailed to me his grand scheme. He wished to put himself at the head of an insurrection in Asia Minor, and, acquainted with the country as he was, and passing for a Mussulman – for he was known as Hussein Bey – he felt confident of giving a shock to the Ottoman Empire which might even destroy it.
>
> As he went on to detail his scheme, it came out that he was the instrument of a Turkish intrigue, the main figure being Mustapha Fazy Pasha, brother of the Viceroy of Egypt, and at that time one of the Cabinet Ministers at the Porte. This man [Mustapha], of course, had aims of his own. He wished to make Syria impossible for the Porte to govern, to have it joined to Egypt, and himself to be somehow or other made Viceroy.
>
> O'Reilly's plans were not absolutely cut and dried, the details being left for the future; but his idea was to undertake some kind of surveying scheme, to work his way to the Bedouins, and from there to commence operations. As soon as O'Reilly developed his plans to me, I saw that such an opportunity would be excellent for Servia to take advantage of. I therefore wrote off immediately to a Servian friend, asking him to come to Wales and meet a friend on a matter of great importance. He at once took my letter to the Prince,[470] who sanctioned his journey, so he arrived after a few days, and we had a conference together.
>
> At this time Crete was in open revolt, Servia was urging upon the Porte the evacuation of her fortresses, and the Prince had formed a sort of alliance with Montenegro, Greece, and Roumania. My Servian friend telegraphed in cypher O'Reilly's proposal and was instructed passively to encourage it, not to lose sight of it, but not absolutely to commit himself.[471]

In June 1867, the Khedive of Egypt, Ismail Pasha, arrived in Paris. He was followed some weeks later by the Sultan, who arranged a meeting with Mustapha, at which fences were patched, if not entirely mended.

---

[470] Prince Mihailo Obrenović III of Serbia.
[471] Ward, *Humphry Sandwith: a memoir*, pp.211-212.

Anticipating difficulties in Egypt, the Sultan pardoned Mustapha for his support of the Young Turkey movement, and Mustapha subsequently informed Eugene that he was pulling out of their speculative venture in the Hauran. It was a devastating blow. The project needed a strong Moslem figurehead behind whom the tribes could rally. Without one, the scheme was doomed to failure.

In the spirit of forgiveness, the Sultan had also included amongst his travelling party Mustapha's uncle, Prince Halim, who had likewise been exiled from Egypt following an unsuccessful coup. Halim had since settled in Constantinople, where he had been kept under constant surveillance. Shaken by Mustapha's withdrawal, Eugene turned instead to Halim, who, at least initially, appeared supportive, albeit similarly reluctant to commit himself.[472]

From Paris, Eugene travelled with the Sultan's retinue to London, where he combined his role of aide-de-camp to Fuad with occasional duties as royal interpreter. On one occasion, he accompanied the Sultan's ten-year-old son, Şehzade Yusuf Izzeddin Efendi, on a visit to the circus; on another, he translated for the Mayor of Liverpool when he called upon the Sultan.[473] He was still with Fuad when the Sultan's retinue departed Dover on 23 July.

Upon his return to Constantinople, his confidence shaken by Mustapha's volte-face, Eugene decided to hedge his bets and expand his 'surveying activities' to investigate the feasibility of building a railroad from the Mediterranean to the Euphrates and from there to the Persian Gulf. On whose behalf this survey was taken and exactly how much official sanction it had remains unclear to this day, but should it be completed, and found to be feasible, it promised even

---

[472] Seyhan, Ahmet. "Said Halim Pasha (1865–1921)" in *Islamist Thinkers in the Late Ottoman Empire and Early Turkish Republic*, Brill, Leiden, 2015, p.147; *New Albany Daily Ledger*, 19 May 1869, p.4.

[473] *Lady's Own Paper*, 20 July 1867, p.3.

greater riches for those who would be commissioned to build what would effectively be an alternative to the Suez Canal. A previous attempt to find a route, undertaken in 1862 by the Irish colonel, Francis Rawdon Chesney, had ended in failure, but the commercial interest was still there.[474]

As to whether the expanded scope of his survey was covered by the terms of his Ergani concession, whether he was simply hoping to attract new investors, or whether the survey was just an excuse to allow him to move into the Hauran without raising suspicion, reports varied.[475] All that is known for certain is that, by the time he returned to Turkey, he had secured a promise of support from Halim and sufficient financial backing to press forward with confidence.

---

[474] *New Albany Daily Ledger*, 19 May 1869, p.4; (Evidence in) Report from the Select Committee on Euphrates Valley Railway. With the Proceedings of the committee. Ordered by the House of Commons to be printed, 22 July 1872.

[475] *New Albany Daily Ledger*, 19 May 1869, p.4.

PUTTING THE TEAM TOGETHER

UPON HIS RETURN to Turkey, Eugene began to assemble an international engineering team about him. First to be recruited was his old friend E.W. Ward. Appointed as commissary general and chief bookkeeper to the surveying expedition, Ward immediately resigned from his official post.[476]

Next to be recruited was Andrew Romer, an 'expert draughtsman and an engineer of much ability'.[477] Romer had fled the U.S. after the American Civil War and enlisted as a colonel in the Ottoman Army.[478] Having served as an ordnance officer in the Austrian Army and as a Major at the U.S. Army arsenal at Watervliet,[479] he was sent to Trieste to procure arms and munitions for the 'protection' of the survey team.[480]

Another early recruit was the Irish physician, freemason and Anglican clergyman Doctor E.W. Dillon. Dismissed from the Royal Navy for drinking,[481] Dillon had served on and off as chaplain to the British Embassies in Basle and Berne between 1862 and 1867,[482] during which time he also studied for a degree in medicine.[483] Eugene would later claim to have hired

---

[476] *New York Herald*, 4 July 1870, p.11; .
[477] *Montreal Weekly Witness*, 12 December 1878, p.1; *Neue Freie Presse*, 20 May 1869, p.9; *New Albany Daily Ledger*, 19 May 1869, p.4.
[478] *New York Herald*, 4 July 1870, p.11.
[479] Crane, *From South Britain to Bagdad*, p.21.
[480] Romer would later be part of a second conspiracy in 1878, see *Evening Mail*, 18 December 1878, p.5.
[481] Crane, *From South Britain to Bagdad*, p.21.
[482] *Dunfermline Press*, 15 October 1862, p.4; *Leeds Mercury*, 1 August 1867, p.2.
[483] *Leeds Mercury*, 27 November 1868, p.4; Bradshaw, George. *Bradshaw's Continental*, Vol. 2, June 1847 - Oct. 1939, pp.360, 362.

him as much for the confidence he had in his reliability under fire as for his surgical expertise.

Next to be recruited was Cecil Armine Jenner, a major in the Turkish service.[484] Cecil was a brother of George Francis Birt Jenner, who, in April 1862, at the age of twenty-three, had been appointed as third secretary to the British Embassy in Athens.[485] The brothers, nephews of Lord Salisbury, the Secretary of State for India, were residing together at this time.

In Athens at the same time as the Jenners was twenty-three-year-old American diplomat Henry Monroe Canfield, a native of Hartford, Connecticut.[486] Canfield was perhaps the most interesting of Eugene's recruits. Known since childhood as an impulsive thrill seeker, he been sent in 1861 to his uncle, George J. Baker, the American Consul in Athens, in the hope of finding him a place at a European medical school and keeping him out of harm's way during the American Civil War.[487] Canfield would eventually enter the University of Göttingen to study medicine, only to be persuaded, after just two semesters, to abandon his medical studies and return to Athens, where his uncle had procured for him the post of consul.[488]

Moving in the highest diplomatic circles in Greece, Canfield soon encountered the Jenners, with whom he grew so close that he would be the only guest at George's wedding to Stephanie Emilianova, daughter of Russian civil servant Alexis Emilianoff of Ragatova. He

---

[484] Melville, Amadeus. *The Plantagenet roll of the blood royal, being a complete table of all the descendants now living of Edward III., King of England*, Melville, London, 1911, p.203.

[485] *Globe*, 7 October 1863, p.4; Hertslet, Edward. *The Foreign Office List*, Harrison, London, 1863, pp.14, 109.

[486] *Baltimore Daily Commercial*, 31 October 1865, p.4; *Morning Chronicle and Commercial and Shipping Gazette*, 5 January 1869, p.2.

[487] Crane, *From South Britain to Bagdad*, p.3.

[488] Ibid., p.7; *Journal of the executive proceedings of the United States of America, From December 1, 1862 to July 4, 1864*, Government Printing Office, Washington, 1887; *New York Times*, 21 January 1863, p.1; *New York Tribune*, 21 January 1863, p.1.

also found his way into a secret society supportive of Italian unification and became particularly friendly with Domenico Menotti Garibaldi, the eldest son of the Italian revolutionary Giuseppe Garibaldi.[489]

While in Athens, Canfield developed an interest in archaeology and antiquities, dabbled briefly in smuggling,[490] and pursued a lifestyle so far beyond the salary of a consular official, he had to supplement his income with private translation work.[491] His 'eccentricities' openly criticised as unbecoming the dignity of his office, he became the subject of various intrigues by embassy cliques anxious to see the back of him.

In June 1865, Canfield left Athens for Paris, intending to travel home on an unauthorised vacation, during which he hoped to employ family influence to secure a promotion to Charge d'affaires. Stopping in Paris to register his presence with the American Ambassador, he was persuaded to engage in espionage, by obtaining employment as a workman at the navy arsenal in Cherbourg, from where he would survey the strength of the French fleet being prepared to sail for Mexico in support of the Emperor Maximillian. Having delivered his report to Paris, Canfield spent Christmas in Connecticut with his family before returning to Athens in January 1866, where the intrigues against him had intensified in his absence.

It was about this time that Canfield and the Jenners became involved, in as much as their diplomatic roles would permit, in the rebellion of the people of Crete. With Crete blockaded by the Turkish fleet, the trio became involved in provisioning the island. Despite their subversive activities, or perhaps because of them, Canfield was transferred to the American consulate at Piraeus and, one week later, George Jenner to the British Embassy in Constantinople.[492] George's brother, Cecil,

---

[489] Ibid., p.4.
[490] Crane, *From South Britain to Bagdad*, pp.8-9.
[491] Ibid., p.5.
[492] *The Hereford Journal*, 13 July 1867, p.6.

would travel with George to Turkey, where he would enlist in the Ottoman Army at the rank of *binbashi* or major.

In September 1867, Canfield added to the list of his eccentric indiscretions by abandoning his post at Piraeus to smuggle munitions to Crete. Mission completed, he returned briefly to Athens in October where, realising that he had by now become too deeply implicated in the revolt to keep his diplomatic post, he jumped before he was pushed. Returning next to Piraeus, he made out a false passport in the name of Charles Lamar, authorised it with his own signature, then locked up the consulate and boarded a blockade runner heading for Crete. Suspected by the crew of espionage, he was landed on the island of Syros, where he met with Andrew Romer.[493]

Impressed by Canfield's linguistic abilities and subversive contacts, not the least of whom was Domenico Menotti Garibaldi, Romer recruited Canfield to the 'survey' team and the pair combined to arrange the smuggling of arms from Brindisi to Alexandria under false invoices. Three vessels, according to Canfield, were bought or borrowed for this purpose, amongst them the private yacht of Emperor Maximillian, which had been loaned to the cause through the intercession of Domenico Garibaldi. Despite having been left in sole charge of this phase of the operation,[494] Canfield would, for many years after, deny having had any knowledge of the survey's ulterior purpose.[495]

Everything was moving in the right direction, but moving so slowly that Eugene was soon struggling financially. Apart from funding the survey missions and paying the salaries of his recruits, he was also being pressed to repay the loan of £1,400 he had secured in 1863 from the moneylender 'Levi', who was now petitioning the British Consul for help in

---

[493] *New York Herald*, 4 July 1870, p.11; Crane, *From South Britain to Bagdad*, pp.13-15, 21.
[494] Crane, *From South Britain to Bagdad*, p.21.
[495] *Chicago Tribune*, 4 December 1868, p.2.

recouping it. With sufficient funds to keep those already employed through the winter but no further, Eugene next sailed for Alexandria to negotiate a lucrative contract to supply mules to the British Abyssinian Expedition.[496]

Angered by the refusal of other Christian nations to assist him in resisting a native revolt and increasing encroachment by Turkey and Egypt, the Ethiopian Emperor, Tewodros II, had seized several British missionaries and diplomats. Attempts to secure their release through diplomatic channels had failed and so, on 21 August 1867, the British sent a military expedition to rescue them. In early October, O'Reilly signed a contract worth several thousand pounds to deliver 1400 mules to Suez,[497] then promptly set out for Aleppo, where he delegated control of the operation to Ward who, while scouring the countryside for serviceable animals, could sound out the attitude of various Bedouin chiefs towards Eugene's plans.[498]

Some weeks later, accompanied by Romer, Eugene returned to Alexandria, to attend a meeting of Abyssinian Expedition staff and meet Canfield when he arrived with armaments left over from the Cretan Insurrection. Here the weapons were transferred to a smaller another vessel and taken to the island of Arwad off the Syrian coast, where Eugene had established a base.[499] O'Reilly, Romer and Canfield then returned together to Constantinople, from where Canfield was sent to assist Cecil Jenner with the engineering survey that was scouting a potential route for a railway line linking the Lebanese port of Tripoli to the Iraqi capital, Baghdad and gathering intelligence on Bedouin and Army movements in the region.

---

[496] *The Scotsman*, 18 Oct. 1867, p.2; *Greenock Advertiser*, 22 Oct. 1867.
[497] *New Albany Daily Ledger*, 19 May 1869, p.4; *Pall Mall Gazette*, 17 October 1867, p.8; *Glasgow Herald*, 18 October 1867, p.5; *New York Herald*, 28 December 1868, p.6.
[498] *Home News for India, China and the Colonies*, 18 October 1867, p.4.
[499] Crane, *From South Britain to Bagdad*, p.25.

A CONSULAR WEDDING

IN THE AUTUMN of 1867, Eugene proposed marriage. A single man approaching his fortieth birthday, his motivation was conventional and understandable. Mathilde's decision to accept him, on the other hand, is not quite so easily explained. She was young enough to be his daughter.

In 1848, the number of Hungarians resident in Constantinople were significantly swollen by the arrival of hundreds of refugees from the failed war of independence, typically single men in their late twenties of predominantly bourgeois or noble origin. Since then, on any given evening, an educated Hungarian girl could easily find a host of age-appropriate suitors at the *Kis Campó* coffee house, a popular Hungarian haunt in Constantinople.[500]

It is not known for certain when Mathilde Solymassy's family arrived in Turkey. In later years, she would claim that she and her father had been born in Turkey and her mother in Hungary.[501] Then again, she would also describe herself as Catholic and Hungarian. The fact that she was literate and fluent in French suggests a bourgeois upbringing, but the Solymassy name does not appear in either the Hungarian consular lists or the Feriköy cemetery database, making it unlikely that

---

[500] Kovács, Nándor Erik. "Hungarian Turkophils in 19th Century Istanbul and Their Bequests in the Library of the Hungarian Academy of Sciences," in *Uluslararası Osmanlı İstanbulu Sempozyumu-IV*, Eötvös Loránd University, Budapest, 2016, p.454; The *Kis Campó* coffee house in Galata was the most popular meeting place for Hungarian ex-pats in Constantinople.

[501] U.S. National Archives and Records Administration, Census, 1900, Manhattan, New York City, New York, Election District 7, Ward 21, ED 522, T623, Sheet Letter:A, Household Id:281, Sheet No.11, p.248.

they were of the nobility.[502]

The death of a 'Károly Solymosi' is noted in the minutes of the Hungarian Society on 2 February 1851. If this was Mathilde's father, his passing may have left his family in straitened circumstances and explain Mathilde's rush into a marriage she would later claim to have been sheathed in an illusion of legality.[503] Many years later, claiming to have been fourteen at the time of her marriage, she would assert that she had:

> ... formed the acquaintance of Eugene O'Reilly, at Constantinople in the year named and, at his earnest solicitation, consented to marry him and a marriage ceremony was, as the girl then believed performed by a person said to be the English Consul at that place, by which she firmly believed she became the wife of Mr. O'Reilly...[504]

Those claims, however, must be treated with caution, for on the birth certificates of her children, her stated age would later place her year of birth between 1845 and 1846, making her twenty-one on her wedding day. As the years progressed, she would also, at various times, claim to have been born in 1848, 1850, and 1855.[505] Whatever her age, Mathilde

---

[502] My thanks to Gábor Fodor, former Director of the Hungarian Cultural Institute in Istanbul, for checking these sources for me.

[503] Csorba, Gyorgy, "Hungarians in Constantinople in the mid-19th Century: Socio-Economic Background and Careers" in Fodor, Gabor ed., *Between Empires – Beyond Borders, the Late Ottoman Empire and the Early Republican Era through the lens of the Kope Family*, Research Centre for the Humanities, Budapest, 2020, p.65; Csorba, Gyorgy & Fodor, Gabor, *Magyarok A Kelet Kapujában – A Konstantinápolyi Magyar Egylet története (1850-1861)*, Pro Minoritate, Nyár, 2021, p.6.

[504] Unsent/draft letter from Mathilda, 7 March 1893, Bankhead/Guest family archives (privately held) courtesy of Sarah B. Guest Perry.

[505] *U.S. Naturalization Record Index*, Soundex Index to Petitions For Naturalizations Filed in Federal, State, and Local Courts in New York City, 1792-1906 (M1674), vol.53, rec. no. 299-298; *New York, U.S., State and Federal Naturalization Records, 1794-1943* for Matilda Massy, Circuit Court, Southern District Vol A, 1, 1 Sep 1845 - 27 Oct 1894, M-160; M-200 (Vito); *1871 Census, London*, Folio 15, p. 24, Mathilde Hassan.

A Consular Wedding

believed herself to be married, as indeed did Eugene, who would refer to her during one tribunal appearance as the 'wife that I love and whose love I cherish'.[506] As for the 'ceremony', it was probably performed by George Jenner, who worked at the embassy and whose brother, Cecil, was heavily involved in Eugene's filibustering scheme.

Since 1849, the *Consular Marriages Act* had given overseas consuls the right to celebrate civil marriages, details of which would then be sent to the Registrar General in London. If the wedding *had* been a charade, then it was a peculiarly elaborate one, requiring the collusion of a celebrant and witnesses. To have knowingly hosted an illegal ceremony at the embassy, George Jenner would have been risking both his reputation and his career, an unlikely scenario. A more benign interpretation of the illegal nuptials can perhaps be found in the circumstances that prevailed at the embassy at the time.

Back in July of 1867, as Eugene was returning with Fuad to Constantinople, Lord Lyons, the British Consul, was recalled to London and sent to Paris to replace Lord Cowley. At roughly the same time, the Hon. Henry Elliot was appointed to Constantinople as his replacement.[507] Elliot had earlier travelled from Paris with the Sultan's party but, following the Sultan's departure, had remained in London to be sworn in as a member of the Privy Council.[508] He had yet to arrive in Turkey at the time of Eugene's 'wedding', and would not do so until 19 October 1867. The embassy, meanwhile, functioned under the direction of his subordinates. On the day in question George Jenner may simply have been the most senior diplomat on duty.[509]

Consular weddings were quite common by 1867, but only the Consul was legally authorised to officiate,

---

[506] *La Liberté*, 13 December 1868, p.4.
[507] *Norwich Mercury*, 13 July 1867, p.5.
[508] *Evening Mail*, 21 August 1867, p.5.
[509] *Levant Herald*, 19 Oct 1867, p.1.

and Jenner was a third secretary. It is not impossible that he wrongly assumed himself entitled to deputise and believed the matter would be regularised upon Elliot's arrival. It would not. So, whether through a grievous error in judgment or deliberate deception, the wedding was never officially registered. As for Jenner, he was soon after transferred to the British Embassy in Tehran, though not before involving himself in Eugene's mischief.[510]

> About £5,000 worth [of arms] had been sent from England. Everything was prepared, but unfortunately, he [O'Reilly] had been indiscreet in his choice of confidants. Among them was, I am told, a British Consul, who entered eagerly into O'Reilly's schemes, which he highly applauded and then regularly wrote home full accounts of them to the Foreign Office.[511]

That 'British Consul' was never explicitly identified, whose brother, Cecil, was heavily involved with Eugene than James Henry Skene, the British Consul at Beirut. Skene, in fact, was so blind to the Irishman's intentions that, while Eugene was delivering arms to the Bedouin, he would send a tourist intent on travelling to Palmyra to meet with him in the desert.

Canfield and Romer returned to Constantinople shortly before Christmas, whereupon Canfield briefly and unsuccessfully set his sights on a bigger payday than the thousand lira a month he was receiving from Eugene. Through the intercession of Augustus Hobart-Hampden, the former Royal Navy captain who now commanded the Ottoman Fleet, he secured an introduction to Mustapha Pasha and attempted to pitch a scheme of his own regarding petroleum drilling in Iraq.[512] He also secured introductions to Halil Bey, whom he believed was secretly providing funds to Mustapha, and to three anonymous brothers involved who were 'well

---

[510] *The Morning Post*, 18 September 1868, p.5.
[511] Ward, *Humphry Sandwith: a Memoir*, p.214.
[512] Crane, *From South Britain to Bagdad*, p.22.

supplied with money'.[513] Sent to Aleppo to assist Ward in transporting the mules and horses across the Sinai Desert, a trip that took three months, he would arrive in Alexandria to find Eugene waiting with 'more money than he could carry'.[514]

It was about this time that Canfield introduced Eugene to Julius Franz, a former corporal in the Austrian Army whom Canfield had first met when he arrived in Alexandria aboard the Emperor Maximillian's yacht.[515] Eugene hired Franz on the spot,[516] and then sent Canfield to assist one of his survey teams, which by now had advanced from Arida on the Syria-Lebanon border to the city of Homs. Canfield was ordered to join the survey and remain with it until all of the arms and munitions had arrived at Arwad.

As he accompanied the survey team across the desert towards the village of Salamiyeh, Canfield would make copious notes on the ruins and architectural features he passed, notes that formed the basis of a paper published later that same year in the Journal of the American Oriental Society.[517] That he had the time to do so speaks volumes for his lack of involvement in the engineering survey and remains at variance with his later claims that he was oblivious to Eugene's subversive activities from the start.

---

[513] Ibid., p.23.
[514] Davison, Roderic H. "Halil Serif Pasa, Ottoman Diplomat and Statesman" in *Journal of Ottoman Studies II*, Istanbul, 1981, pp.209-210; Crane, *From South Britain to Bagdad,* pp.22, 24.
[515] Crane, *From South Britain to Bagdad*, p.25.
[516] *New Albany Daily Ledger*, 19 May 1869, p.4; See also H. Frantz-Bey, "Cairo's Neubauten," *Zeitschrift fur praktische Baukunst*, no.31, 1871, pp. 193-198, 325-330, in which Franz describes himself as the Ober-Baudirektor des Khedive.
[517] *Journal of the American Oriental Society, 1868-1871*, Vol. 9, p.lxv.

JANE DIGBY

EARLY IN 1868, approximately three months after the survey team had set out from Beirut,[518] Andrew Romer turned up Trieste, where he hoisted the American flag on a recently purchased yacht,[519] renamed it the *General Sherman*, and loaded it with two mortars and 200 carbines bought earlier in Vienna. The yacht would dock in Beirut in February, where Romer would deposit his papers at the American consulate claiming to be engineer surveying a railway route from Tripoli to the Euphrates.[520] He had been ordered, he would claim, to wait in Beirut for a communication from the head of his company, a Turkish official by the name of Hassan Bey.

When questioned by customs about the needle rifles his ship was carrying, Romer would claim them to be for the protection of the survey team, local officials having refused them an escort. While waiting for Eugene to arrive, he would also invite some American tourists to travel with him to Palmyra, thus avoiding 'the usual £300 blackmail to Sheikh Medjuel and his hungry Arabs'.[521]

Eugene, meanwhile, remained in Constantinople, where he continued to cultivate the impression that the long-hoped-for railroad from Tripoli to Baghdad was not only feasible but probable. It was noticed, however, that for a project of this scale, he appeared to be keeping an unusually low profile and no longer socialised with the various consuls he used to meet on a regular

---

[518] *La Liberté*, 13 December 1868, p.4.
[519] *New York Herald*, 28 December 1868, p.6.
[520] *Morning Chronicle and Commercial and Shipping Gazette*, 5 January 1869, p.2.
[521] *Chicago Tribune*, 4 December 1868, p.2.

basis. His behaviour, however, was attributed to the pressure of work and political disagreements.[522]

It was about this time that Eugene received a fresh injection of funds, alleged by some to have come from Prince Halim, and by others to have come from the French, who were believed to favour his railway project on account of the disastrous effect it would have on British interests in the Suez Canal.[523] Eugene himself would claim the investors to have been a party of British entrepreneurs,[524] a claim seemingly corroborated years later by a French journalist, who would identify one of those entrepreneurs as:

> ... an Englishman whom we do not want to name, because he has settled down and is now engaged in serious business...[525]

Whoever that person was, it is unlikely to have been Humphry Sandwith, who, having grown impatient at Eugene's refusal to accept any money from him until Mustapha's commitment had been assured, had long since pulled out of the enterprise. With regard to Russian involvement, Sandwith would later write that:

> I was anxious for O'Reilly to succeed, as I hoped to see the beginning of the end of that organisation of brigandage, the Ottoman Empire. General Ignatieff, Russian Ambassador at the Porte, was one of his confidants, and aided him without committing himself.[526]

In April 1868, Canfield and the survey team reached the outskirts of Hama.[527] Two months later, on 18 June, Eugene left Constantinople for Beirut, travelling

---

[522] *New York Herald*, 4 July 1870, p.11.
[523] *New Albany Daily Ledger*, 19 May 1869, p.4.
[524] *Belfast Weekly News*, 19 December 1868, p.7; Davison, Roderic H. *Reform in the Ottoman Empire*, Gordian Press, New York, 1973, pp.197-198; *New York Herald*, 4 July 1870, p.11.
[525] *Le Peuple français*, 28 September 1881, p.1.
[526] Ward, *Humphry Sandwith: A Memoir*, pp.214-215.
[527] *Journal of the American Oriental Society, 1868-1871*, Vol. 9, p.lxv.

in the company of the new governor of Lebanon, Franco Pasha.[528] During the journey, Eugene requested an armed guard to protect the survey team in the desert.[529] Franco refused, as Eugene expected he would, thus affording him the perfect excuse to enlist a 'private security' corps of some eighty Circassians, all former members of the Damascus gendarmerie. This unit was then placed under the command of Julius Franz, whose role within the expedition was, like Canfield's, officially recorded as an 'engineer'.[530]

Upon his arrival in Beirut, Eugene recalled Canfield from Hama,[531] and then moved to the Lebanese port of Tripoli,[532] where he collected the muskets, mortars and munitions that Romer had smuggled through customs labelled as railway irons. The weapons were then ferried to the island of Arwad and added to the cache that had earlier arrived from the UK and Alexandria.

> From there they were carried across to the shore in row-boats, and taken inland by caravans of camels, and disposed to the Arabs. The shipment across to the mainland from the island, and the landing of the goods, were carried out under an elaborate system of flash signals between the main-land, the boats, and the island, and there was probably some collusion between the local Turkish officials for enabling them to get away with it as well as they did. The enterprise lasted seven months...
>
> None of the money received from the Arabs for these goods had to be turned over to anyone, or even accounted for. The men in the party kept it for themselves, and divided it as they chose. From the slopes of the Lebanon, by flashing powder from a cartridge, signals were given to the bay. Henry [Canfield] got his bearings by daylight from

---

[528] Ward, *Humphry Sandwith: a memoir*, pp.211, 213.
[529] *New York Herald*, 4 July 1870, p.11; Kemal H. Karpat. *Studies on Ottoman Social and Political History – Selected Articles and Essays*, Brill, Leiden, 2002, pp.790-791.
[530] Klutschak, Franz and Bernhard Gutt, *Bohemia: ein Unterhaltungsblatt*, Prager Zeitung, January 1868, p. 3618.
[531] *Chicago Tribune*, 4 December 1868, p.2.
[532] *Boston Pilot*, 9 January 1869, p.2.

these slopes with fine glasses. Then at night, opening cartridges, he strung powder along over the rocks at intervals, and set it off by flashes timed by his watch. When the flashes were returned, they could communicate by code, and decide on the landing.[533]

A few days after Romer's return, the group moved the heavy weapons to Beirut, where Eugene released those members of the engineering team who had not been privy to his military plans. The remaining team, along with their Circassian escort, then set out for Homs, stopping only when they reached the edge of the desert. Here Eugene received word that representatives from several Bedouin tribes had set out from Hama to find him. The sheikh of the first tribe declined to join him, but Suleiman al Murshid, one of the most powerful sheikhs in the Hauran and ruler of a tribe of approximately 60,000 Bedouin, was more than willing to do so. And with that, ironically, the Irishman's problems began.

The Bedouin lived by the camel. Their lives and movements revolved about the feeding and care of these animals. Routes to and from seasonal pastures determined tribal boundaries, just as the camel markets of the Middle East determined tribal prosperity and population. But the desert scrub could only feed so many and competition for pasture bred quarrels, border disputes and raids.

Eugene had planned for every eventuality but the intensity of tribal rivalries. The Bedouin did not trust the government, did not trust outsiders, and did not trust each other.[534] And yet, if he was to take his team into, or across, the desert, he needed camels and Jane Digby, or, more accurately, her husband Medjuel, was ideally placed to supply them. Medjuel, for several years, had been a fugitive from Turkish justice, and

---

[533] Crane, *From South Britain to Bagdad*, p.25.
[534] Lawrence, T.E. *The Seven Pillars of Wisdom*, Jonathan Cape, London, 1935, p.44.

Jane, deprived of her British citizenship, a stateless woman. Their support would have been guaranteed, but for the involvement of Murshid.

In his negotiations with the Bedouin, Eugene had agreed on the monies and land that each would get if their joint enterprise proved successful.[535] In return, Suleiman al Murshid of the Qumusa branch of the Seb'a had promised to supply men, while Medjuel el Mezrab to supply camels for the enormous sum of £10,000.[536] Eugene's biggest mistake was to have paid Jane Digby in advance.

Back in 1861, Jane's husband, Medjuel, had purchased a large flock of sheep from the Seb'a on the understanding that the Seb'a would winter them with their own. When Medjuel came to collect them, however, he was told that they had perished during an unusually severe winter. Medjuel did not believe the story and, to restore his loss and his honour, he determined to recover either his sheep or an equivalent compensation through the traditional means of *divan* (arbitration) or *ghazou* (an armed raid on camels).[537] Desert justice was swift. The nature of Bedouin life was not conducive to slow legal processes.

During this conflict, a certain Faris Ibn Meziad, an ally of Murshid, went to the Governor of Homs and accused Medjuel of causing trouble in the desert. The complaint led, in January 1862, to Medjuel's arrest and imprisonment. As Jane was still a British citizen at the time, her husband enjoyed certain protections under British law. Following pressure from the British consul, he was released on bail and promptly fled into the desert.[538]

At the start of the current enterprise, Jane had

---

[535] *New York Herald*, 4 July 1870, p.11.
[536] Burton, Isabel. *The Inner Life of Syria, Palestine and the Holy Land, from My Private journal*, vol. 2, Henry S. King & Co., London, 1875, pp. 12-13.
[537] Ibid.
[538] Ibid., p.210.

22. Jane Digby, Lady Ellenborough.

introduced Eugene to Medjuel, the nominal head of the Mezrab, and persuaded her husband to provide camels and safe passage across his territories.[539] Upon learning of the involvement of al-Murshid and el-Meziad, however, Medjuel withdrew his support and

---

[539] Ward, *Humphry Sandwith: A Memoir*, p.211.

refused to hand over the camels that Eugene had already paid for. Deciding to take by force what was rightfully his, Eugene allowed al Murshid to attack Medjuel's camp with mortars, killing a Bedouin woman and wounding two of Medjuel's. Reprisals inevitably followed. Writing to Eugene's brother, James, an anonymous witness would later recall that:

> The sheikh refused to give up the camels, nor would he refund the money which Mrs. Digby had pocketed. Thereupon your brother joined a tribe of Bedouins hostile to that of Mrs. Digby, attacked and routed them, took several thousand camels, of which your brother only retained those he had bought and paid for.[540]

Raids between rival tribes were not uncommon. The Wuld Ali and Seb'a had gone to war as recently as 1864, and all the major tribes had gone to war in December 1865.[541] Jane herself had been subjected to a camel raid in 1862 when the Wuld Ali stole 250 camels and £2000 worth of goods.[542] On not one of these raids had Jane herself been present, nor was she for the latest raid. In Homs at the time, she noted the following in her diary:

> Cannon and musketry was heard in the morning, and about twelve dozen Arab horsemen rushed into the town with the too true news that Hassaim Bey had indeed attacked our camp with Ebn Merschid, and after pouring a volley of balls into our tents, had carried off all our camels, but, thank God, had killed none of our men.[543]

Having been armed by Eugene with mortars, Murshid was never going to stop there. In the same

---

[540] Ward, *Humphry Sandwith: A Memoir*, p.211.
[541] Lovell, Mary S. A Scandalous Life – The Biography of Jane Digby, e-book, Richard Cohen Books, London, 1995, p.225.
[542] UK National Archives, Rogers to Foreign Office, FO78/1686, FO78/1751, XC 11848.
[543] Blanch, Leslie. *The Wilder Shores of Love*, e-book, Bookblast e-publishing, London, 2015.

23. A Bedouin of the Hauran.

diary, Jane noted that throughout the month of May:

> ... ebn Merschid, allied with Hassan Bey, was attacking the summer encampments and plundering them.[544]

Early reports were supportive of Eugene and believing of the story that the attack on Medjuel's camp was simply a feud between two Bedouin sheikhs.[545] A report in the *Levant Herald* on 1 October was typical of the public reluctance to believe Jane. In publishing a letter from her, the editor cautioned his readers that:

---

[544] Lovell, Mary S. *A Scandalous Life, The Biography of Jane Digby*, Harper Collins E-Books, London, 2012, p.229.
[545] *Glasgow Evening Citizen*, 27 October 1868, p.2.

In printing it we deem it right to say that information from another source states Col. O'Reilly to have bought and paid Mrs Digby herself for the camels referred to, but that her husband, Sheikh Medjuel, afterwards refused to deliver the animals, though retaining the cash – a not improbable Arab trick.[546]

Though Jane had not been present when Medjuel's camp was attacked, her letter read as though she had:

> The first result of Col. O'Reilly's "road scheme" has been a most treacherous, and I say cowardly, raid upon our tribe and tents, especially. I call it cowardly for the immense advantage they had in newly invented arms and ammunition and the safe distance at which they poured a perfect hailstorm of balls into the tents, and treacherous because up to the moment O'Reilly removed from Selamieh[547] and made alliance with a rival tribe, he appeared to be on the most friendly footing.
>
> Aided by the Ebn Merchid Arabs, and Faris el Meziâd they carried off our camels, while he continued covering them with his fire, and was afterwards presented with 75 as his share of the booty, which he still retains; 30 more were shot or hacked with their swords, and for several days Homs and the neighbouring villages held a feast on their flesh; others were driven off by the Arabs, and are still in the desert, but those we hope to recover.
>
> I make no comment upon this extraordinary and shameful proceeding: it were useless. If some Government or other is really giving him aid and support, there is nothing to do but wait events, and such appears to be really the case; or from whence and how could he procure such quantities of arms – 2 cannons and 2 cases of bombshells, one of which fell into the hands of our tribe, and *sert de piece de conviction* – and men of all nations, including Circassians, English gentlemen, Americans, Hungarians, Turcomans, and Christians of Kesrouan.
>
> There is a great *enquête* at Hamah, and various sheikhs of tribes have been summoned, Sheikh Medjuel among the

---

[546] *Levant Herald,* 1 October 1868, pp.2-3.
[547] Now called Salamiyah.

rest; but although O'Reilly had promised Ebn Merchid full protection from all pursuit on the part of the Government, and given him, they say, a sum of money, he has left him and gone into the desert. All this took place an hour and a half from Homs, at our encampment. Afterwards he went and attacked the Ressalimen tribe, some hours further on, quite unconscious and unprepared as they were; of course with the same success.

Now I should like to hear what is the public opinion of Beyrout on Hassan Bey's action, and what are likely to be the consequences. Some days after O'Reilly left Homs, a Russian telegram arrived for him here, and some talk of others being a party concerned. I should think the Ottoman Government cannot, for its own sake, allow such acts to pass unnoticed. Colonel O'Reilly's intention is to work his way down to the Euphrates, if allowed; he has already begun to take grain and barley from Selamieh without payment. I am grieved that he and his band are chiefly Englishmen.[548]

Fearing for their lives, Medjuel and Jane raced to Damascus to warn the Governor General of Syria, Mehmed Rashid Pasha. Rashid, at first, was reluctant to believe them. O'Reilly, after all, was a pasha, the recipient of the Order of Merit, the Order of Valor, and the Order of the Medejie.[549] And yet, the raid on Medjuel's camp had been criminal enough in its own right to warrant an arrest, even without the dangerous proliferation of modern weapons. After much deliberation, Rashid telegraphed the Governor of Homs and ordered him to capture the insurgents and seize their weapons.

Meanwhile, back in Egypt, an assassination attempt was made on the Khedive during a visit to the Cairo illuminations. As his carriage passed through a narrow street, a steel ball with sharp spikes was dropped at his head. It missed, and the suspect escaped undetected. Suspicion was rife that the attack had

---

[548] *Levant Herald,* 1 October 1868, p.3.
[549] Curtis, Georgina Pell and Benedict Elder. *The American Catholic Who's Who*, NC News Service, 1911, p.497.

been fake, a ruse by the Khedive to elicit popular support and cast suspicion on his uncle, Prince Halim, whose popularity with all classes of Egyptian society had been a constant thorn in the Khedive's side.[550] Government papers, as a result, were instructed to withhold news of the alleged assassination attempt until 2 October, at which time they were encouraged to hint darkly at 'treason'. But, as of yet, nobody had any reason to link the unrest in Syria to the unrest in Egypt. That was about to change.

---

[550] *Levant Herald*, 3 October 1868, p.1; Ibid., 16 October 1868, pp.3-4.

CAPTURE!

LIONEL MUIRHEAD, AN English adventurer in his early twenties, was a close friend of the poets Gerald Manley Hopkins and Robert Bridges. Having graduated from Corpus Christi College, Oxford, in 1867, he and Bridges had been travelling in the Middle East until Bridges, in June 1868, decided to return to England.[551] Blind in one eye and unable to continue his studies, Muirhead remained in Syria to prolong the adventure. He arrived in Aleppo three months after Eugene had departed, intent on visiting the ruins at Palmyra. Reluctant to pay Medjuel's extortionate fee, he sought the advice of the British consul, James Henry Skene.

> The Sheikh who usually escorts travellers asks at least £80 for a single traveller – a terrible item in our account book – so Mr. Skene kindly undertook to enable me to reach Palmyra without any bakshish, or very little. A party of engineers had landed at Tripoli 3 months previously to make plans for a line of railroad from Tripoli to the Euphrates: the head of this expedition, Colonel O'Reilly, being a great friend of Mr. Skene's, I started from Aleppo with a letter of introduction to him. Their camp was then pitched in the desert amongst the Arabs, with whom they were on good terms, at no great distance from Palmyra ...
>
> At Hamah I applied to the Pasha for an escort to Hassan Bey's camp, and after much delay was refused. So I hired a common Arab and set out to take my chance without escort. All night under the clear moon we travelled over the stony tract and at daybreak reached a small collection of huts, the farthest civilized settlement eastward till one arrives at the Euphrates. 40 Mowali – a marauding expedition

---

[551] Bridges, Robert. *The Selected Letters of Robert Bridges*, vol. 2, University of Delaware Press, Newark, 1984, p.933; Ibid, vol.1, 1983, p.83.

– passed us in the night a mile off; two men met us who had been robbed. I fortunately escaped.

From this village I went on to Colonel O'Reilly's camp. Here I stayed 5 days enjoying myself mightily, galloping about the great plains with quaintly shaped hills bounding them, and seeing Arab life unadulterated. The great Sheikh Suleyman Ebn Meerched, who rules over 60,000 Ansaçh, spent a day or two at the camp negotiating an escort for Colonel O'Reilly and Company to the banks of the Euphrates. Before I arrived at this camp the engineers – a force of 100 men in all, Circassians, Hungarians, Syrians etc. – had a fight with a tribe and came off victorious. The beaten tribe happened to be under the wing of the Turkish government, while Suleyman Ebn Marshed, who defied the Turks, was an outlaw.[552]

That, at least, was how Muirhead would describe his adventure to others, and how he would portray his innocent presence in the Hauran. But he was, it would appear, being somewhat economical with the truth. Canfield would later describe Muirhead's activities in a very different light:

During the presence of the party in the vicinity of Hamath, an Englishman appeared on the scene who announced that he wanted to go to Bagdad to join the party of the Marchioness of Elly-Butte, but that he had missed them and wanted to go on to Palmyra alone. Henry [Canfield] volunteered to accompany him, and they went to Palmyra, and thence to Bagdad. They were accompanied by a party of fifteen or twenty Esbaa, and a few of the Mesrab tribe. The trip to Palmyra occupied three days. From Palmyra on, they had only three Arabs with them to Bagdad.

The Marchioness of Elly-Butte [Jane Digby] was an English woman, married to a sheik of the Mesrab tribe who controlled the right to get into Palmyra... Henry met her ... at Homs on his way to Bagdad with his English companion. They were given a fine feast, and rewarded their hospitality by stealing 40 camels from their host's caravan before breakfast.

After the Bagdad trip Henry joined his party again, and

---

[552] Bridges, *The Selected Letters of Robert Bridges*, vol. 2, pp.95-96.

Capture!

the smuggling operations went on. The Esbaa were the principal customers. Howitzers, shells etc. were supplied in great abundance. He never knew where the Arabs got their money with which to pay for this material, but he knew that no accounting was to be required of his party for the disposition of it. His own share was deposited at the Ottoman Bank at Beirut.[553]

By the time Canfield and Muirhead returned, Eugene had taken possession of the camels he had paid for and was now camped slightly to the north of Salamiyeh, a small agricultural village 33km southeast of Hama. The village consisted of no more than a few cottages built to form a small fort within the ruins of ancient Irenopolis.[554] Populated almost exclusively by Isma'ili Muslims, it occupied a strategic location between mountain passes.

Between the raid on Medjuel's camp and Canfield's theft of Digby's camels, the veil of secrecy had by now been rendered, and the surveying expedition exposed as little more than a Trojan horse. A response was bound to follow, if not from Medjuel himself, then from the Ottoman authorities. At full strength, Eugene's motley assembly of mercenaries and Bedouins could easily have defeated the paltry forces of the Pasha of Homs. But with the Bedouin princes now coming to him, rather than he having to seek them out, Eugene opted to stay put, leaving himself vulnerable to attack when Murshid left to take care of business elsewhere.

Truth be told, Eugene's plans had begun to unravel weeks earlier when his mercenaries demanded to be paid in advance. Many of them had worked for him as part of the Damascus Gendarmerie and had suffered financial losses as a result. And while their failure to be paid during that debacle had not been Eugene's fault, they were understandably wary of a repeat.

---

[553] Crane, *From South Britain to Bagdad*, p.22.
[554] Skene, James Henry. *Rambles in The Deserts of Syria and Among The Bedaweens*, John Murray, London, 1864, p.158.

Eugene, who had not carried a large amount of money with him for fear of losing everything to a raid, promptly sent Ward to Aleppo to withdraw the necessary funds. Ward, alas, was waylaid by his attraction to the young wife of an elderly diplomat – a British Consul, according to Canfield.[555] The liaison delayed him several days, during which time the mercenaries began to desert. And so, when the Governor of Homs ordered his cavalry to ride out in support of the Governor of Hama, the military force at Eugene's disposal was significantly diminished.[556]

The night the Ottoman cavalry left Homs, Canfield was sent by Eugene to Salamiyeh to invite the mayor, Mahamoud Aga, to meet with him. While there, Canfield fell into conversation with the commander of a bashi-bazouk regiment who let slip that three thousand troops were due to arrive the next day. Suspecting a raid on Eugene's camp was imminent, and there being no writing materials to hand, Canfield sharpened a bullet, engraved a message on a cartridge belt and sent an orderly with the message to O'Reilly's camp at Taladah. He then rode through the night to Hama, passing the Ottoman troops along the way.[557]

Word of the expected raid had by now reached Constantinople, and upon his arrival at Hama, Canfield was informed by Cecil Jenner that Prince Mustapha had withdrawn his support and was pleading with them to abandon the enterprise and return to Constantinople.

The pair spent that night at the French consulate. Rising during the night and finding Jenner gone and Ottoman soldiers standing guard outside, Canfield shoved a plank across a narrow outside passage and crawl undetected to the stable where, having quietly saddled his horse, he knocked out the back wall of the stable and rode out into the Orontes River, from where

---

[555] *New York Herald*, 4 July 1870, p.11.
[556] *Boston Pilot*, 9 January 1869, p.2; *Levant Herald*, 3 October 1868, p.1.
[557] Crane, *From South Britain to Bagdad,* p.26.

Capture!

he headed for Taladah.[558]

Ward, meanwhile, returned to Eugene's camp during the night carrying a keg of whiskey and funds to pay the men. He, too, had received a telegram from Mustapha and relayed the news to Eugene, who had already received a similar message but was reluctant to break camp while engaged in discussions with the prince of an independent tribe of Arabs, who had camped nearby. At first light, however, the Arabs folded their tents and disappeared.[559] Anticipating a battle, Ward, too, decamped and fled.

Fear of Eugene's mortars had thus far kept the Governor of Hama's forces at a safe distance, but early the next morning, before the lanterns were quenched, the governor's troops found themselves reinforced by several hundred horsemen and eight pieces of field artillery newly arrived from Homs. In the early exchanges of artillery Julius Franz was wounded and another of the Europeans, described variously as a Pole or a Hungarian, was killed.[560] With only eighty to a hundred men at his disposal, Eugene had little option but to seek terms.[561] His surrender was described by Muirhead in a letter to Robert Bridges:

> Suddenly, on the morning of the fifth day, 1100 troops appeared at 4 a.m. before our camp. Colonel O'Reilly rode at once over to the pashas and said he was quite willing to surrender without resistance if they would agree to allow him and his engineers to keep their private arms, to make no one a prisoner, and to touch no private property. The pashas agreed instantly. So all the camp was struck and away moved men, horses and camels on the way back to Hamah: I and Mohammed,[562] and my muleteer going with

---

[558] Ibid.
[559] Ibid., p.27
[560] *New York Herald*, 28 December 1868, p.6; *New York Dispatch*, 30 January 1870, p.3.
[561] *Glasgow Evening Citizen*, 27 October 1868, p.2; *New York Herald*, 4 July 1870, p.11.
[562] His personal guide.

them.

> We all halted to encamp that first night near a spring of water. No sooner had we dismounted than the pashas' conduct changed entirely. Colonel O'Reilly, his officers and myself were made close prisoners in a tent, 14 armed sentries being placed over us. That night the pashas had very little to eat apparently and sent to ask us for dinner as we had potted meats and other savoury messes in tins; I need scarcely add that after the scurvy treatment we had received, it was refused. Next morning at 3 a.m. by moonrise we started for Hamah, the muleteers and camel drivers being manacled two and two.[563]

The following day, Canfield, who had ridden through the night, glimpsed a cloud of dust on the horizon. Tying up his horse, he climbed a nearby hill to get a better look. A body of men were approaching on horseback, led, it seemed, by his companions, recognisable by their distinctive hats. Assuming that Eugene had managed to win over, or bribe, a detachment of Ottoman forces and was now marching on Hama, Canfield remounted.

> He went back to his horse, and rode into the bunch. Colonel O'Reilly and Romer, with a Turkish guard on each side of them were in front. Henry saluted, and said, "I have orders to return to Constantinople." The answer was "Shut up you damn fool, we are all prisoners!"[564]

If Cecil Jenner was still in Hama when the prisoners arrived in the town, he didn't hang around. Along with a naturalised Pole by the name of 'Voniky', he fled to Constantinople. They would be the only members of the European contingent to escape arrest. Ward would later be apprehended at İskenderun, waiting to catch a steamer for Europe.[565] According to Muirhead:

> After a long march over desert hills, we reached the town: a

---

[563] Bridges, *The Selected Letters of Robert Bridges*, vol. 1, pp.95-96; *New York Herald*, 4 July 1870, p.11.
[564] Crane, *From South Britain to Bagdad*, p.27.
[565] Then called *Alexandretta*.

Capture!

grand procession was then formed, the pashas riding in front and military music playing "Cut off their heads! Cut off their heads!" as I afterwards heard. Having arrived at Hamah after looking as innocent and unconcerned as possible while the crowd were hooting us and crying in Arabic "*Vive le Sultan! À bas les infidèles*" we were all clapped into close confinement in the barracks. I cannot tell you all our little adventures while therein immured, but generally we got next to nothing to eat as our servants (Mohammed included) were all in quad like ourselves. Here I remained for 2½ days...

I was at length let out, Mr Skene having written to the French Vice Consul at Hamah, but for 5 days I was detained within the walls of Hamah. During these days I learnt that the Turkish government suspected Colonel O'Reilly and his engineers of being engaged in a plot for the subversion of the government, rather a serious charge. At the end of this time, I was ordered to Damascus, and the engineers were to go too.[566]

What Muirhead failed to mention in the above account, perhaps because he had not witnessed, or failed to understand it, was a moment, later recounted by Canfield, during which their lives had apparently been spared by the use of a masonic symbol:

On the eleventh of September, 1868, I had rode out of Hamath to meet our surveying party, consisting at that time of Cols. Eugene O'Reilly and Andreas Romer, Dr. E.W. Dillon, Mr. Muirhead, an English artist, and Mr. E.W. Ward, with Julius Franz, wounded. I met them north of the village of Selamieh, returning under agreement to Hamath, not as prisoners, but to investigate the charter under which we were working, followed and accompanied by some fifteen hundred regular army, and several hundred irregulars.

Within a half hour of the time I joined them, we encamped by a large pool just north of the great castle, on the hill west of Selamieh. After we had dismounted, our horses were picketed a little ways from us, the tents pitched, and we were all collected and taken one side,

---

[566] Bridges, *The Selected Letters of Robert Bridges*, vol. 1, pp.95-96; *New York Herald*, 4 July 1870, p.11.

where we were surrounded by a guard three deep, and disarmed. I then heard distinctly the order, "Bayonet them!" given in Turkish by Osman Bey, commanding colonel, when the three in front of me – viz., Colonel O'Reilly, Colonel Romer, and Dr. Dillon – made together a sign, which seemed to cause a great deal of confusion among the Turks; after which we were led back to the tents, and in the morning taken to Hamath.

I was convinced at that time that it was a Masonic sign given by them which saved our lives, then and there; since, I am still more convinced, because I am certain that the order was given from Constantinople to dispose of us there and then. Not being myself a Mason, I cannot say, with certainty, what the sign was, or its meaning. But as I knew the gentlemen to be Masons, and saw the simultaneous movement which alone prevented our being butchered then and there, I could not help my own conjectures.

Fearful of meddling with what was none of my business, I have never mentioned the above circumstance excepting to my most intimate friends. Believing you to be a Mason, I know of no harm which can result in repeating it to you, especially as you know something of the history of our capture. I have heard Dr. Dillon mention that he had given Masonic signs to several Sheiks of the wild tribes in the desert, and been recognized by them.[567]

Canfield would also claim that, during their detention at Hama, orders were received from Constantinople to hang them, but he could not account for why they were ignored. In the above account, he claimed not to have recognised the masonic symbols used by O'Reilly because he himself was not a mason, only to contradict himself in later years when he would admit to having joined the Masonic lodge at Taladah during his early days in Aleppo. On 8 October 1868, the *Levant Herald* published the following letter, dated 'Hamah, Sept. 14':

---

[567] *New York Dispatch*, 30 January 1870, p.3;Masonic signs being recognised by Arab chieftains also reported in 1862, by James Henry Skene in his *Rambles in The Deserts of Syria and Among The Bedaweens*, John Murray, London, 1864.

Capture!

The commission of engineers, which, under the direction of Hassan Bey (Colonel O'Reilly), had previously completed the plans and sections of a line of railway from Tripoli to Homs, having been refused by the local authorities an escort across the desert to the Euphrates, enrolled men on their own account, and started about six weeks ago.

The well-known Sheikh Medjuel, of the Mezrab tribe, and more famous still as the husband of Mrs Digby, who has made a small fortune out of travellers to Palmyra, having broken his engagements with Hassan Bey, the latter entered into an alliance with Suleiman Ibn Merchid, the great chief of the Isbaa Bedouins. The latter happened to be on bad terms with the Turkish authorities and refused to go to the Euphrates till he had tried a little moral – and metallic – persuasion with some fractions of his tribe which had so far forgotten their Arab immunities as to pay tribute to the Turks.

Being in the desert, of course, O'Reilly was in honour bound to obey desert law and help his friend. The result was some fighting, in which Sheikh Suleiman, aided by the Bey and his escort – they say O'Reilly's travelling equipment included an ample supply of breech loaders and four mountain guns – adequately chastised his apostate clansmen, and levied a fine, in camels, for their weak recognition of any sovereignty but his own.

The latter did not take their beating kindly, but appealed to the Governor of Homs, who, with his colleague of Hamah, mustered a force of Arabs and other irregulars to attack Suleiman Ibn Merchid and Hassan. Fear of the latter's sniders and howitzers, however, kept these from approaching the Sheikh's encampment till reinforced by several hundred horsemen and eight field pieces, sent by the Governor of Damascus. Thus strengthened, they attacked Suleiman's camp during the night when only about a hundred men were in the tents – the rest being absent with the Sheikh himself on an excursion elsewhere.

O'Reilly, too, had in the meantime disbanded much of his escort, and offered only as much resistance to the assailants as sufficed to obtain favourable terms of surrender. But these were speedily violated by the chiefs of the attacking force, and the Bey, his European companions, and the few Arabs in the camp were made close prisoners and sent in hither to Hamah. Here most of the Bedouins were released, but O'Reilly and his friends are kept in rough durance, and are to be sent on tomorrow to Damascus, for an investigation of the charges against them.[568]

According to Canfield, Eugene had been accompanied in the desert by a 'Circassian' woman whom he appeared to trust implicitly and whose identity has never been established. According to Jeremiah Augustus Johnson, the U.S. Consul in Beirut:

> While making their way to Arab camps, and before gathering under their standard any considerable number of detached and outcast Bedouins, they passed a convoy of Arabs and soldiers, who were escorting the hareem, or wives, of a local governor on their way to Damascus. The women were riding on camels in the *tahut dewan* – the Pullman car of the country for women of distinction, with all curtains closed. In passing, however, curiosity of the Pasha's women induced them to pull the curtains aside and a beautiful young Circassian let her veil fall in such a way as to show her face and form.
> Col. O'Reilly, while armed to the teeth for fighting his foes, had no armor proof against her charms, and at once wheeled into line to follow her to her next camp in the desert. Romance replaced rebellion in his chivalric and gallant nature to the extent of arousing the guards of the hareem into angry expostulation and later on to armed intervention.[569]

During their transportation from Hama to Damascus, the Turkish commander, Yusuf Pasha, was somehow made aware that the Circassian woman who had been travelling under Eugene's protection and detained along with the others, was concealing about her person Eugene's private papers.

> It was a Turkish custom not to interfere with women or their baggage. The papers which were the principal

---

[568] *Levant Herald*, 8 October 1868, pp.1-2.
[569] Johnson, *The Life of a Citizen at Home and in Foreign Service*, pp.177-179.

incriminating evidence against them were in the possession of a Circassian woman camp-follower under the protection of Colonel O'Reilly. The officer took good care that these were not tampered with, but did not take possession of them. They were very incriminating and involved many people higher up, including many Turks.

The commander of their captors, Jussuf, after many a midnight conference over the camp-fire, in bargaining and dickering, finally agreed to permit the destruction of the papers for ten thousand pounds, which was, of course, to be his personal graft. The reason this sum was agreed upon was because he was finally convinced that this was all they had. The other members of the party had saved very little out of all they received.

Henry [Canfield] had accumulated six thousand pounds, and he insisted on retaining one thousand pounds for his own use thereafter, preferring to take his chances on hanging or anything else, rather than to be reduced to complete poverty again. So he put up five thousand pounds of his own six thousand, and the rest of the party contributed another five thousand pounds, and in the presence of the entire party, the incriminating documents were destroyed.[570]

At Damascus, as the prisoners were handed over to Rashid Pasha, Jane Digby was forced to deny reports of her own involvement in the affair. A letter from her to the British Ambassador, Henry Elliot, denying the rumours, was leaked to the press.[571]

Muirhead, released on bail following Skene's intervention, was obliged to remain for ten days in Damascus for questioning, during which time he lodged at the British Consulate. When finally allowed to proceed with his travels, he returned to Damascus to thank Skene, then spent three months in a convent at Urfa. Cecil Jenner fled to Constantinople only to find that his brother, George, was no longer in a position to assist him, having been recently transferred

---

[570] Crane, *From South Britain to Bagdad*, p.28.
[571] *The Scotsman*, 14 October 1868, p.3; *Pall Mall Gazette*, 12 October 1868, p.8.

to Iran where, on 6 October 1868, he assumed the post of acting Consul-General at Tabriz.[572] Cecil, therefore, sought the protection of Henry Elliot, the British Ambassador, who advised him to get out of Turkey as quickly as possible.[573]

By 18 October, the newspapers were reporting that Eugene, described as an English soldier of fortune, had been arrested. For his family at home, that would have been embarrassing enough in its own right, but the papers also went on to describe him as the bastard son of a great lord.[574] Fuad, by this time, had left Turkey in search of expert medical care, leaving Eugene friendless at the Porte.[575] As for Romer's yacht, the *General Sherman*, it left Beirut immediately word of Eugene's arrest became known. It headed initially to Cyprus and then to Syros in the Aegean Sea, before disappearing completely.[576]

---

[572] Hertslet, Edward. *The Foreign Office List*, Harrison, London, 1874, p.120.
[573] *New York Herald*, 28 December 1868, p.3; *New Albany Daily Ledger*, 19 May 1869, p.4.
[574] *La Presse*, 18 October 1868, p.4.
[575] *Levant Herald*, 15 October 1868, p.2; *The Times*, October 19, 1868, p.8.
[576] *New York Herald*, 28 December 1868, p.6.

A DIPLOMATIC STORM

HIS GRAND SCHEME as much bungled as thwarted, Eugene and his co-conspirators were detained for over a month in a Damascus prison, immured in tiny fetid cells next to the latrines and questioned daily as to their motives and objectives.[577] At first, the charges related only to the theft of camels – serious enough in its own right – but it was only a matter of time before the matter of treason was raised.

As the interrogations progressed, reports began to emerge of several thousand stands of arms found near the coast awaiting O'Reilly's orders, and of a significant number of functionaries in Syria waiting to join the insurrection at a moment's notice. Rumours also abounded of enormous sums of money allegedly placed at Eugene's disposal by various actors in England, France, and Egypt.[578] The British government, it was further reported in the American press, even possessed documentary evidence concerning the plot that was 'not for newspaper publicity'.[579] And as if all that wasn't bad enough, allegations insulting to Eugene's late mother were now reprinted in the Dublin papers.

> The supposed leader of the insurrection is Colonel O'Reilly, otherwise Hassan Bey, an Irishman, who ... went into the Turkish service at the outbreak of the war of 1863 with the rank of major, having evidently influence at his back in high quarters in England. He was commonly reported to be an illegitimate son of Lord Palmerston; every young man who had "interest" with the Government at that time, and of whose origin nothing was known, used to be fathered on

---

[577] *New York Herald*, 4 July 1870, p.11.
[578] *New Albany Daily Ledger*, 19 May 1869, p.4.
[579] Ibid.

the lively old lord, who accordingly had an immense family of dashing adventurers all over Europe.[580]

Throughout his detention, Eugene persisted in his military hauteur, distancing himself from his Turkish interlocutors as though he were a prisoner of war and not an independent actor likely to be executed for treason. At every twist and turn he demanded that he and his colleagues be released in accordance with the terms of their surrender.

> He bore himself, indeed, with such *sang froid* that the Pasha at last believed that the revolt had really been hatched by the Porte itself, for purposes of its own. Such things had often happened, and at a not very remote period. He therefore ceased to bully the prisoners, lodged them well, and fed them royally.[581]

The Porte was not in the habit of beheading pashas, but Eugene was not a Turk, nor had he familial ties to influential Turkish families. So, from exactly what well did he draw such extraordinary confidence? It was almost as if he knew that he had an ace up his sleeve and, though reluctant to play it too early, was artful enough to hint at its existence.

And then the diplomatic storm broke. The Greek and Russian ambassadors applied to have their citizens tried before a mixed commission of Turkish judges and delegates from their own embassies.[582] Romer and Canfield followed suit by claiming American citizenship and forcing the American Consul, Jeremiah Augustus Johnson, to send his brother, Lorenzo, to represent them.

> My brother attended the investigation on behalf of the imprisoned Americans and conferred with them in their prison as to their defence. He found they had been confined

---

[580] *Nation*, 19 November 1868, p.407.
[581] *New York Herald*, 4 July 1870, p.11.
[582] *London Morning Post*, 12 October 1868, p.5; Who the Russian was, I have been unable to ascertain.

A Diplomatic Storm

in separate cells, not too far apart for communication with each other by taps on the wall, and concealed messages in exchanges of pipes and innocent looking envelopes, and that they had no defense. Caught with arms in their hands, in flagrante delicto, they could only claim that they were tourists, but as they had no passports and no excuse for their six pounder they could only rely on pull, or such influence as could be used in their behalf. Fortunately we found a way out of this trouble by pleading *insanity* on the part of the Americans, a plea which in Turkey is accepted for any eccentricities.[583]

The American Secretary of State, William Seward, refused to intervene, but Edward Joy Morris, the US Minister Resident to the Ottoman Empire, surprised his government by demanding that the two Americans be handed over to *him*. His arguments were based on what would later become the standard American interpretation of Article 4 of the Turco-American Treaty of 1830 – that American citizens should be tried by their own consuls, even in cases involving the Ottoman state or subjects.

The argument was spurious. The treaty of 1830 only allowed for the presence of an interpreter during the trials of Americans in Ottoman courts. A clerk of the Consulate General in Beirut, nevertheless, was subsequently permitted to participate in the interrogation of the Americans, a concession not extended to the other prisoners.

Not all of Eugene's papers, it appears, had been incinerated and those that had survived were incriminatory.[584] Unable any longer to pretend he had been engaged solely in a railroad survey, he offered to provide a written confession if Yusuf would release his companions. The Pasha agreed, and Eugene signed the following lengthy statement, absolving his co-conspirators of prior knowledge of his intentions:

---

[583] Johnson, *The Life of a Citizen*, pp.177-179.
[584] *New Albany Daily Ledger*, 19 May 1869, p.4.

I commence by stating that I am here a prisoner contrary to the laws of nations, having surrendered the arms and munitions of war that I possessed, under certain conditions made between me and Hassan Pacha, General of Brigade, in the presence of his Excellency, Youseff Pacha. These conditions were as follows:

First – That a safe conduct and sufficient escort be given to Colonel Romer Elias, sometimes known as Omar Bey so that he should be able to continue the survey of the proposed road to the Euphrates.

Second – That I and my companions be permitted to retain all such arms and munitions of war as personally belonged to us.

Third – That each man should be free to go home and that each man should retain his own horse.

All these conditions having been broken, despised and unrecognised by the authorities, and a number of persons totally ignorant of my intentions being in prison, I have consented to write the following in order to facilitate their discharge:-

I declare that the origin of this enterprise was a speculative one, formed several years ago while I was in Stamboul, Constantinople, suffering from the results of intrigues successfully set on foot against me. Later – that is to say, last year – I had interviews with several persons with the view of securing the pecuniary means of commencing this speculative movement in Syria. Our ultimate aim was to force the Ottoman government to consent to certain conditions which we intended to demand.

These conditions would have been the creation of a viceroyalty in Syria, with his excellency Fazil Mustapha Pacha as Viceroy, followed by a recognition of his right to the succession to the Viceroyalty of Egypt. Once in arms we should have made a definite arrangement with Mustapha Pacha, such, for instance, as a cession of land for the purposes of colonisation, and the payment of a sum of money. The latter part of the programme (the money part) only to be insisted on in case that his right to the succession to the Viceroyalty of Egypt should be recognised. This scheme was, in short, one of those affairs in which money was intended to be employed for the overturning of a government, such as has been successfully done in Naples and South America. It must be remembered also, by the

A Diplomatic Storm

way, that at this time, Fazil Mustapha Pacha was an exile.

Shortly after his Majesty, the Sultan, during his visit to Europe, having shown his goodwill towards Mustapha Pacha, the execution of this project, in the autumn of last year was arrested by the positive refusal of that nobleman to enter into the affair. I had, however, sufficient means to continue in my employment the men I had engaged through the winter: and, further, finding other persons in England ready to aid me I prepared to set out from Constantinople in the month of June. I ought to say here upon a point of honour, that I resigned my commission as an officer in the Ottoman service as soon as I had resolved to enter into this affair. I ought now to speak of the persons who accompanied me in this expedition.

The first whom I engaged was Colonel Romer. I told him nothing of the ultimate aim of the enterprise; I simply commanded him to prepare transportation for arms and munitions of war for a secret expedition. He consented to serve under me on condition that the munitions having been once landed where I wished, he should have the right to demand the object of the enterprise, and that if he did not approve of it, or should find it contrary to his principles, he should be at liberty to retire.[585]

While waiting I also engaged Mr Franz and Mr Lamar (Mr Canfield, who goes by this alias), telling them that I should require them to make the survey of a railroad to Homs. I had already the pecuniary means to make this survey, in view of a concession from the government for the transportation of minerals from the mine of Arghana to the Mediterranean coast.[586]

At this time I engaged also Mr. Ward, who had given up his position as superintendent of bridges in the Ottoman service, having the autumn previous taken part in furnishing mules and horses for the expedition in Abyssinia. I also engaged Dr. Dillon as physician to accompany the surveying party for the railroad to the Euphrates. Having recognised in him a man of honour and of courage, I knew well that he would not retire when he should find himself in the face of danger, and in consequence

---

[585] The suggestion that Romer might have had moral principles elicited hilarity in court. See *New York Herald*, 4 July 1870, p.11.
[586] Now called *Ergani*.

I said nothing to him of my speculative projects.

I have also to say of the Circassians and others whom I had enrolled as escort, that none of them knew anything of my ulterior aims. When they fought and when they wounded persons (as stated in the charge) they did so simply because I ordered them to do so, and without knowing why or for what they were fighting.

My other associates, who are not in Syria and speak Turkish and Arabic better than myself, and who know the country better, had again and again written to me, asking permission to accompany the expedition. One of the old officers of the Anglo-Turco contingent [Humphry Sandwith], a man very rich, retired from the affair, because I had positively refused his aid, as I did not wish to engage too positively in the affair until I was in possession of the money of which the participation of Mustapha Pacha at the outset had given me assurance.

Such being the position, I pass on to recent events. The day after the affair with Ibn Aide, I received final notice that nothing was to be expected from Mustapha Pacha, and immediately I separated myself from Suleyman Ibn Meerscheed. I then awaited the arrival of Mr. Ward from Aleppo, in order to set out upon the line of the railroad to the Euphrates and complete the survey. I intended also to give leave of absence to the greater part of the men who were with me.

I had given an order to one of my men to go to Mahamoud Aga, at Salamieh, in order to invite him to meet me, so that I might say to Youssef Pacha, that I was going. During the following night I heard the news that the tribes had set out from Hamah to find me. When the tribes presented themselves upon the hill, at the distance of about twelve hundred yards from our encampment, upon the invitation of the two Pachas, I went to see them, and we made a convention, the conditions of which I have given at the commencement of this statement.

His Excellency, Reschid Pacha, has expressed suspicions that this affair had some relation to the revolution in Crete, having received information that a vessel loaded with munitions of war had set out from Syra lately for the Syrian coast.[587] I give now to his Excellency the most positive

---

[587] Greek port, now called *Syros*.

assurance that I have had relations neither with the Greeks nor with the insurgents in Crete, and that I never expected to receive from that side assistance of any kind, neither in men nor in munitions of war.

The cannon we have had in the desert were only a few days at Syra, where they were cast. One of the most distinguished of my associates indeed wrote to me, requiring that I should have nothing to do with Hellenism or Panslavism, and I gave him, as I now give his Excellency, the most solemn assurance that the friends of neither cause aided us in this enterprise.

I desire to terminate this statement by demanding the execution of the convention I have referred to. That is to say, I demand the immediate liberation of myself, of my employees, and of all others induced by my influence to join this expedition, and I demand further that their horses and all their personal property be restored to them. I declare now that all I have here said and stated is the truth and nothing but the truth.[588]

Despite the confession, none of the prisoners were released. The rumoured involvement of international figures had made the Sultan fearful of exposing the participation of 'foreign diplomats',[589] especially now that all manner of conclusions were being drawn from Eugene's trips to Alexandria.[590] The papers found in his possession and seemingly signed by the heir to the Ottoman throne, Mohammed Mourad Effendi, as well as a number of fatwas signed by several Muslim muftis, were promptly declared to be forgeries,[591] and after a brief trial in Damascus, the foreign prisoners were transferred to Constantinople.

> The local trial of Col. O'Reilly and his party, for their attack on the Mezrab Arabs near Homs, ended last week at Damascus. The native rank and file of the party have been sentenced to imprisonment here in Syria, and O'Reilly

---

[588] *New York Herald*, 4 July 1870, p.11; Nat. Archives UK, FO195/806.
[589] *New York Herald*, 4 July 1870, p.11.
[590] *The Times*, 19 October 1868, p.8.
[591] Ibid.

himself and his immediate staff are to be sent to Constantinople for further investigation of the affair...It has been remarked, however, with regret, that whilst the foreigners have received almost indulgent treatment, the natives concerned in the affair have been kept all along in chains, and were even chained during the trial.

H.M. Consul at Damascus, attended to watch the proceedings for the British subjects implicated, and to this fact, doubtless, much of the easy treatment may be ascribed. The American Consular agent rendered similar service to the two Americans mixed up in the affair, – so, altogether, the foreigners have had no reason to complain. They will probably be sent to Constantinople by the steamer which takes this.[592]

The *Levant Herald* carried the official line, which suited the diplomatic purposes of the British, French and Ottoman governments. The American newspapers, however, were less constrained:

> It remains to be seen whether O'Reilly will now settle the long pending controversy as to the relative strength of the pen and the sword. His sword has been taken from him, but he has ingeniously interwoven into his confession certain names and hints, provoking suggestions that he may yet secure his liberty as the price of revealing more...
>
> The prisoners have now been ordered to Constantinople, where, no doubt, by the magic power of intrigue and gold they will all find means to open their prison doors; for, whatever may be said of the patriotism and honesty of the Ottoman officials who are high in office, yet men are found in subordinate conditions in this, as in every country, who are not impervious to bribes. There is evidently a considerable fund of money at the disposal of O'Reilly in the Ottoman Bank, which he will find more powerful, if he can recover it, than all the needle guns with which he so stupidly blundered with his armed escort and party of surveyors.[593]

It wasn't to be quite so straightforward. Further

---

[592] *Levant Herald*, 26 November 1868, p.2.
[593] *Morning Chronicle and Commercial and Shipping Gazette* (Quebec), 5 January 1869, p.2.

A Diplomatic Storm

searches would unearth letters from Eugene to Halim, indicating that the insurrection was never intended to be confined to Syria, but extended to Egypt, where a contingent under the command of European officers was to be armed with all means necessary to overthrow the Egyptian government.[594] Another letter, addressed simply to *Altesse*,[595] discussed the landing of guns, muskets and munitions.[596]

As it conformed so closely to official suspicions, the *Altesse* was assumed to be Halim,[597] and the assumption used by the Khedive as an excuse to send Halim into exile. On 9 November, Halim set sail for Constantinople, determined to plead his case before the Supreme Court.[598] Upon his arrival he demanded that an official inquiry prove his complete ignorance of O'Reilly's plot. The Grand Vizier, however, dismissed the matter as a trifle and offered him the post of Ambassador at the Court of Vienna. Halim refused the appointment, as it too would have taken him into exile, but he accepted instead a seat on the Ministerial Council.[599] The Porte, it seemed, was anxious to brush the affair under a heavy Turkish carpet.

---

[594] *Le Temps*, 11 December 1868, p.2.
[595] Lüttke, Moritz. *Aegyptens Neue* Zeit, F.A. Brockhaus, Leipzig, 1873, pp.89-90.
[596] Jerrold, Blanchard. *Egypt under Ismail Pacha*, Samuel Tinsley & Co., London, 1879, pp. 101-102.
[597] *L'Émancipation*, 4 January 1869, p.5.
[598] McCoan, James Carlisle. *Egypt Under Ismail: A Romance of History*, Chapman and Hall Ltd., London, 1879, p.79; *Morning Herald* (London), 11 November 1868, p.4; *Otago Witness*, 13 February 1869, p.18; *The Montreal Witness*, January 6, 1869, p.3; *The Times*, 11 November 1868, p.5; *Wrexham Advertiser*, 28 November 1868, p.8.
[599] Jerrold, Blanchard. *Egypt Under Ismail Pacha: Being Some Chapters of Contemporary History*, Samuel Tinsley & Co., London, 1879, pp. 101-102.

THE ZAPTIEH PRISON

PLACED ABOARD A Turkish naval vessel, the prisoners were transported to Beirut, from where Eugene alone was rushed to Constantinople. Arriving on 30 November,[600] he was detained at the Zaptieh Prison without trial or representation while the Porte decided what to do with him.[601] The other prisoners would not leave Beirut until the morning of 3 December.

Confusion appears to have reigned in official circles as to what had actually happened in the desert and the extent to which each of the various prisoners had been involved. As a result, the 'surveying team' were treated with kid gloves, with Romer even being allowed to bring with him his groom and Arabian stallion.

Shortly after they left Beirut, the ship carrying the 'engineers' dropped anchor off Tripoli, where the local governor, at that time travelling on a Turkish man-of-war, sailed over to dine with them, or rather to enjoy the good food and wine that was not available to him as a Muslim on a Turkish naval vessel. The prisoners were then transferred to a prison on shore, before also being taken, several days later, to Constantinople. They arrived on 7 December.[602]

> The British prisoners have entrusted their defence to a member of the local English bar, who on Monday proceeded to the Zaptieh, accompanied by a consular dragoman, to see his clients and receive their instructions. The Minister of

---

[600] *The Shields Daily News*, 2 December 1868, p.3.
[601] There were two principal prisons in Constantinople. The Zaptieh Prison, used for simple detentions and located at the Police Department, had a capacity of about 2000. The Central Prison could accommodate over 10,000.
[602] *La Liberté*, 11 December 1868, p.4.

The Zaptieh Prison

Police, however, refused the necessary permission, and on further application to the Grand Vizier, his Highness also declined to permit the interview. As "freedom defence" is one of the most boasted modern reforms of Turkish jurisprudence, it is difficult to understand why, in this instance, the privilege should be refused.

The effect, however, of the vizierial inhibition can only be temporary, as a demand for the transfer of the whole of the British prisoners to our own gaol has since been addressed to the authorities. This being a clear treaty right, it will no doubt be insisted by the embassy, and, once in the custody of Mr. Judge Francis, the militant Bey and his fellow unfortunates will be sure of fair play. The further question of their trial may then arise.

In this again, the strict letter of the treaty gives the jurisdiction to our own court; and in the cases of the two Americans of the party, Porte rumour says that Mr. Morris has already claimed the right for his own consulate. The lax custom of recent years has suffered this particular privilege to fall into abeyance, and for obvious reasons, the Porte may possibly resist its revival. The case, however, promises to be a "leading" one in capitulation law, and we shall therefore note its incidents carefully.[603]

A commission of enquiry with a distinctively European flavour was now convened: a nod, perhaps, to international interest in the case. It was scheduled to operate under the presidency of Ikiades Effendi, a member of the Council of State, with the guidance of Husni Pasha, the Minister of Police. Ikiades was a Greek, and Husni, though Turkish by nationality, was said to be 'Italian in spirit and deed'.[604] Married to the Sultan's niece, Béhigé Sultana,[605] he enjoyed a reputation as a brutal and unregenerate hardliner.[606]

Proceedings against Eugene, Romer and Canfield

---

[603] *Cambridge Independent Press*, 19 December 1868, p.3.
[604] Anderson, Lisa. "Nineteenth-Century Reform in Ottoman Libya" in *Int. Journal of Middle East Studies*, vol. 16, no. 3, 1984, p. 343.
[605] Martin, Frederick. *The Statesman's Year-Book*, Macmillan & Co, London, 1871, p.451.
[606] Gibb, E.J.W. *A History of Ottoman Poetry*, Luzac, London, 1907, p.72.

24. Turkish Commission of Enquiry.

began on 12 December with a preliminary hearing at the Zaptieh Prison. Under the Ottoman judicial code, preliminary hearings were intended to allow judges to hear the written record of police interrogations and to facilitate the prosecutor in translating the evidence into bills of indictment. The accused was not represented by counsel.

Initial exchanges between Eugene and Husni were hostile and curt:

— Accused, your name, your age and your qualifications?
— I am an O'Reilly by birth, subject of Her Majesty Queen of Great Britain and Ireland. I served in Her Majesty's Army, and after the Crimean War and the brilliant defeat of Kars I took service in the Turkish Army. The protection with which I was honoured by the late Lord Palmerston, more than my own feeble merits, afforded me a warm welcome. The Seraskier, Riza-Pasha, preserved my rank as an officer and in 1860 Fuad-Pasha made me a colonel. But the 'tolerance' of the Sublime Porte obliged me to change my name, as a symbol of my alleged conversion to Islamism. It is only a symbol; but as I have a wife, that I love and whose love I cherish, I am happy for you to call me Hassan Bey. I am thirty-nine years of age.[607]
— You are accused of...
— Excuse me, Mr. President, I could, as a colonel, meet your first question. You were, ten years ago, Chibouktchi, under the orders of the present Grand Vizier. As Chibouktchi you suddenly became provincial governor. You

---

[607] *La Liberté*, 13 December 1868, p.4.

The Zaptieh Prison

governed so well that you became Minister of Police with the rank of Marshal. Nothing prevents your former superior, the Grand Vizier, from calling you today to command the army. I therefore risk at any moment finding myself under your orders, without either of us knowing how it happened.

In consequence, General, I must decline to respond to your request. For when I am interrogated as an accused, I am no longer Hassan-Bey, but become O'Reilly again, a subject of Her Britannic Majesty; and, under the legislations and treaties, I will refuse to answer until I see next to me a dragoman from the British embassy.

— You speak Turkish well. We don't need a dragoman for you to understand us.

— I know the process of Turkish justice well. I persist in my refusal to answer.

— Did you answer the Damascus Valley interrogation correctly?"

— I was answering as a military leader.

— We are going to read the minutes drawn up in Damascus.

— Useless! I dispute its authenticity, as no consul or dragoman was present at the interrogation.

— We will move on to your co-defendants. Canfield, Romer, tell us about your trip to Syria.

— We are citizens of the United States. Where is the dragoman of our legation? [608]

Uncertain of the legality of their refusals, Husni adjourned the proceedings and sent for the English dragoman, Vincent Alishan, who was occupied in another council of the ministry. When Alishan had taken his place, proceedings resumed.

> — Hassan Bey, you are accused of having fraudulently smuggled weapons of war into the empire; of having formed gangs for the purpose of revolutionising Syria; of having stolen camels from Sheik Medjuel; of having caused the death of a Muslim woman in the firefight you engaged in with the Megrab tribe, with the assistance of the Esb'a tribe. What do you have to say?
>
> — Whoever stole the camels must answer that. Arabs at

---

[608] Ibid.

war with one another plunder one another, it's as old as the sun, and it will last at least as long as the crescent claims to dominate them. The Esb'a plundered the Mezrab yesterday; tomorrow the Mezrabs will plunder the Esb'a, until the end of the centuries, or until they unite against a common enemy. Moreover, in these circumstances, the thieves were not the Arabs. They fled upon the approach of Chibli, the Pasha of Urfa, leaving their loot behind them. Chibli-Pasha had everything removed and carried home by his soldiers. As for him, when he came to arrest us, we made no resistance. The Muslim woman who was killed in the fight, her blood falls on the Arabs.

Regarding the import of weapons of war – it was about fifty breech-loading rifles and two howitzers – Chibli Pasha confiscated those. In that the law obtained satisfaction and did not pronounce that the confiscation of weapons seized from the foreigners had violated any recognized monopoly by treaties. But hold on! Who keeps these weapons which are mine? Who guards them? And let there be no more question of this whole business of revolution in Syria. Who would lead us? To discover who would take you too far and too high.

— What do you mean by this reticence, these half-confessions? Justice here needs to know everything.[609]

Too far and too high! Eugene was at it again, hinting at a wider conspiracy than may ever have existed in fact. Uncertain of what the Irishman was referring to, Husni sought clarification from the British dragoman, Vincent Alishan. Though speaking in hushed tones, the pair were overheard by a French journalist discussing a memo confidentially delivered to the British ambassador concerning Fuad's decision to recall O'Reilly to service. In the letter announcing that recall, Fuad had mentioned the possible resumption of certain projects abandoned in 1860.

Though never explicitly stated, the possibility was left hanging that one of these projects concerned Lord Dufferin's suggestion that the only way to bring lasting peace to the region was to create a viceroyalty or

---

[609] Ibid.

The Zaptieh Prison

pashalik with Fuad installed as Viceroy.[610] Husni was incensed.

> — What were these plans? The letter doesn't say it. The railroad project from Homs to Tripoli? To exploit the copper mines? To ensure the safety of the caravans against the looting of the Bedouins? To make conscription possible among the sultan's Arab subjects? This project, or another even more dear to Fuad personally? All that is certain is that O'Reilly returned to Turkey at the request of Fuad-Pasha and that after three months of errands and bribes at the Sublime Porte and Imperial Palace, he left for Beirut, accompanied by a few engineers, bearing a railway concession and carrying a firman from the Grand Vizier, Ali Pasha, instructing all civil servants to allow Hassan Bey's machines to pass without inspection or dues of any kind.[611]

Reluctant to risk further discussion in a public arena, Husni adjourned the hearing, called for his horse and went to brief the Grand Vizier. An article published in the following day's *La Liberté* predicted that the court, faced with the latest British insinuations, would almost certainly choose to decide the case quickly and deport the defendants.[612] How Fuad's letters came to be in the possession of the British Ambassador remains a mystery, but his possession of them changed everything.

Canfield's father, meanwhile, having heard nothing of his son since he left Greece, had travelled to Washington to plead with the Turkish Ambassador, Edouard Blaque. Blaque wrote a strongly worded letter in his favour, and in January 1869, Mitchell Canfield and his wife, Eliza Jane, left the U.S. intent on presenting it to the Grand Vizier in person. The American press reported the appeal as being on the premise that his son

---

[610] Zachs, Fruma. "'Novice' or 'Heaven-Born' Diplomat? Lord Dufferin's Plan for a 'Province of Syria'': Beirut, 1860-61" in Middle Eastern Studies, vol. 36, no. 3, 2000, pp. 160–76.
[611] *La Liberté*, 13 December 1868, p.4.
[612] Ibid.

was suffering from a mental illness.[613]

On the afternoon of 11 December, the last Friday before Ramadan, the ladies of Constantinople began their annual exodus to the Sweet Waters of Europe, a pleasure resort and picnicking spot at the head of the Golden Horn, a traditional holiday that was no less observed by the staff of the local embassies. The following morning, normal diplomatic service having resumed, Edward Joy Morris wrote to the Ottoman Minister of Foreign Affairs, Safvet Pasha, demanding the release of the American prisoners.

Wary, perhaps, of British involvement in the affair being extracted from O'Reilly, the British ambassador, followed suit. Just two months earlier he had publicly abandoned O'Reilly and his colleagues to the consequences of their conduct.[614] Now he was pleading on their behalf.[615] The irony notwithstanding, his demands, like those of the Americans, fell on deaf ears.

> The case of Colonel O'Reilly has made no progress since our last. The Porte has not yet formulated the charge on which he is to be tried, and, pending that preliminary, no steps have been taken by Mr Elliot to obtain his removal to our own consular prison, nor has his advocate yet been allowed access to him at the Zaptieh. It is said, however, that his right to removal into British custody will he insisted on…[616]

On Christmas Eve, when the hearings resumed, a solicitor by the name of James Carlile McCoan was sent by the British Embassy to represent Eugene. From Dunlow in Co. Tyrone, McCoan had spent the

---

[613] *Philadelphia Daily Evening Bulletin*, 25 March 1869, p.5; *Philadelphia Enquirer*, 29 December 1868, p.1; Feyizoğlu, Öznur. *Osmanlı Arşiv Belgelerine Göre Sultan Abdülaziz Dönemi Osmanlı Amerika İlişkileri (1861-1876)*, Master's Thesis, Kocaeli University, Institute of Social Sciences, department of International Relations, Political History Program, 2009, pp.229-231.

[614] *La Presse*, 18 October 1868, p.4.

[615] *Le Public*, 29 December 1868, p.1; *The Irishman*, 2 January 1869, p.3; *The Times*, 26 March 1869, p.7.

[616] *The Times*, 18 December 1868, p.3; *Le Public*, 29 December 1868, p.1.

latter part of the Crimean War reporting for the *Daily News* before relocating to Constantinople and accepting an appointment as a barrister at the Supreme Consular Court. More significantly, he was the founder and owner of the *Levant Herald*.[617]

Welcoming McCoan, the commission president, Ikiades Effendi, insisted that, though free to attend as an observer, McCoan could not act as counsel. To do so would set a precedent not hitherto recognised by Turkish courts. McCoan replied that if no precedence currently existed in Turkish Law for the presence of a defending counsel, then this was exactly the kind of case in which it *should* be set. As no agreement could be reached, the hearing was adjourned until the matter could be decided by the Grand Vizier, at which point Eugene was briefly brought back from the cells to receive a private message from Alishan.[618] He was questioned again on 16 January but refused to reveal anything more.[619] By that time many foreign newspapers had begun to raise doubts as to his guilt.[620]

On Monday, 18 January, two steamers of the Egyptian Company collided off Izmir, one of which sank with all hands. The following day, the *New York Herald* reported that amongst those lost were several members of Eugene's 'Syrian expedition', Romer and Canfield included. The reports were false – Romer and Canfield were already in Constantinople – but Mitchell and Eliza Jane Canfield, who had recently arrived in Paris, could not know that. Until letters from friends in Athens brought them up to date, the Canfields lived under the assumption that their son was dead.[621] On hearing that Henry was alive, they raced through

---

[617] Murphy, David. *Ireland and the Crimean War*, Four Courts Press, Dublin, 2002, pp. 170,172,185.
[618] *Levant Herald*, 26 December 1868, p.2; *The Foreign Office List*, Harrison, London, 1865, pp. 69, 242.
[619] *Le Messager du Midi*, 16 January 1869, p.1.
[620] *L'Émancipation*, 7 January 1869, p.5.
[621] *New York Herald*, 19 January 1869, p.4.

Switzerland to Athens, where an exhausted Eliza Jane was left in the care of friends and relatives while Mitchell carried on to Constantinople.

On Wednesday, 20 January 1869, Eugene's final pre-trial examination took place at the Zaptieh. It turned out to be a protracted round of protests and recriminations, during which an exasperated Eugene finally gave up trying to defend himself and refused to answer any more questions until his trial, at which point he would be allowed the benefit of counsel. Three days later, Dillon, Ward, Romer and Canfield were also examined,[622] but no concrete evidence could be found to implicate them beyond the fact that Eugene had employed them for engineering survey. A British consular report of their interrogation suggested their continued detention was based on the hope of prising from them some damning evidence against the Irishman.[623]

On 5 February, Dillon was released. The following day Mitchell Canfield arrived in Constantinople. With the help of the American Secretary of Legation, John Porter Brown, he began an interminable round of visits, passed from one official to the next, gaining sympathy but little success. Four days later, however, the atmosphere surrounding the case changed radically when news of the death of Fuad Pasha reached Constantinople and shone an international spotlight on the latest British insinuations. Suddenly, the potential complications of a public trial began to outweigh the benefits, and the Sultan promptly decided to drop the matter.[624] Rumours that he had ordered the release of the prisoners leaked to the press three days later.[625]

In the meantime, on 4 March, Eliza Jane Canfield, tired of waiting in Athens, arrived unannounced in Constantinople. So desperate was she to see her son that, despite the heavy rain, she immediately made her

---

[622] *Levant Herald*, 21 January 1869, p.2.
[623] *Levant Herald*, 25 January 1869, p.2.
[624] *Levant Herald*, 13 February 1869, p.1.
[625] *La Liberté*, 14 February 1869, p.4.

way to the prison. When next she and Mitchell visited Henry, on 8 March, they would find his spirits greatly improved and expectant of a 'speedy turn of the case'.

After months of winter nights and prison rations, Ward's period of incarceration came to an end on 11 March when he succumbed to a serious illness and was released into the care of the British Hospital at Galata.[626] Six days later, the Canfields, whose funds were by now all but depleted, left Greece.[627] Three days later, Henry was set free. He fled initially to Greece, from where his parents took him first to Paris and shortly thereafter to the United States.[628] Upon hearing of his impending release, he made a promise to Eugene.

> Colonel O'Reilly entrusted Henry with a message to deliver to some colleague in Paris, on his way to America, telling him of the failure of the expedition, and requesting help. Henry had to make this trip through the outskirts of Paris, and cautiously hunt up this party, who was apparently very much incognito, but he delivered the message.[629]

Later that year, Henry Canfield would submit a paper to the American Oriental Society on the Syrian surveying mission but would not attend the reading.[630] He would settle in South Britain, Connecticut, join a local masonic lodge, get married and return to farming.[631] The fate of the lone 'Austrian', Julius Franz,

---

[626] *Levant Herald*, 13 March 1869, p.2.
[627] Crane, *From South Britain to Bagdad*, p.19.
[628] Feyizoğlu, Öznur. *Osmanlı Arşiv Belgelerine Göre Sultan Abdülaziz Dönemi Osmanlı Amerika İlişkileri (1861-1876)*, Master's Thesis, Kocaeli University, Institute of Social Sciences, department of International Relations, Political History Program, 2009, pp.229-231.
[629] Crane, *From South Britain to Bagdad*, p.20.
[630] *Journal of the American Oriental Society, 1868-1871*, Vol. 9, p.lxv.
[631] *Levant Herald*, 18 March 1869, p.3; *Anglo American Times*, 3 April 1869, p.21; Erhan, Cagri. "A Slice of Ottoman-American Relations" in *Yeniden Ergenekon*, 941, 23 October 2017; *Proceedings of the most Worshipful Grand Lodge of Ancient Free and Accepted Masons of the State of Connecticut 1866-1870*, Wiley, Waterman & Eaton, Hartford, 1870, p. 399.

was never reported, but, like Canfield, he was assumed to have been released without charge.

On 23 March 1869, Eugene heard the final jangle of the gaoler's keys and discreetly dragged his louse-bitten limbs out into the world again. His sudden and ignominious emergence was attributed to the influence of Lord Palmerston,[632] though the upcoming visit of the Prince and Princess of Wales, due to arrive in Constantinople three weeks later, may also have been a factor. Any revelation by Eugene of the involvement of British entrepreneurs would have embarrassed both countries.[633]

Of all the conspirators, only Dillon was permitted to remain in Turkey. The others were ordered to leave and never come back.[634] The enforcement of this decree, however, appears to have been somewhat lax, for as late as 30 April, Eugene had yet to leave.[635] Was it only now, as he applied for a British passport for his 'wife', that he discovered his marriage had never been registered? Was that the reason for his delayed departure? If it was, then he was careful not to inform Mathilde. All that is known for certain is that, on the morning of 15 May 1869, travelling as Mr and Mrs Hassan, Eugene and Mathilde left Turkey on an Austrian steamer bound for Trieste.[636]

---

[632] Johnson, *The Life of a Citizen at Home and in Foreign Service*, p.178; Canfield was actually a grandnephew to Lewis Cass. His uncle Augustus was married to Cass's daughter, Mary Sophia.

[633] *Morning Herald* (London), 30 April 1869, p.5.

[634] Kuneralp, Sinan. "Ottoman Diplomacy and the Controversy over the Interpretation of Article 4 Of The Turco-American Treaty Of 1830" in *The Turkish Yearbook of International Relations*, XXXI, 2000, pp.10-11; *Kilkenny Moderator*, 27 March 1869, p.3; *The Times*, 26 March 1869, p.3; In 1878, Romer found his way back into Ottoman service, only to again be charged with conspiracy against the Sultan. See *Montreal Weekly Witness*, 12 December 1878, p.1.

[635] *London Evening Standard*, 30 April 1869, p.5.

[636] *Levant Herald*, 15 May 1869, p.2.

LE GRAND HOTEL DU LOUVRE

WITH THE GATES to his imagined future firmly closed behind him, Eugene arrived in Paris, his military hauteur undented by the taint of ignominy and failure. Pride demanded that he be seen; that he rise above the discomfiture of dispossession and deportation and stand as proud and defiant as the blameless victim of some foreign bankruptcy. Necessity, on the other hand, demanded a degree of humility, and that he begin to leverage those international connections that might still be willing to receive him.

Determined to announce his 'innocence' as much as his availability for work, he took up residence at the Grand Hôtel du Louvre, an outlandishly expensive choice of accommodation for a man whose only sources of income now were the dividends of some unidentified investments.[637] Lest his arrival in Paris should pass unnoticed at home, he had his brother, James, place an announcement in the Irish papers:

> 'Colonel O'Reilly has arrived at the Grand Hotel, Paris, from Constantinople. From certain circumstances connected with Colonel O'Reilly's recent imprisonment, his brother, Mr. O'Reilly, is anxious that his present movements should have every publicity'.[638]

Commissioned by Napoleon III in 1855, the Grand Hôtel, with its 700 rooms and 1,200 staff, was the ultimate in luxury accommodation. A palatial building with spectacularly opulent common areas, it catered to

---

[637] *Freeman's Journal*, 31 May 1869, p.3.
[638] *Drogheda Argus and Leinster Journal*, 5 June 1869, p.7.

the elite of European society and occupied an entire block between the Rue de Rivoli and Rue de Marengo. The ground floor was entirely given over to a giant department store, encapsulating a luxurious reading room and more than forty boutiques and jewellers.

25. Interior Courtyard of the Grand Hôtel de Louvre, Paris.

The largest and most modern hotel in Europe, the Grand Hôtel should have been beyond the pocket of a recently released prisoner with limited prospects of employment. Then again, with a youthful bride on his arm and an uncertain future ahead of him, it was as good a time as any to lay the bricks of a future nostalgia. He owed her that. That, and a fashionable European wardrobe. This was, after all, a place where people dressed formally for dinner. Indeed, it says much of her bourgeois upbringing that Eugene felt comfortable parading Mathilde as his wife.

The couple spent almost three weeks in Paris, where Eugene had much to show his new bride and old acquaintances to look up. The city was abuzz with excitement following a rare appearance of the Aurora Borealis, the opening of the newest sensation in entertainment – the Folies Trèvise (later the Folies

Bèrgere) – and the forthcoming legislative elections. The highlight for most tourists, however, was a visit to the Palace of Versailles. It only opened to the public on the first Sunday of every month, but, for most, it was a wonder worth the expense of an extended stay.[639]

26. The table d'hôte dining room circa 1870

Versailles would next open to the public on 6 June, a date just happened to coincide with the second round of parliamentary elections. With the threat of violence hanging over the city, getting out of Paris for the weekend was probably not the worst idea. But while the timing of Eugene and Mathilde's exit suggests a visit to Versailles, it could equally have been to the mysterious individual to whom Canfield had carried a clandestine message some weeks earlier.

Wherever it was they went, upon their return, on the morning of Monday, 10 June, they found Paris in turmoil. For the previous two nights the city had been

---

[639] Khān, Sir Sayyid Ahmad. *A Voyage to Modernism*, Primus Books, Delhi, 2011, p.134.

beset by riots, forcing the Prefect of Police to deploy both cavalry and infantry to the streets. Fearful, perhaps, of where the violence could lead, Eugene made immediate arrangements to leave. As he caught up on the weekend's newspapers in the reading room of the Grand Hôtel, however, he caught sight of a familiar name among the social notices. Sir Henry Bulwer had arrived in Paris.[640] Eugene immediately went to call on him, but Bulwer was not at home.

> Grand Hotel du Louvre,
> Monday evening,
>
> Dear Sir Henry Bulwer,
>
> Having been outside Paris and only returning this afternoon, I could not have written to you in time. So I called myself, but did not find you at home. I leave Paris for Ireland tomorrow morning, but wherever you go in the meantime I will make you out, as I want at least to thank you personally for past kindnesses.
>
> Believe me Sir,
> Ever Yours Most Sincerely,
> Eugene O Reilly.[641]

Having failed to find Bulwer, Eugene left shortly afterwards for London, where his name was promptly linked with that of George Francis Train, the American railway tycoon.

> Col. O'Reilly (Hassan Bey), the hero of a thousand and one raids, recently arrived in England, and will probably soon join George Francis Train in an Irish raid.[642]

Train had been arrested the previous March in Cobh

---

[640] *La Liberté* (Montpellier), 11 June 1869, p.2.
[641] National Archives UK, Norfolk Record Office, O'Reilly to Bulwer n.d., BUL1/374/8.
[642] *The New Berne Times*, 18 June 1869, p.3; *The Daily Standard*, 18 June 1869, p.2; *Daily Southern Cross*, 31 March 1868, p.3.

on charges of possessing subversive speeches in support of Irish independence. He had been released after four days on the condition that he would not promote or support the Fenian movement while in the United Kingdom. Despite their mutual interest in railways, there is, however, no evidence that Eugene and Train ever met.

Six weeks after he arrived in London, Eugene took the boat to Dublin. Arriving on 29 July 1869, he took rooms at the Gresham. *Saunders's News-Letter* would record the arrival of one 'Hassan Bey O'Reilly' but would make no mention this time of a wife or 'suite'. Why he would choose to leave Mathilde alone in London is unknown.

Eugene's younger brother, Matthew George, was newly dead, having shuffled off this mortal coil on 17 June 1868 – just as Eugene was beginning his ill-fated desert adventure. He had left behind him a wife and a son, the latter of whom had been christened Eugene, after the famous uncle who had been registered, in absentia, as the child's godfather.[643] The child and his mother were possibly in Dublin as early as this date, but there is no evidence either of them having met Eugene or of him having assisted them.

As for James, Eugene had not seen his elder brother since 1867. Given his recent imprisonment and the extensively published, and never denied, allegations that he was the illegitimate progeny of Lord Palmerston, the reception he received must surely have been strained, for after a short stay, Eugene bid farewell to his family and set sail for London. He would never return.

---

[643] N.L.I., Catholic Parish Registers, Cork and Ross, Kinsale, 1859-1880, 3 May 1864.

BOULOGNE-SUR-MER

HE TOOK HER next to Boulogne-sur-Mer, a picturesque fishing village and ferry port on the northeast coast of France. Mathilde was pregnant and, at just five and a half hours from London and three hours from Paris, the town was ideally situated for their needs and as healthy a place as any to raise a child.

They had hardly known each other when they married, having been together for less than a year, but had been tightly bound by romantic affection, the exigencies of travel, and a purposeful and conjugal *esprit de corps*. With a child on the way, they needed now to become a family in a more conventional sense.

They took up residence at number 40 Boulevard des Tintelleries, a tree-lined avenue popular with English tourists.[644] Lying midway between the upper town with its aristocratic appearance and medieval ramparts, and the lower town with its seaside entertainments, their new home was also convenient to Merridew's bookshop, a well-known institution whose Reading and Conversation Rooms came fully stocked with English language newspapers and magazines. The house was similarly within walking distance of those other stalwarts of anglophone sociability – the Hotel Folkestone, Hotel du Rhin, Hotel Meurice, Hotel du Nord, and the Éstablissment (a popular bathing establishment and casino).

All in all, Boulogne was an ideal place to network, even in winter, when three out of every forty inhabitants would be British. For a young woman more comfortable speaking French than English, it was also a more

---

[644] Since renamed Boulevard de Clocheville; Merridew, H.M. *Plan of Boulogne-sur-mer*, 1873.

convenient location than London or Dublin to prepare for the arrival of a baby. It was here, at ten minutes past midnight on 9 June 1870, that Eugénie Caroline was born.[645] The name 'Eugénie' was an obvious choice, reflecting both her father's name and that of the Empress Eugénie, the popular wife of Napoleon III.

27. Boulogne-sur-Mer.

In the early afternoon of the following day, Eugene took a ten-minute stroll through the cobbled streets of the old town to the imposing red-bricked Hôtel de Ville. Here he took his place in the queue to register his daughter's birth. Waiting alongside him were a local carpenter and a grain merchant on similar missions. Stretching fraternal hands across the social divide, each happily witnessed the signature of the others.

On Eugénie's birth certificate, Eugene gave his occupation as an 'annuitant', the source of which remains unknown. He gave his surname as Hassan. This was not the name that Mathilde had expected to see on her daughter's birth certificate – she had expected to see 'O'Reilly' – and it was only now that she discovered their marriage had not been legal. To

---

[645] Etat Civil A.C, Pas-de-Calais Archives, Boulogne-sur-mer, no.604, Hassan, Eugénie Caroline, FRNC06200, 9 June 1870; 1871 Census, London, St. George Hanover Square, Belgrave, 51, 17 Ranelagh Grove, Folio 15, p. 24, Mathilde Hassan.

Mathilde, it felt like the breach of an inviolable trust.

One can imagine her fury. By design or by neglect, Eugene had made a bastard of his daughter and a pariah of her mother. He promised to sort it out, but until he got around to doing so, Mathilde had no choice but to continue living as Mrs Hassan. In his private correspondence, he continued to sign himself as O'Reilly, but publicly and officially, the couple were known as the Hassans, and that was more than sufficient during the winter months when the couple lived quasi-anonymously in their little apartment. Summer, however, was another matter entirely.[646]

28. Boulevard des Tintelleries.

Taking its name from the valleyed stream that ran through the town, the Boulevard des Tintelleries linked the old town to the new and gave its name to the public park that sat just a short walk from their home. Here, on pleasant days, nursemaids would sit with their upholstered wicker prams in the cool shade of the plane trees while toddlers gambolled on the lawns. Summer evenings would see balls, concerts and

---

[646] Clarke, Henry Hyde. "On the Progress of the Through Railway Route to India", in *Journal of the Society of Arts*, No.992, Vol. XX, London, 24 November 1871, pp.21-28.

firework displays, most especially during the Boulogne Féte, which was held every July in the Jardin des Tintelleries.

For the duration of the Féte, the surrounding streets would be packed with British tourists, any number of whom might recognise Eugene. How long would it be before questions were asked? How long before one or other of the Jenners gaily recounted the circumstances of their 'marriage' at some private dinner or in some private correspondence? How long before their marital status became a public scandal?

Eugene had promised Mathilde time and again that he would put matters right, but as he clung to a festering dream of restoration, the task of putting food on the table had assumed a greater priority than the official recognition of what was already a lived reality. One can only speculate as to his reluctance, but perhaps it was as much a matter of practicality as it was of pride or shame. To go to a priest would mean having banns published, and there could be social and economic consequences to that kind of exposure. It might even cost them their home should the landlord refuse to sanction the presence of an immoral couple.

Having grown strangely small in the eyes of the world for having lost the trappings of authority, Eugene found the prospect of having to earn a conventional living abhorrent. Plagued by an increasingly intemperate sense of entitlement, a return to military life was likewise out of the question. Such a path, given his recent history, would have entailed a degree of demotion and subordination. Not even the outbreak of the Franco-Prussian war in July 1870 could tempt him back into uniform.

And so, no sooner had his young wife regained her girlhood than they were off again, joining the masses of refugees who, in September 1870, were fleeing the advancing Prussians. They sailed initially to Folkestone, from where they made their way to London. Here they took rooms at Emily Paine's lodging house at 17

Ranelagh Green, then a working-class district of Chelsea.[647] Given Eugene's recent stays at the Gresham and the Grand Hôtel du Louvre, a London lodging house represented a significant change of circumstances.

Following the end of the war, in May 1871, the Hassans returned to Boulogne and settled at 38 Boulevard des Tintelleries, next door to their previous residence. It was almost as if nothing had changed. And yet it had. The notion of creating a rail link to India via the Levant was attracting a lot of commercial interest and, given his experience of railway construction in the Levant, Eugene's experience in the field was highly prized, not least by the engineer, philologist, and founder of the London and County Bank, Henry Hyde Clarke.

From 1845 to 1847, Clarke had been editor of the *Railway Register* and, in the early 1860s, had worked in Constantinople as an agent of the Smyrna-Aidin Railway Company, a company promoting the cultivation of cotton. In 1862, when the Porte established the Imperial Cotton Commission, he became its vice-president.[648] With Lancashire cotton manufacturers fearful of becoming dependent upon supplies from the United States, entrepreneurs like Clarke were busily searching for alternative sources in Turkey and India.

On Friday, 24 November 1871, at the Society of Arts on John Street, London, Clarke read a paper titled *On the Progress of the Through Railway Route to India*. In this paper, Clarke made frequent reference to Eugene, with whom he had been in regular correspondence, and appended to his paper a report compiled, at his

---

[647] *Globe*, 16 September 1870, p.6.
[648] Calhoun, Ricky-Dale, *Seeds of destruction: the globalization of cotton as a result of the American Civil War*, PhD dissertation, Dept. of History, Kansas State University, 2012; Valenzuela, Francisco Javier. *The Construction of the Smyrna-Aidin Railway – A Discussion*. M.A. Seminar Paper, University of Texas, El Paso, 30 Nov 1975; Wilson, David. *Hyde Clarke (1815-1895)*, 2015, retrieved from http://www.levantineheritage.com/pdf/Hyde-Clarke-by-D-Wilson-2015.pdf on 1 November 2022.

Boulogne-Sur-Mer

expense, by the Irishman. This report offered a detailed analysis of the conflicting political, military, social and economic considerations that would determine the route of any Asiatic railway hoping to travel through Turkey.[649] It did not go unnoticed.[650]

On 13 January 1872, just two months after Clarke presented his paper, Eugene arrived unexpectedly in Constantinople. Exactly what brought him back is unknown. He may simply have been attempting to access the funds he had deposited in the Ottoman Bank, but it was most likely connected to the work he was doing for Clarke. His arrival was quickly noticed, and he was ordered to leave on the next Trieste steamer, a departure he contrived to miss. Following the issue of an arrest warrant, he was forcibly deported on the Marseille packet of 17 January, having been in the city for just five days.[651]

On 3 April 1872, Mathilde gave birth to a son. Formally christened Mathieu Henri, after Eugene's younger brother, at home he was only ever called Henry.[652] Shortly after his birth, the family left France for destinations unknown. They do not appear in the French census of that year, and when at length they returned, it was not to Boulogne but to Bordeaux and an apartment at 3 Rue Guiraude, where Eugene may have been attempting to establish himself as a wine merchant.[653] They had no sooner moved in, however, than Eugene found work elsewhere.

---

[649] Clarke, "On the Progress of the Through Railway Route to India", pp.21-28; *Civil and Military Gazette (Lahore)*, 23 Sept. 1872, p.5.
[650] *Allen's Indian Mail*, 5 December 1871, p. 1162.
[651] *Echo* (London), 2 February 1872, p.5.
[652] Etat Civil A.C, Pas-de-Calais Archives, Boulogne-sur-mer, no.402, Hassan, Eugénie Caroline, FRNC06200, 5 April 1872.
[653] Glasnevin Cemetery Records, 1874, record no. BGLV12813.

BELGRADE TO FEZ

IN JULY 1873, the Serbian government issued a call for tenders to build a system of railways and other public works in Serbia. The modernisation project was to begin with the construction of a line from Belgrade to Aleksinac,[654] where it would connect to the Constantinople line.[655] The successful bidder would win a lucrative fifty-year concession with a government option to buy it out after twenty.[656]

British interest in the project saw Eugene hired as a railway consultant, most likely through the influence of Humphry Sandwith, who for years had been an adviser to the Serbian National Party in Western European matters. Leaving a pregnant Mathilde in Bordeaux, Eugene travelled to Belgrade, where he was put to work on behalf of a British consortium. Alas, though well-respected within the Serbian National Party, with whom he wielded considerable influence, Sandwith's relationship with the prime minister, Jovan Ristić, was barely cordial, and a decision on concession was continuously delayed.[657]

> Suffice it to say that, as usual in these cases, he found himself at Belgrade in the midst of a network of cross interests and of contending intrigues, and that after success had often seemed within his grasp, and promises

---

[654] Then called Alexinatz.
[655] Ward, *Humphry Sandwith: A Memoir*, pp.216-218; *Lloyd's List*, 10 January 1873, p.5; *Liverpool Daily Post*, 13 January 1873, p.6; *Week's News* (London), 12 July 1873, p.17.
[656] *Daily Telegraph & Courier* (London), 28 April 1873, p.3.*Times of India*, 01 August 1873, p.4; *The Railway News*, 5 July 1873, p.11.
[657] *Sheffield Daily Telegraph*, 23 July 1873, p.3.

had been made and all but signed and sealed, he had the mortification of finding that the work was to be put into other hands, and that the English capitalists who were hoping to undertake it were to be disappointed.[658]

Despite the failure of the British bid, Eugene was dispatched soon after, most likely by the same consortium, to Morocco, an industrial terra nullius with little or no rail infrastructure. Back on 16 September, the Sultan of Morocco, Muhammad IV, had died, and his son, Hassan I, was shortly to be crowned. With half the industrial world anxious to seek an audience with the new Sultan, Eugene was quickly despatched to Casablanca. He arrived on 25 September at the head of a four-man delegation.[659] His presence was quickly noticed by the press and the cause of much confusion. Some papers alleged him to be travelling on an 'industrial mission' at the behest of a 'London firm' or as the emissary of 'some large English capitalists'.[660] Others claimed him to be carrying 'special despatches from the Sublime Porte'.[661] Of the two, the former seems most likely.

Eugene and his team waited in Casablanca for the arrival of the new Sultan for almost two months, and it was an uncomfortable stay. The previous November, the Irish physician, Arthur Leared, was scathing in his description of the town.

> The streets and open spaces were covered with fetid pools of stagnant water; and in these, as elsewhere, was every species of abominable filth ... Just outside the gate on the land side was the slaughtering-ground, where the offal of animals festering in the hot sun added to the pollution of

---

[658] Ward, *Humphry Sandwith: A Memoir*, pp.216-218.
[659] *York Herald*, 2 April 1874, p.3.
[660] *Cosmopolitan*, 11 June 1874, p.3; *Enniskillen Chronicle and Erne Packet*, 02 April 1874, p.4.
[661] *Morning Post*, 11 November 1873, p.5; *Hour* (London), 9 & 11 November 1873, p.3; *Shipping and Mercantile Gazette*, 11 November 1873, p.6.

the town. Fortunately it was well supplied with water, though this was also sadly polluted.[662]

Four years had passed since a cholera epidemic had engulfed Casablanca and carried off 563 victims, and lessons had yet to be learned.[663] To make matters worse, the British delegation had arrived at the start of Ramadan. Eating, drinking, smoking and bathing were prohibited during daylight hours and would remain so until the rise of the next moon. With the majority of the local population striving to keep themselves awake during the night so that they might sleep for much of the day, little work was done. Even had they wanted to move, little could be done to assist them.

Setting off alone was not an option. The kidnapping of Europeans for ransom was so common in Morocco that the Ironmongers Company of London held in trust a 'large sum of money for the redemption of slaves in Barbary'. Indeed, one James Butler, a Spanish citizen of Irish parentage, was currently in his eighth year of captivity at the hands of the Sheikh of Wadnoon.[664]

Ramadan came to an end on 21 November. One week later, with the new Sultan yet to arrive, Eugene gathered his delegation and set off across the flat and marshy hinterland for Rabat, where they rested for several days before crossing the mountains to Fez, the spiritual and cultural capital of Morocco.[665]

The 'Mecca of the West' or the 'Athens of Africa', Fez was a sheltered hamlet surrounded by mountains on all sides but the west. The impossibly narrow streets, the frenetic and labyrinthine souks and the way the winter sun would gild the medluk-rendered walls of its historic medina had been a draw to tourists for centuries.

Back in October, riots had arisen in Fez as a result

---

[662] Leared, Arthur. *Morocco and the Moors*, Sampson, Lowe, Marston, Searle, & Rivington, London, 1876, pp.56-57.
[663] Ibid.
[664] Ibid., pp.362-365; *The Morning Post*, 7 October 1874, p.5.
[665] *Hour* (London), 09 December 1873, p.7.

Belgrade to Fez

29. Grande Rue Cherabliane, Fez.

of the levying of non-Islamic taxes, and when the inhabitants met to plan their ceremony of allegiance to the Sultan, groups of artisans threatened to boycott the ceremony and forced the suspension of the taxes. Only when the Sultan promised an amnesty for those involved in the riots did the protests come to an end.[666] The situation remained tense, and there was still no sign of the new Sultan arriving. The weather was wonderfully pleasant, which was more than could be said for the water:

> The houses in the upper part of the town ... get fairly pure water. A few suits of dirty clothes may have been washed in it before coming to them ... but the water supply of the lower town is simply the sewage of the upper.[667]

Within days of his arrival, Eugene fell prey to dysentery, possibly as a result of having contracted cholera. Whether he had contracted the disease in Casablanca, Rabat, or Fez is difficult to say, but over the succeeding twenty-six days, the colour drained from his brow, and his health slowly deteriorated. Unlike Casablanca, Fez at least possessed a decent hospital – the famous Maristan of Sidi Frej – and Eugene would have had access to medical care. Nevertheless, tortured daily by fever, dehydration and bloody diarrhoea, he slowly wasted away.[668] He probably deserved better than to suffer an undignified bedridden withering, but it was not to be, and, on 29 December 1873, the dashing *sabreur* of Kalafat and Oltenitza lost his final battle and was laid to eternal rest in a place where none would remember him.[669]

---

[666] Dennerlein, Bettina. "Legitimate Bounds and Bound Legitimacy. The Act of Allegiance to the Ruler (Bai'a) in 19th Century Morocco" in *Die Welt Des Islams*, vol. 41, no. 3, 2001, pp. 287–310.

[667] Colville, Sir Henry Edward. *A Ride in Petticoats and Slippers*, Sampson Low, Marston, Searle & Rivington, London, 1880, pp.143-144.

[668] *Indian Statesman*, 08 Apr 1874, p.4; *Boston Pilot*, 14 Feb 1874, p.3.

[669] *The Irishman*, 24 January 1874, p.13; *Drogheda Argus and Leinster Journal*, 31 January 1874, p.7; *Freeman's Journal*, 14 February 1874, p.8; *The Levant Times*, 28 January 1874, p.2.

A WIDOW SCORNED

DECLARATIONS OF FOND remembrance were few and far between and eulogies slow in coming. When eventually they did, they had been cobbled together from newspaper headlines and half-remembered stories. For each that was flattering, there would be another, indifferent to the conventions of solemnity, in which Eugene would be painted as a faintly ludicrous figure, his character occluded by caricature and cast in a picaresque or traitorous light.

> Of the sincerity of earlier professions of patriotism there are good reasons for doubt, seeing that during the latter part of his career he "went over to the enemy" and maligned his countrymen in the congenial columns of the English *Times*. As we are proverbially counselled to speak of the dead nothing but good, we will content ourselves with saying that while in his youth he appeared to love his country, in his maturity he maligned and doubted her.[670]

Even in death, rumours that he had converted to Islam continued to dog his reputation.[671] Those who had known him personally, however, described him as a 'gallant colonel', a man whose career had been marred by a tendency to be oversanguine, and yet a man, for all of that, who was extremely likeable.

> With a military bearing, rather above the middle height, lithe in form, fair-haired, frank, and handsome-faced, Eugene O'Reilly had a winning manner and a generous heart, and gained the cordial liking of all with whom he

---

[670] *The Drogheda Argus*, 31 January 1874, p.7; *The Irishman*, 24 January 1874, p.477.
[671] *Boston Pilot*, 7 February 1874, p.4.

came in contact.⁶⁷²

Not a single mention was ever made in these brief eulogies of the wife and children he had left destitute in Bordeaux. Not one consoling platitude would be thrown their way, and with few friends and fewer family to support them, their lives began to disintegrate.

Mathilde was seven months pregnant when she received word of Eugene's death, and the disruption and uncertainty that followed his passing would slowly yield to an ulcerative bitterness that would plague her for the remainder of her life. Having put off for too long the humiliation of having to regularise his marriage, he had left her with no more rights than a casual mistress.

It was four in the afternoon of 28 February 1874 when Mathilde gave birth to her second son, Armand Ernest Hassan.⁶⁷³ Overwrought and alone, with a new baby and no means of supporting herself, she was forced to appeal to the charitable instincts of a local consul, whose identity and nationality she would never reveal. He gifted her the funds to book passage on a merchant steamer to Dublin. And so, just weeks after she had given birth, she set sail for Dublin, intent on appealing to the better nature of Eugene's only surviving brother, James.

On this voyage, Mathilde took with her only her three-year-old daughter, Eugénie. The boys, still infants, she left with Madame Aren, the midwife who had nursed her through pregnancy.⁶⁷⁴ Merchant vessels did not offer family rooms, and the cabins of paying passengers tended to be somewhat niggardly. Lurching about a steamship on a winter sailing would have been challenging enough with one child, let alone

---

⁶⁷² *Indian Statesman*, 08 April 1874, p.4.
⁶⁷³ Archives Municipales de Bordeaux, Cote du document – 1 E 300, Etat Civil, Section 2, no. 265, Hassan, Armand Ernest, 9 June 1870.
⁶⁷⁴ Aren lived at 49 Rue D'Ares, Bordeaux.

three, two of whom still had to be carried.

But why bring Eugénie at all? She was just three years old. Was it, perhaps, to elicit the sympathy of the O'Reillys in a manner that could not be done in a letter? Or was it simply for the company? Eugénie had been her firstborn, the beneficiary, for a while, of her undivided love and attention. There was a bond between them unlike any she could have with her sons.

Mathilde and Eugénie arrived in Dublin towards the end of March 1874 and made immediately for the home of the O'Reillys.[675] It did not go well. Struggling financially and dedicated to the sanctification of his brother's memory, James refused to recognise Mathilde as Eugene's wife. To James, she was simply his brother's mistress, the mother of his illegitimate children, public knowledge of which could only justify the kind of outlandish rumours he had spent half his life battling to disprove. He would not allow his brother's memory or his family's reputation, to be sullied in such a manner. Or at least that was how Mathilde would later choose to tell it.

There was, however, possibly more to James' reticence than simply concern for his family's reputation. He had recently become the primary breadwinner for not just his own family but that of his youngest brother, Matthew George. Matthew's widow had recently fallen on hard times and had recently travelled to Dublin in the hope of getting her son, Eugene, accepted as a boarder at the newly opened Masonic Orphan Boy's School in Sandymount, at least until she could raise the fare to take them both to Australia, which she would eventually do in 1879.[676] James, as a result, was financially stretched.

---

[675] A clipping of Eugene's Obituary from the *Dublin Evening Mail* of 28 March 1878 was found amongst Mathilde's papers when she died.

[676] *Irish Times*, 14 May 1875, p. 5; *Belfast News*-Letter, 15 May 1875, p.4; *Irish Times*, 16 April 1880, p.2; Stuart, Thomas. *Masonic Female Orphan School of Ireland: Grand Centenary Celebration*, Wilson Hartnell, 1892, pp. 26-31.

Mathilde was forced to rent a tenement flat in Summerhill, the largest red-light district in Europe, where more than 1,600 prostitutes plied their trade. She herself was blessed with a hardy constitution, but the cramped and unsanitary conditions quickly told on Eugénie. At first, it appeared as though the child had caught nothing more than a common cold, but after about a week, she began to suffer bouts of intense coughing and was subsequently diagnosed with whooping cough, an epidemic of which had recently engulfed the city.[677]

Eugénie died on 17 April 1874 and was buried two days later at Glasnevin Cemetery under the name of Eugénie Hassan.[678] On her burial certificate, she was described as the daughter of a 'wine merchant'. James took care of the burial and registration but would not permit her to be buried with the O'Reillys. In death, as in life, she was to be denied her father's name.

Eugénie's death took a heavy toll on Mathilde, who lapsed into a suicidal depression, her condition so desperate that the O'Reillys were forced to swallow their distaste and take her in. Their belated altruism came at a price. Mathilde's 'illegitimate' relationship with Eugene was never to become public knowledge or allowed to become fuel for the predatory piety of the pulpit bashers. She would also have to abandon all claims to kinship or to the O'Reilly name. In no position to refuse and in no shape to be sent home to France, Mathilde consented.

James, by now, had ten children to feed, shelter, and educate – Edward and Gertrude having been born since he last saw his brother.[679] He could not afford to

---

[677] *Eleventh Detailed Annual Report of the Registrar General of Marriages, Births and Deaths in Ireland 1874*, Alexander Thom, Dublin 1874, p.20.
[678] Glasnevin Cemetery Records, 1874, record no. BGLV12813.
[679] Ancestry.com. Ireland, Select Births and Baptisms, 1620-1911. Provo, UT: Ancestry.com Operations, Inc., 2011; N.L.I., *Irish Catholic Parish Registers*; Microfilm: 09155/01.

take on Henry and Armand, even had he been willing to do so. Were he to send for them, questions would also arise regarding their parentage. And yet, that is precisely what he promised Mathilde he would do as soon as she was well enough to care for them. Their absence, however, simply added two great boulders of guilt to the sum of what was already an inexpressible and paralysing grief.

Changing her surname to Massy, at James' insistence (the name of Hassan Bey being only too well known in Dublin), Mathilde moved in with the O'Reillys, presumably in the guise of a governess, and Susan began the slow task of nursing her back to health.[680] But she lived now in a kind of social limbo, not quite servant and not quite family, financially dependent upon James and receiving little in the way of income, except for certain 'personal services' she provided to the family.

On 28 March 1875, the *Dublin Evening Mail* reprinted Eugene's obituary from the London *Times*. Mathilde cut it from the paper and kept it: a memento, perhaps, to share one day with her sons. God knows their father had left them little else. A year, two years, four years slipped past, and Mathilde's sons grew up without her. To Mathilde it seemed as though James' promise of reunification would never be kept; to the O'Reillys as though they would never be rid of her.

What prompted Mathilde's eventual awakening is unknown, but it appears to have been the counsel of a Jesuit priest to whom she one day confessed the fear that she was losing her battle with despair. The Jesuit warned her that, for as long as she lived with the O'Reillys, she would never be free of that feeling. The best course of action, he advised, was to make a new life for herself somewhere else. She was still young.

---

[680] Unsent/draft letter from Mathilda to her son dated 7 March 1893, Bankhead/Guest family archives (privately held) courtesy of Sarah B. Guest Perry.

She could start afresh. Given time, she might even be able to provide a home for her sons.

Her hopes of having her marriage retrospectively legalised, the priest further advised, was beyond any level of influence she was ever likely to exert. Indeed, were she to take steps in that direction, she would almost certainly lose the goodwill of the O'Reillys. And so, taking the Jesuit's advice, she left Dublin for Paris, where she landed herself an apprenticeship as a dressmaker. Another two years slipped by – two years of squinting eyes and calloused fingers – but in the early summer of 1881, She bid adieu to Paris and sailed to New York as Madame Massy, dressmaker.

MADAME MASSY

WHY MATHILDE CHOSE New York above Bordeaux is anyone's guess, but in New York, a French-trained dressmaker could easily pass for middle class and move in circles that might well have been closed to her in France. Indeed, not long after she arrived, she appears to have caught the eye of a wealthy American cotton broker. His name was James Bankhead Guest.

Mathilde and James would never marry or have any children, but they would live together until Guest's death on Christmas Eve 1892.[681] Throughout that time, Mathilde would keep Susan O'Reilly appraised of her whereabouts, just in case one or other of her sons might attempt to seek her out. But, as the years slipped by and the dream of a reunion remained unfulfilled, her heart hardened against the memory of the man she blamed for that estrangement, her late 'husband', Eugene O'Reilly.

Twelve days before he died, James Bankhead Guest amended his will, and instead of leaving everything to his nieces, he left everything bar the contents of his safe to Mathilde so that she might live comfortably after his death.[682] Some weeks later, financially secure for the first time in her life, she sat down and composed a letter to her son Henry. Whether the letter was ever sent is unknown. Littered with inaccuracies and redolent of an unforgiven past, she recounted details of her life with Eugene from the emotional security of the third person:

---

[681] Warren, J.E. "The Bankhead Family" in *The William and Mary Quarterly*, October 1929, Vol. 9, No. 4, p. 308.
[682] Codicil currently in private collection of Sarah B. Guest Perry.

SHAMROCK, CROWN AND CRESCENT

New York City,
March 7, 1893.

My Dear Son,
    There are some peculiarly sad histories in life the relation of which are at times more painful, more deeply painful, than can be pictured by anyone. The one to which it has become my duty to call your attention is such, in essence and minutest detail. In the year 1867, in the military service of the Turkish Government, at the City of Constantinople, was an Officer of rank equivalent to what is known in the British Armies as Lieutenant Colonel, his military title being "Hassan Bey", his real name "Eugene O'Reilly". He was of Irish parentage but had selected as his profession that of a soldier.
    In this same year, there resided in the same city a girl of fourteen years of age bearing the name of Mathilde Solymassy, she had formed the acquaintance of Eugene O'Reilly, at Constantinople in the year named and at his earnest solicitation, consented to marry him and a marriage ceremony was, as the girl then believed performed by a person said to be the English Consul at that place by which she firmly believed she became the wife of Mr. O'Reilly, bearing the name of Hassan, which as I have before stated was part of the military titles which the man then bore.
    In the year 1870, a female child was born to them and christened "Eugenie". As it became necessary to register the birth of this child, the mother requested of the father that the names of the parents be stated as Eugene O'Reilly and Mathilde O'Reilly. It was then for the first time, that this girl mother learned from the lips of the man who had sworn to love and cherish her that the ceremony which had been performed at Constantinople was not a legal ceremony, and that she was not in law a wife.
    At this time Eugene O'Reilly gave his solemn promise, that what may be characterized as a great mistake, if not a wanton act, should be rectified by him and the woman made his lawful wife; but the vicissitudes of the man's life, separating him for long intervals from the woman, the promise was never redeemed – the reparation never made. In 1872 at Boulange Ser Mer, France, a son was born to them and christened Henry Hassan and in the latter part of 1873 at Bourdeaux, France, another son was born to them and christened "Armand Hassan". Colonel O'Reilly having

Madame Massy

died at Fez the woman was left at Bourdeaux with these three children, absolutely penniless, thrown upon the world without a name.

My son, I cannot convey to you in words, the condition of absolute desperation this placed me in. My life and good name had been placed in the keeping of your father Eugene O'Reilly, and my confidence in the integrity of his word had only tended to make my lot the more bitter and myself and children homeless and nameless.

When Armand was three months old, Eugénie was dangerously ill, and everything seemed so disheartening that I determined to appeal to Colonel O'Reilly's relatives in Ireland for aid. Through the kindness of a consul I secured passage on a merchant vessel and a small sum of money, and leaving yourself and Armand in the care of the nurse who had attended me in my last confinement, with my rapidly dying daughter I went to Dublin, Ireland and appealed to Colonel O'Reilly's brother James for help in my distress. I was told that they would receive me into their house, but only upon the express condition that I should be known by another name, and at their suggestion I chose the name which I have ever since borne "Massy", the word being the latter portion of my maiden name.

Not very long after my arrival at Dublin, your sister died and was buried. I had been promised that Armand and yourself should in no very long time be restored to me, but for four years I remained entirely dependent upon the family of James O'Reilly save what personal services I rendered them, and you were not restored to me. At this time, I was in a most disturbed state of mind and sought the counsel of a Jesuit Father at Dublin, telling him frankly my position and stating to him that I was unable any longer to bear the great mental strain from which I had been suffering for four years.

He told me the circumstances of my case fully justified the inference that it was the intention of Mr. O'Reilly's relatives to securely preserve from the world what might prove, if it was brought to light, a great blot upon the name of a family of social standing, and respected in the community, and that unfortunately I did not have it in my power if I took any steps in the direction of seeking to prove myself the wife of Colonel O'Reilly to either do so or avert a great scandal, and advised me to go out into the world alone and seek my own living.

Relying upon the value of this advice I went to Paris, and there after working assiduously for twenty-two months became thoroughly conversant with dressmaking and in the year 1880 came to New York City where I have since been earning my living by my labor in the business. I have married and am respected by all who know me. Mrs. O'Reilly of Dublin, for years after my coming to this city, knew where I resided, and she felt that either she or her children, should have acquainted you with it so that you might have been at liberty to write me. For nearly nineteen years I have been practically hidden from the world and separated from society.

Has it been because of my own wish? Could I when a child in 1867, having placed my life in the hands of your father, foreseen that I was to be dishonored as I was, and even to say unable to give you the name that by everything that is sacred belongs to you...[illegible]. I know your heart will say that no girl of the age of fourteen years could have been wilfully guilty of so gross an act. So my son, you have heard the truth from me and I want you to believe that no matter what circumstances may seem to be against me, that I have been pure in heart and life and more than that, that my mother's heart goes out to both Armand and yourself and that it is my most earnest desire to hear from you both.

Could I but give you a name – the name that is yours, my years of toil and suffering would seem as nothing, but how powerless I am – how totally unable to set right another's wrongdoing. I have briefly, very briefly, told my story. Oh believe me, believe me, it is true and do not judge me harshly for my sorrows have been great. Have I done wrong in this placing before you facts that may on your own account make your heart and that of Armand bleed? I could no longer refrain. Circumstances have led me directly to the conclusion that this was a solemn duty and I beg of you to write me when you have received and calmly read this letter.[683]

The following year, Mathilde attempted to resume her career as a dressmaker, only to find the profession

---

[683] Unsent/draft letter from Mathilde to Henry, 7 March 1893, Bankhead family archives, courtesy of Sarah B. Guest Perry.

rendered all but redundant by the growth of department stores and mail-order catalogues that were now offering ready-to-wear dresses.[684] It all went downhill from there.

In 1894, James O'Reilly died at his home at 2 Gardiner Place in Dublin.[685] Following his death, his wife, Susan, moved in with her unmarried daughter, also called Susan, then resident at 34 Mountjoy Square. She died there on 7 August 1898. With Susan's death whatever hopes Mathilde had of reuniting her sons all but vanished and she fell prey to 'nervous neuralgia' – a debilitating nineteenth-century disorder common in overweight or diabetic women. Caused by the streptococcus bacterium, the symptoms included various combinations of rashes, headaches, dental, facial and leg pain.

Forced by her infirmity to move out of her apartment at 142 West 91st Street, she moved into a more manageable flat in a boarding house at 213 West 120th Street. Still in possession of many of James' possessions and knowing that, as she became increasingly debilitated, she would no longer be able to prevent them from being stolen, she asked his siblings to take them.[686]

Mathilde survived on her own for several more years, but her physical and mental health was slowly deteriorating. In June 1901, she was admitted to the Central Islip State Hospital, at that time the second-largest psychiatric hospital in the United States. She would spend the next twenty-six years of her life in

---

[684] *New York City Directory*, Trow, New York, 1891, p.916; Amnéus, Cynthia. *A Separate Sphere: Dressmaker in Cincinnati's Golden Age, 1877-1922*. Cincinnati Art Museum, 2003, pp.1,37.

[685] Irish Death Register 1864-1921, Dublin North. General Register Office, Vol. 2, p.326; Calendar of Wills and Administrations 1858-1922, 1894, p.711; Calendar of Wills and Administrations 1858-1922, 1899, p.390.

[686] Mathilde Massy to Frank B. Guest, 7 June 1900; Mathilde Massy to Mrs Honora Newhall, 19 June 1900, Mathilde Massy to Mrs Honora Newhall, 2 July 1900, Guest Family Private Papers.

that institution and would eventually die there, on 22 August 1927, from a combination of biliary calculi and chronic endocarditis.[687] Death would pierce her privacy, and amongst her papers would be found a draft of the letter she had written thirty-four years earlier to Henry and a clipping of Eugene's obituary, taken from the *Dublin Evening Mail* in 1878.

The sons of Eugene O'Reilly never knew their father and never bore his name. Henry grew up to be a humble roofer and a private in the French reserve. He never left France and married twice, firstly to a Mme. C. Carrieta in Bordeaux and then to a Léonie Carrére.[688] He outlived them both. I could find no record of where or when he died.

Armand would spend his whole life in France, marrying Alida Marguerite Wuillame, a native of Cateau, a village close to the Belgian border. He would survive both world wars to die at Houilles, 20km north of Versailles, on 26 May 1965, at the age of ninety-one. Syria would become an independent country in 1946, three years after Lebanon.

---

[687] New York State Death Index, 1852-1956, Death Certificate No. 50044, 22 August 1927, Massy, Matilda.

[688] Archives Municipales de Bordeaux, Cote du document – 2 E 355, Etat Civil, Section 2, Hassan-Carrére, 11 January 1902, p.25.

ACKNOWLEDGEMENTS

I should like to thank the librarians and staff of the Manuscript Reading Room at the National Library of Ireland for their assistance and patience while I transcribed Luby's account of the Blanchardstown Affair, and also the staff of the UK National Archives for providing me with copies of diplomatic communiques concerning Eugene's time in Lebanon and Syria.

Special thanks are also due to Sylviane Vaucheret for assisting me with the French language translations and to Sarah Guest Perry who graciously provided me with copies of Mathilde's letters and shared documents from her family's private archive. I am also indebted to Melinda Elliott of Southbury, Connecticut, for the time and effort she put into finding and procuring for me a copy of Augustin Crane's extremely rare memoir of his cousin Henry M. Canfield.

My gratitude is also due to Gábor Fodor, former Director of the Hungarian Cultural Institute in Istanbul, for checking the Hungarian Consular lists for members of Mathilde's family. Finally, as ever, I am grateful to Cliona and Eleanor, for their encouragement and patience. Words alone cannot express my gratitude.

LIST OF ILLUSTRATIONS

1. Attack on the Widow McCormack's House on Boulagh Common, 29 July 1848. From a lithograph by N. Currier, New York, c.1848. Image courtesy of Library of Congress, control number: 90708823.
2. Barricades rue Saint-Maur, avant l'attaque des troupes du général Lamoricière, dimanche 25 juin 1848 à 7 h du matin. Daguerréotypes. Musée d'Orsay (Paris) - Référence de l'image: 02CE10881/PHO2002-41 --- 02CE10879/PHO 2002-42.
3. Richmond Bridewell, Dublin, Harper's Weekly, Vol. X, No.484, New York, 7 April 1866, p.210 (front cover).
4. Lord Palmerston. Nadar (Gaspard-Félix Tournachon, known as) (Paris, 06–04–1820 - Paris, 21–03–1910), Museum of Romantic Life, Paris. CC0 1.0 DEED/CC0 1.0 Universal.
5. Constantinople, from Bruun, Malthe Conrad. *Géographie complète et universelle. Nouvelle edition*, vol.6, Morizot, Paris, 1856, frontispiece. Public domain.
6. The Yüksek Kaldırım, in Shepp, D.B., *Shepp's Photographs of the World,* George V. Jones & Co., Boston, 1891, p.265.
7. Shumla Street Scene, *Illustrated London News*, 5 April 1856, p.364.
8. Omer Pasha in audience with British visitors, Shumen, 1854. *Illustrated London News,* 4 March 1854, p.1.
9. Balkan travellers in early 1854. *Illustrated London News,* 15 April 1854, p.1.
10. Vidin, 1854. *L'Illustration: journal universel*, No. 574, v.23, June 1854, p.1.
11. Calafat, 1854. *Illustrated London News*, 21 Jan 1854.
12. Turkish Bashi Bazouks 1876 Anonymous. Free Art Licence via http://www.vokrugsveta.ru/vs/article/3104/. Accessed 22/1/2023.
13. William Ferguson Beatson. Steel engraving by Stodart from a photograph by Mayall, published by James S Virtue, circa 1850.
14. Richard Francis Burton in his tent in Africa. From Burton, Isabel. *The life of Captain Sir Richard F. Burton,* vol. 1, Chapman & Hall Ltd., London, 1893 [Public Domain].
15. Massacre of Christians: Damascus. *L'Univers illustré.* 1859-1860, t. 3, p.281.
16. Italian States in 19th Century. Via Wikimedia Commons: https://commons.wikimedia.org/wiki/File:Italia_1843-es.svg
17. Jumblatt Palace, Moukhtara, 1861. From Harvey, Annie Jane. *Our Cruise in the Claymore, with a visit to Damascus and the Lebanon,* Chapman and Hall, London, 1861.
18. Map of the Hauran Region via Wikipedia. Amitchell125, CC BY-SA 4.0 https://creativecommons.org/licenses/by-sa/4.0.
19. Abd el Kader. Photograph by Etienne Carjat, 1865. Public domain via Wikimedia Commons. https://commons.wikimedia.org/wiki/File:Abd_al-Qadir.jpg

20. Yūsuf Bey Karam, Saroufim1, CC BY-SA 4.0, via https://commons.wikimedia.org/wiki/File:Young_Youssef_Bey_Karam.jpg
21. Humphry Sandwith. Stipple engraving by D.J. Pound, Image courtesy of the Wellcome Collection, via Wikimedia Commons, Reference: 8365i, https://wellcomecollection.org/works/r2fyzyfy.
22. Jane Digby, Lady Ellenborough. Public domain photograph from *Forty Years in Constantinople. The Recollections of Sir Edwin Pears 1873-1915*, Herbert Jenkins Limited, London 1916, pp.72-73
23. Dorot Jewish Division, The New York Public Library. "A Bedouin of the Haurân." New York Public Library Digital Collections. 1881 - 1884. https://digitalcollections.nypl.org/items/510d47d9-5f05-a3d9-e040-e00a18064a99
24. A Turkish Commission of Enquiry, by Horace Harral, for *Illustrated London News*, 1877. Mid-Manhattan Library/Picture Collection, NYPL Call Number: PC TRI-18. Public Domain.
25. Cour du Grand Hôtel du Louvre. Rivière, Charles, Lithographer, and Publisher Maison Martinet. Paris. Retrieved from the Library of Congress, <www.loc.gov/item/2016652454/>.
26. The table d'hôte dining room of the Grand Hôtel du Louvre on the Rue Rivoli in Paris, c. 1870, Public Domain via Wikimedia Commons.http://www.cairn.info/resume.php?ID_ARTICLE=AUTRE_CSERG_2008_01_0074, Public Domain. Unknown Author. https://commons.wikimedia.org/w/index.php?curid=31075554
27. Boulogne-sur-mer. Clerc-Rampal, G. *Mer: la Mer Dans la Nature, la Mer et l'Homme*, Librairie Larousse, Paris, 1913, p.271.
28. La Place Saint Michel et le Boulevard de Clocheville (Tintelleries), Stevenard, Boulogne-sur-mer, Postcard c.1900.
29. Grand Rue Cherabliane, Fez, c.1900, old postcard, Joseph Bouhsira, edit. Author's private collection.

INDEX

Abd el Kader, 166, 172, 173, 174, 176
Abdulaziz, Ottoman Sultan, 128, 154, 178, 183, 187, 190, 194, 197, 198, 207, 237, 239
Abdulmedjid I, Ottoman Sultan, 52, 53, 56, 57, 88, 119, 120
Abro Sahak Efendi, 137, 141, 148
Aghawat, 168, 169, 170, 174, 175, 176
Ahmed Köprülü Pasha, 127, 138, 141
Aleppo, Syria, 100, 175, 204, 221, 224, 238
Algeria, 172, 174, 187
Ali Bey, Metuali Chieftan, 134, 175
Âli Pasha, Mehmed Emin, 241, 247
Alishan, Vincent, 245, 249
Ballingarry, Co. Tipperary, 20, 21
Bankhead Guest, James, 275
Barkley Family, Railway Entrepreneurs, 189
Barry, Michael Francis, 6, 12, 162
Barry, Patrick Joseph (P.J.), 2, 5, 6, 8, 12, 13, 2-15, 16, 162
Bashi Bazouks, 60, 71, 72, 73, 74, 75, 76, 79, 82, 83, 102, 108, 111, 178
Beatson, William Ferguson, 63, 101, 84-113, 116, 117, 164
Bedouin, 162, 169, 170, 172, 177, 178, 204
Béhigé Sultana, 243

Beirut, 125, 128-37, 141, 144, 153, 163, 177, 208-13, 219, 232, 235, 242, 247
Beirut International Commission of Inquiry, 137
Beit Meri, 125
Belfast, 23, 43, 44, 52, 161
Belvedere College, 51
Bentivoglio d'Aragon, Stanislas Prosper Philippe, 130
Berkeley, Captain, 104, 107, 111, 115
Blanchardstown, i, 2, 3, 14, 42, 45, 46, 162
Blaque Bey, Eduoard, 247
Bordeaux, 263, 264, 270, 275, 280
Bosnia, 57
Boulogne-sur-Mer, 258-63
Brett, Brigadier General De Renzie James, 107, 116
British Abyssinian Expedition, 204
British Osmanli Cavalry, 117, 164
British Turkish Contingent, 86, 94, 96, 106, 108, 112
Bucharest, 76, 78, 79, 80, 84, 122
Bulwer, Sir Henry, 128, 138, 142, 154, 175
Burton, Richard Francis, 92, 93, 94, 95, 104, 105, 107, 108, 110, 111, 113, 116, 117, 120
Buxton, Edward, 166
Büyükderé, 106
Buzău, 81

Calafat, 64, 67, 68, 69, 70, 72, 73, 74, 75, 76, 77, 163, 268
Calvert, Frederic William, 108
Çanakkale, 86, 91, 92, 97, 99, 100, 104
Canfield, Henry Monroe, 201, 203, 209, 211, 234, 237, 243, 245, 247, 250, 251
Canfield, Mitchell M., 247, 251
Cannon, General Robert, 79
Casablanca, Morocco, 265
Castelfidardo, 140
Catholic Relief Act, 25
Central Islip State Hospital, 279
Chesney, Francis Rawdon, 199
Chibli Pasha, 246
Churchill, Alfred Black, 128, 182, 183
Circassians, 71, 86, 178, 230
Ciupercenii Vechi, 74
Clarendon, George Villiers, 4th Earl of, 101
Clongowes Wood College, 27, 28
Constantinople, 53, 54, 85, 94, 95, 100, 118, 119, 121, 150, 151, 153, 156, 163, 177, 182, 187, 194, 198, 202, 207, 232, 236, 241, 262
Court of Exchequer, 25, 30, 40
Cowley, Henry Richard Charles Wellesley, 1st Earl, 207
Crean, Lt. Michael Theobald, 140, 141
Crimean Banquet, Dublin, 118
Damascus, 123, 126, 127, 128, 129, 130, 132, 134, 136, 137, 138, 148, 154, 155, 156, 162, 164, 167, 169, 171, 172, 174, 176, 177, 178, 219, 227, 229, 230, 231, 233, 240, 245

Damascus Extraordinary Tribunal, 137, 138, 148
Damascus Gendarmerie, 195
Dardanelles, 86, 88, 99, 103, 110, 111, 112, 114
Davud Pasha, 184, 185, 186
Deir el Qamar, 125, 132, 138
Dickens, Charles, 260
Digby el Mezrab, Jane, 112, 165, 166, 167, 213, 214, 215, 217, 219, 231
Dillon, Dr. E.W., 157, 200, 237, 250, 252
Dillon, John Blake, 39
Drogheda Tavern, 5
Druze, i, 124, 125, 126, 132, 133, 134, 135, 138, 143, 144, 147, 148, 149, 153, 155, 167, 184
Dublin Remonstrants, 3
Dufferin and Ava, Frederick Temple Hamilton-Temple-Blackwood, 1st Marquess of, 128, 130, 138, 148, 177, 246
Duffy, Charles Gavan, 42, 43, 45
Dunshaughlin, 3, 7, 9
Dupuis, Lieutenant-Colonel, 65, 72
East India Company, 85, 101
Ellenborough, Lady Jane. *See* Jane Digby el Mezrab
Elliot, Sir Henry George, 207, 208, 231, 248
Eloquentia Perfecta, 27, 28
Emilianoff, Alexis, 201
Emilianova, Stephanie, 201
Ergani Copper Mines, 180, 190, 237
Erskine, Edward M., 171, 175
Esb'a Tribe, 246
Eupatoria, 88
Evelyn, George Palmer, 64, 65, 66, 70, 71, 72, 73, 74, 76, 77
Farley, James Lewis, 137

Fenton, Sophie. *See* Sophie O'Reilly
Fenton, Thomas, 121
Fez, Morocco, 266, 268, 277, 286
Franco Pasha, 212
Franz, Julius, 212, 237, 251
Fraser, Major A.J., 148
Fuad Pasha, Mehmed, 121, 122, 128, 129, 130, 132, 134, 135, 136, 137, 143, 144, 146, 147, 148, 149, 153, 154, 155, 162, 168, 169, 170, 171, 172, 177, 182, 183, 186, 187, 194, 195, 198, 232, 244, 246, 247, 250
Galata, 251
Gardino, Lieutenant, 69, 72, 73, 78, 81, 82, 83
Garibaldi Domenico Menotti, 202
Garibaldi, Giuseppe, 138
Giraud, Lieutenant-Colonel, 104, 114
Giurgiu, 78, 79
Glascott, Dr. John Nassau, 53
Godkin, Edwin Lawrence, 71, 78
Grand Hotel du Louvre, 253
Grand Hôtel du Louvre, 262
Grattan Club, 3, 41
Grattan, Henry, 162
Gresham Hotel, 190, 192, 195, 257
Habeas Corpus Suspension Act, 20, 42
Hajj, the, 168, 177
Halim Pasha, Governor of Damascus, 163, 170
Halim, Mohammad abd al, Prince of Egypt, 211, 220, 241
Halim, Muhammad abd al, Prince of Egypt, 187, 190, 198
Halpin, Thomas, 20

Hama, 219, 221, 225, 226, 227, 228, 229, 238
Hama, Syria, 211, 213, 224, 225
Hasbaya, 126, 130, 132, 133, 134, 135, 136
Hassan Bey. *See* O'Reilly, Eugene
Hassan I, Moroccan Sultan, 265, 267
Hassan, Alida Marguerite Wuillame, 280
Hassan, Armand Ernest, 270, 273, 276, 277, 278, 280
Hassan, Eugénie Caroline, 259, 270, 271, 272, 277
Hassan, Henry. *See* Mathieu Henri Hassan
Hassan, Léonie Carrére, 280
Hassan, Madame C. Carrieta, 280
Hassan, Mathieu Henri, 263, 275
Hassan, Mathilde. *See* Mathilde Solymassy
Hauran Desert, 132, 133, 168, 169, 170, 171, 177, 195, 216
Henry Pelham-Clinton, 5th Duke of, 85, 88, 90
Heraclius, Byzantine Emperor, 125
Hollywood, Edward, 36
Homs, Syria, 180, 213, 215, 218, 219, 224, 225, 229, 237, 239, 247
Hotel d'Angleterre, 55, 120
Hungarian War of Independence, 47–48
Husni Pasha, 243, 245, 247
Hyde Clarke, Henry, 262, 263
Ignatyev, Count Nikolay Pavlovich, 211
Ikiades Effendi, Joseph, 243, 249
Iliński, Antoni Aleksander, 71, 77, 79, *See* Iskander Bey
Inniskilling Dragoons, 50

International Criminal Court, i
Irish Confederation, The, 20, 32, 33, 35, 41, 42
Iskander Bey, a.k.a. Antoni Aleksander Iliński, 71
Ismail Pasha, Khedive of Egypt, 187, 190, 197, 219, 220, 241
Izmir (Smyrna), 138, 180
Jenner, George Francis Birt, 201, 207, 208, 231, 232, 261
Jezzine, 133
Johnson, J. Augustus, 230, 234
June Days' Revolt of 1848, 41
Karachi Brothel Report, 94
Karam, Yusuf Bey, 184, 185, 186
Kenyon, Father John, 46
Khurshid Pasha, 129, 132, 138, 143
Kirwan, Captain Martin, 140
Kmety, György, 121, 132, 146, 147
Kurshid Pasha, 141
Laing, Samuel, 181
Lakeman, Sir Stephen, 80, 81, 84
Lamartine, Alphonse de, 35, 36, 37, 38, 39
Latas, Mihajlo. *See* Omar Pasha
Ledru-Rollin, Alexandre Auguste, 36
Leonard, John Patrick, 38, 39
Levi, Mr., Money Lender, 171, 203
Lloyd, St Vincent, 89
Louis IX, King of France, 125
Luby, Catherine, 4
Luby, Rev. James, 4
Luby, Thomas Clarke and Blanchardstown Affair, 1

visit to Father John Kenyon, 46–47
Mahmud II, Ottoman Sultan, 122
Maidstone Barracks, Kent, 49, 51
Mallouf, Nassif, 113, 114, 115
Maranite, 153
Maronites, i, 124, 125, 126, 128, 129, 142, 144, 184
Martin, Admiral Sir William Fanshawe, 132
Massy, Mathilde. *See* Mathilde Solymassy
Mazzini, Giuseppe, 138
McCarthy, Dr. Justin, 52
McCoan, James Carlisle, 248, 249
McDermott, Martin, 36
McDonnell, Alexander, 50
Meagher, Thomas Francis, 28, 32, 33, 36, 37, 39, 41
Meagher, Thomas sen., 36
Mehmed Emin Ali, 194
Mercier, Colonel, 65, 72, 73, 74
Meri Ayume, 135
Merton, Louis, 182
Metuali Tribe, 134
Meyler, Walter Thomas, 161, 162
Meziad, Sheik Faris el, 215, 216, 218
Mezrab Tribe, 165, 177, 239, 245, 246
Mezrab, Medjuel el, 165, 210, 213, 215, 216, 217, 218, 219, 221, 223, 229, 245
Mihailo Obrenović III, Prince of Serbia, 197
Mirès, Jules, 181
Mitchel, John, 34
Mitilini, 98
Mohammed IV, Moroccan Sultan, 265
Mohammed Mourad Effendi, 239
Mola, Kececizade Izzet, 121
Moldavia, 57

Molly Maguires, The, 2, 8
Money, Edward, 101
Moore, Lewis, 43
Moore, Niven, 131, 132, 133
Morris, Edward Joy, 77, 235, 243
Moses, Louis. *See* Louis Merton
Moukhtara, 144, 145, 147, 148, 153, 154
Mount Lebanon, 122, 128, 148, 154, 168, 175, 184, 185
Mufti of Beirut, The, 141, 142, 143
Muheidden Bey, Colonel, 104
Muirhead, Lionel, 231
Murshid, Sheikh Suleiman al, 215, 216, 217, 218, 219, 222, 229
Murshid, Suleiman al, 214, 217
Murtagh, James, 193
Mustapha Fazil Pasha, Prince of Egypt, 190, 195, 196, 197, 198, 211, 236, 237, 238
Napoleon III, Emperor of France, 130, 174, 194, 253
Nasrallah Coussa. *See* Franco Pasha
Navan, Co. Meath, 3, 5, 6, 7, 12, 13, 24, 25, 26, 30, 42
Neill, Brigadier General James, 97
New York, 13, 45, 47, 51, 179, 193, 206, 274, 275, 276, 278, 285
Newton, Charles Thomas, 98, 99
Nicholas I, Tsar of Russia, 55, 56, 57, 79
Normanby, Constantine Henry Phipps, 1st Marquis of, 36
Novara, 63
Novara, Battle of, 45, 69, 82

O'Brien, William Smith, 19, 20, 32, 33, 35, 36, 39, 41, 44, 156, 162
O'Connell, Daniel, 25, 27, 32, 33, 38
O'Gorman, Richard, 36, 37, 39, 40, 44, 53
O'Hara, Charles, 2, 3, 4, 5, 6
O'Reilly, Anna, 191
O'Reilly, Edward (son of James), 272
O'Reilly, Eugene
  and Freemasonry, 51, 182–83
  and Henry Hyde Clark, 262–63
  as Civil and Military Leader of Syria, 144–51
  as Inspector of Railways, 190
  as Tribunal Judge, 137–43
  at Buzău, 79–84, 79–84
  at Calafat, 67–77
  at Giurgiu, 78–79, 78–79
  at Oltenitza, 58
  at Shumen, 59–65
  Balkan Crossing, 65–66
  Beatson's Mutiny, 106–17
  Birth of Eugénie, 258–59
  Birth of Henry, 263
  Blanchardstown Affair, 26–29
  Castelfidardo Falsehood, 138–41
  Confederate Delegation to Paris, 35–39
  Damascus Gendarmerie, 168–79
  death of, 268
  Desert Uprising, 210–32
  Education, 26–29
  in Belgrade, 264–65
  in Boulogne-sur-Mer, 258–63
  in British 10th Hussars, 49–51
  in *Garde nationale*, 39–41
  in Sardinian Army, 44–45, 48–49

Karamist Rebellion, 186–87
Marriage to Mathilde, 205–8, 252, 259–61
Meets Prince of Wales, 164–67
Rescue of Christians, 123–36
Young Ireland Rebellion, 41–42
O'Reilly, Eugenia (Daughter of James), 191
O'Reilly, Gertrude, 272
O'Reilly, Honoria, 191
O'Reilly, James, 17, 40, 50, 141, 148, 149, 190, 253, 270, 271, 272
O'Reilly, James jun., 191
O'Reilly, Maria, 191
O'Reilly, Mary, 17, 18, 24, 43
O'Reilly, Mary Margaret, 109
O'Reilly, Matthew, 15, 16, 17, 21, 22, 24, 27, 43
O'Reilly, Matthew (son of James), 191
O'Reilly, Matthew George, 29, 40, 121, 257
O'Reilly, Myles, 139
O'Reilly, Rev. Eugene, 24, 26, 30
O'Reilly, Rosa, 191
O'Reilly, Sophie, 121
O'Reilly, Susan, 50, 109, 191
O'Reilly, Susan jun (Daughter of James), 191
O'Rorke, James, 6, 11
Oath of Allegiance, 29
Oath of Supremacy, 25
Oltenitza, Battle of, 58, 163, 268
Omar Bey. *See* Andrew Romer
Omar Pasha a.k.a Mihajlo Latas, 57, 61, 62, 147, 148
Palmerston, Henry John Temple, 3rd Viscount, 38, 45, 48, 49, 51, 53, 55, 90, 116, 117, 118, 233, 244

Palmyra, 167, 208, 221, 229
Panmure, Fox Maule-Ramsey, Lord, 90, 96, 97, 105, 106, 107, 108, 111
Papal States, 138, 139
Paris Revolution of 1848, 35, 41
Pears, Sir Edwin, 165
Peel, Frederick, 112
Pera, 109, 110
Pius IX, Pope, 138, 139, 140
Poiana Mare, 76
Price, Edward, 180
Rabat, Morocco, 266
Raglan, FitzRoy James Henry Somerset, 1st Baron, 85, 91
Rashaya, 126, 132
Rashid Pasha, 231, 238
Rashid Pasha, Mehmed, 219
Redcliffe, Stratford Canning, 1st Viscount Stratford de, 53, 57, 85, 99
Repeal Association, 32
Ressalimen Tribe, 219
Richard Griffin & Co., 121
Richmond General Penitentiary, 43, 44
Ristić, Jovan, 264
Riza Pasha, Mehmed, 55, 121, 244
Rogers, Edward Thomas, 172
Romer, Andrew, 200, 210, 212, 232, 234, 236, 237, 243, 245, 250, 252
Ruse, Bulgaria, 67, 78, 189
Russell, Lord John, 32, 133
Safvet Pasha, Mehmed Esad, 248
Salamieh, 238
Sami Pasha, Abdurrahman, 68, 69
Sandwith, Humphry, 61, 110, 164, 179, 195, 211, 264
Sandwith, Thomas Backhouse, 110, 164
Şanlıurfa, 176

Scarlett, General Sir James, 85
Schwartzenberg, Charles de, 186, 187
Scutari, 100, 116
Seb'a Tribe, 217
Seb'a Tribe, 215
Şehzade Yusuf Izzeddin Efendi, Prince of Egypt, 198
Seraskier, 55, 91, 98, 244
Seward, William, 156, 157, 158, 162, 235
Shelley, Edward, 89, 90, 91, 97, 99, 100, 102, 103, 107, 108, 109, 110, 111, 112, 115, 116, 117
Shirley, Major-General Arthur, 109, 110, 112, 116
Shirwani Pasha, Rushdi, 174, 175
Shumen, 59, 60, 63, 64, 65, 70, 109, 110, 115
Sidon, 130, 132, 133, 134, 135, 136
Simmons, Lintorn, 81
Sinope, 89, 91
Sivas, 90
Skene, James Henry, 100, 110, 117, 208, 221, 227, 231
Smith, Major-General Michael, 107, 110, 116
Smith, Margaret, 109
Society of St Vincent de Paul, 30
Solymassy, Mathilde, 192, 194, 205, 206, 252, 259, 263, 264, 270, 271, 272, 273, 275, 276, 278
Somerville, Sir William, 15, 20, 43
Stamboul, 55, 236
Sublime Porte (Ottoman Government), 63, 130, 138, 144, 149, 150, 151, 170, 176, 177, 181, 183, 186, 188, 189, 196, 197, 211, 232, 234, 241, 242, 243, 244, 247, 248, 250, 262, 265
Suez Canal, 204, 211
Sullivan, Pat, 193
Syria, 125, 130, 141, 147, 149, 154, 155, 156, 166, 168, 172, 175, 176, 177, 179, 181, 190, 197, 198, 220, 236, 238, 240, 241, 245, 246, 280
Tabid, Abdullah, 113, 114, 115
Tanzimat (Ottoman Modernisation Council), 122
Tarsus, 113
Tenant Right League, 30
Tewodros II, Emperor of Ethiopia, 204
Train, George Francis, 256
Treaty of Paris, 1856, 113
Trieste, 200, 210, 252, 263
Trinity College Dublin, 1, 29
Tripoli, Lebanon, 210, 212, 221, 229, 247
Turuk u Maabir Idaresi (Office of Roads and Passages), 179
Varna, Bulgaria, 63, 189
Victoria, Queen of England, 79, 195
Vidin, 65, 66, 67, 68, 72, 73, 75, 76
Vivian, General Robert, 86, 96, 97, 100, 106, 108, 109, 110, 111, 114, 115, 116
Wallachia, 57, 61
Wallscourt, Joseph Henry Blake, 3rd Baron, 36
Wallscourt, Lord, 36
Ward, Mr., Commissary General to O'Reilly Expedition in Syria, 179, 200, 204, 224, 226, 237, 238, 250, 251
Wheeler, Rev. George Bomford, 161

293

Wuld Ali Tribe, 217
Young Ireland Movement, i, 32
Young Ottomans, 190
Yusuf, Ahmad Agha al, 170, 171, 177

Yusuf, Muhammad al, 170
Zaptieh Prison, Constantinople, 242, 244, 248, 250

www.ingramcontent.com/pod-product-compliance
Lightning Source LLC
Chambersburg PA
CBHW070138100426
42743CB00013B/2743